# FROM DUTY TO DESIRE

EDITORS

Sherry B. Ortner, Nicholas B. Dirks, Geoff Eley

PRINCETON STUDIES IN
CULTURE / POWER / HISTORY

# FROM DUTY
# TO DESIRE

## REMAKING FAMILIES IN A
## SPANISH VILLAGE

*Jane Fishburne Collier*

PRINCETON UNIVERSITY PRESS
PRINCETON, NEW JERSEY

Published by Princeton University Press, 41 William Street,
Princeton, New Jersey 08540
In the United Kingdom: Princeton University Press,
Chichester, West Sussex

*Library of Congress Cataloging-in-Publication Data*
Collier, Jane Fishburne
From duty to desire: remaking families in a Spanish
village / Jane Fishburne Collier.
p.   cm. — (Princeton studies in culture/power/history)
Includes bibliographical references and index.
ISBN 0-691-01665-8 (cloth : alk. paper)
ISBN 0-691-01664-X (pbk. : alk. paper)
1. Family—Spain—Andalusia.   2. Social norms.
3. Social control—Spain—Andalusia.
4. Self-realization—Spain—Andalusia.
I. Title. II. Series.
HQ650.15.A53C64 1997
306.85′09468—dc21                                            97-10672
                                                                  CIP

This book has been composed in Galliard

Princeton University Press books are printed
on acid-free paper and meet the guidelines
for permanence and durability of the Committee
on Production Guidelines for Book Longevity
of the Council on Library Resources

http://pup.princeton.edu

Printed in the United States of America

1   3   5   7   9   10   8   6   4   2

1   3   5   7   9   10   8   6   4   2
(pbk.)

**For George, David, and Lucy**

AND IN LOVING MEMORY OF

ELOINA AND CRISTINA FERNÁNDEZ GONZÁLEZ

# Contents

# Acknowledgments

THIS BOOK REFLECTS more than thirty years of conversations with friends and colleagues in Spain and the United States. I owe particular thanks to the people of Los Olivos who welcomed me, my husband, and our baby in the fall of 1963, when we arrived to settle in the village for nine months. Wonderful neighbors such as Isabel and Pepe, Julia and Gumersindo, and Amelia and Esteban invited us into their homes. Other villagers, such as Francisco and Modesta, Lorenza and Esteban, and Pilar of the store offered friendship and advice. My deepest gratitude is to Eloina and Cristina Fernández González, whose presence I deeply miss, and to their sister Magdalena. They and their kin—Loli and Pedro, Cándido, Remedios and Miguel, Emilio and Loli, María and Mariano and their children—have enriched my life in more ways than I can count. On return visits to Los Olivos, new neighbors such as Josefa and Nemesio, Resurre and Baldomero, Juliana and her daughter Angeles, Miguela, Manola, Carmen, and Conce helped me to understand the changes that had occurred during my absence. Antonio and Mercedes offered warm hospitality and intelligent comments on current events, and the storekeepers Mari and Pili shared their insights along with sales advice. Among the emigrants who taught me about the effects of participating in urban job markets, Alfonso and Pepita, Amparo and Francisco, Pepi and Felix, Conce and Luis, Lorenza and Esteban and their children, Miguela and Juan José, Julia and her children, and Florentina, Fernando, and Angeles deserve particular thanks. I also want to thank all those who agreed to interviews. Their kindness and patience made this book possible.

Of the North American friends and colleagues who helped me, I owe particular thanks to those who did field research in Los Olivos and generously shared their findings with me. My husband George Collier not only gave me access to his field notes, census analyses, and historical data but also accompanied and encouraged me through the years of research and writing. Special thanks also go to Richard and Sally Price, who spent the summer of 1964 living with a village family and who later offered detailed and helpful suggestions on an earlier draft of this book manuscript. Michelle Zimbalist and Sally Simmons also shared their field notes from the summer of 1965, and Michelle Zimbalist Rosaldo, as my colleague at Stanford University during the 1970s, worked with me in developing the analysis of gender that informs the story I tell of changing subjectivities in Los Olivos. Her premature death cut short our conversations, but her influence is reflected in everything I have written since we first collaborated in developing an undergraduate course, "Women in Cross-Cultural Perspective."

Spanish colleagues also offered invaluable advice and help. Carmelo Lisón-Tolosana graciously encouraged my husband's and my research. Joan Frigolé R. remains a steadfast friend and insightful critic. Adelina Muñoz Molina shared her experience and analysis of social change in Spain when she visited Stanford University. In Andalusia, colleagues at the Universidad de Sevilla such as Alfredo Jiménez, Salvador Rodríguez Becerra, Isidoro Moreno, and Encarnación Aguilar Criado offered hospitality and advice. In Barcelona, George Collier and I enjoyed Verena Stolcke's company, generosity, and broad knowledge of contemporary anthropology.

Because I spent more than ten years writing this book, I owe thanks to many friends and colleagues who commented along the way. In 1984–85, when I spent a year at the Stanford Humanities Center, Nancy Fraser helped me to formulate my ideas. In 1988–89, when a fellowship to the Mary I. Bunting Institute at Radcliffe College gave me the time I needed to write a first draft, several Bunting Fellows, particularly Sandra Bartky, offered useful comments on some chapters. I also owe very special thanks to Sally Merry, my friend and colleague from Wellesley, who not only read and commented on each chapter as I wrote it in 1988–89 but continued to read revised chapters and to comment on them by E-mail.

After 1989, when I was able to circulate a nearly complete draft of the book manuscript, I received advice from many friends and colleagues. I owe particular thanks to Louise Lamphere, David Gilmore, Richard Maddox, Akhil Gupta, Nancy Donham, and Ruth Behar, whose useful comments I have tried to incorporate. Richard and Sally Price, George Collier, and Bill Maurer offered particularly detailed and helpful suggestions. I also benefited from the advice of Liliana Suárez-Navaz, Rosalva Aída Hernández, Heather Paxson, Helen Gremillion, and Ann Swidler, who read and commented on chapters of the manuscript.

A sabbatical in 1995–96 finally gave me time to revise the earlier manuscript. During the revision process, I benefited particularly from the comments and criticisms of Bill Maurer and Saba Mahmood, both of whom, but particularly Saba Mahmood, helped me to find the language I needed to represent the changes I observed in Los Olivos. Sally Merry offered particularly helpful suggestions for revising the introduction.

The revised manuscript benefited from the comments of Jane Schneider and Michael Herzfeld, the readers chosen by Princeton University Press. Both of them offered many helpful suggestions, and Michael Herzfeld later gave me invaluable advice for revising the final chapter on

Andalusian nationalism. I also want to thank the editors at the Press: Mary Murrell for her skillful management of the review and publication process, and Kim Mrazek Hastings for her thoughtful copyediting.

This book would not have been possible without institutional support for field research. George Collier's and my first stay in Los Olivos in 1963–64 was financed by a Fulbright fellowship, administered by the Fulbright Commission in Spain. In 1980, the Comité Conjunto Hispano-Norteamericano para la Cooperación Cultural y Educativa gave us a travel grant to explore possibilities for conducting a restudy, and the Center for Research in International Studies at Stanford University allowed us to spend the summer of 1981 in Los Olivos. Most of the research on family change was carried out in 1983–84, with support from the National Institute of Child Health and Human Development, grant number R01-HD-17351, for a project titled "Late Marriage, Family Constellation, and Kinship Change." In 1987, Joan Frigolé R., George Collier, and I received a grant from the National Science Foundation, BNS 86-15724, for a project titled "Ethnographic Study of Community Development in Spain: 1900–1986." This grant, combined with another in 1988 from the U.S.–Spain Joint Committee allowed us to compare historical processes of family change in eastern and western Andalusia.

Finally, I would not have been able to write this book without the support of the Stanford Humanities Center and of the Mary I. Bunting Institute at Radcliffe College, both of which provided me with the free time I needed to analyze the data I had collected and to draft chapters.

# FROM DUTY TO DESIRE

# Introduction

Doña Perfecta, a wealthy widow, angrily confronts her
nephew who has just declared his intention to marry her
only daughter in spite of Doña Perfecta's opposition:

> "So, to this wretched atheist," she cried with
> open fury, "there are no social conventions,
> there is nothing but personal whim!"
> *(Pérez Galdós 1960 [1876], 144)*[1]

IN THE SPRING OF 1983, I interviewed a married couple who lived in
Barcelona but who had grown up in the small village of Los Olivos
(pseudonym) in western Andalusia. During the visit, Esteban, the husband, proudly showed me his copy of the recently published multi-
volume *Gran enciclopedia de Andalucía* (1979), which he had bought,
he said, to teach his children about their Andalusian heritage. I was surprised. Not only was Esteban's mother still alive, but she was an active,
intelligent woman who loved to share the knowledge she had accumulated during her long and eventful life. Why had Esteban not asked his
mother to teach her grandchildren about their Andalusian heritage?

This book suggests an answer to that question. I will never know
what personal reasons Esteban and his wife might have had for believing
that their children should learn about their heritage from books rather
than from their grandmother. But I explore why it made sense for villagers of Esteban's generation to agree with the encyclopedia's editors that
Andalusia was a region without usable memories. The encyclopedia's
editors, for example, declared in their introduction to the first volume
that "Until today, Andalusia was only a pure romantic sentiment." The
inhabitants of the region "felt themselves to be Andalusians—but without firm connections to their origins and without elements to focus their
regional identities." "This Encyclopedia," the editors wrote, "begins
the task of 'endowing soul' to the Andalusian region, giving it access to
its own cultural elements. If we do not do this," argued the editors, "we
Andalusians will fall into a dangerous frustration when we realize that
we lack a base of identity for our Andalusian community."[2]

Obviously the *Gran enciclopedia de Andalucía* reflects the rising tide
of regionalist sentiment that accompanied Spain's transition to democracy after General Franco's death in 1975. The editors wanted to define
an Andalusian identity comparable to the national identities being

asserted by Catalonians and Basques. It is also easy to understand why Esteban and his wife might have purchased the encyclopedia for their children. They lived in Barcelona, in the midst of Catalonian nationalists who often disparaged immigrants from Andalusia. Their children needed positive images of their Andalusian heritage in order to counter the discrimination they experienced. What is surprising, however, particularly to an anthropologist, is why neither the encyclopedia's editors nor Esteban and his wife turned to living elders for information about Andalusian culture. After all, anthropologists who wrote about Andalusia before massive emigration emptied rural villages had commonly portrayed the region as replete with "culture" (Brennan 1950, 1967; Gregory 1978; Martínez-Alier 1971; Moreno Alonso 1979; Moreno Navarro 1972; Navarro Alcala-Zamora 1979; Price and Price 1966a, 1966b; Pitt-Rivers 1954). Some even blamed the rural exodus for "ethnocide" (Pitt-Rivers 1976). Why, then, was this rich culture spurned?

Andalusian nationalists have argued that the customs recorded by anthropologists and remembered by living elders were not authentic expressions of the Andalusian soul. Rather, they reflect the effects of Castilian domination (e.g., Acosta Sánchez 1979). Such nationalists are probably right. People do produce culture in historical circumstances that inevitably involve dominations of one sort or another. At this point, however, I will not pursue this explanation.[3] Instead, I plan to focus on the ideas and practices available to people for monitoring, assessing, and regulating themselves and their activities. Drawing on the insights of Antonio, a man born in the late 1930s and about fifteen years older than Esteban, I suggest that villagers and former villagers of Esteban's generation had to reject the customs of their parents and grandparents because, as self-consciously "modern" people, they felt compelled "to think for themselves."

Antonio used the phrase "to think for themselves" in an interview I had with him in his Seville home in 1983, in which he argued that "young people" (meaning those born in Los Olivos after 1945 or so) had a different "mentality" [mentalidad] from their elders. He, like all the villagers and former villagers I interviewed in 1983, was impressed by the changes he had seen in his lifetime. But unlike some of the people I spoke with, he welcomed these changes. His observation about the changed mentality of young people came at the end of a diatribe against the villagers of his youth for having spoiled their rural "paradise" with petty quarrels over "interests." Rather than appreciating what they had, Antonio told me, they constantly accused each other of shirking familial and social obligations. But "young people," he said, have begun "to think for themselves"—implying, of course, that the villagers Antonio knew in his youth did not think for themselves. They had allowed others to think for them.

In this book, I plan to use Antonio's implied contrast between "thinking for oneself" and "letting others think for one" as a conceptual tool for exploring the development of what might be called "modern subjectivity" in the small Andalusian village of Los Olivos. Obviously I do not accept Antonio's contrast at face value. I believe that people always both think for themselves and let others think for them. As possessors of individual brains, we must each think our own thoughts. As animals who become human only within cultures, we inevitably think with concepts that have been developed by others. Nevertheless, my experiences living in Los Olivos for nine months in 1963–64 and returning for a restudy in 1983–84, when more than half the villagers had moved away to cities, convinced me that Antonio's implied contrast not only summarized the changes he experienced but also offered a way of understanding why members of Esteban's generation bought encyclopedias rather than asking living elders for information about their Andalusian heritage.

The title of this book, *From Duty to Desire*, is drawn from another, less celebratory, characterization of Antonio's insight that "young people" had begun "to think for themselves." It comes from a cliché I heard several times during the 1980s: "Ahora que tenemos la democracia, todos hacen lo que quieren" [Now that we have democracy, people do as they please]. Obviously, quoters of this cliché were less than happy that people had begun "to think for themselves." A hitchhiker I picked up near Los Olivos, for example, complained that people now shirked obligations they once accepted without question.[4] He was particularly angry at his mother and sisters for deciding that they no longer wanted to cook his meals and wash his clothes. Quoters of this cliché may have blamed the decline of duty on Spain's transition to democracy, which occurred after Franco's death in 1975, but they actually echoed sentiments expressed a century earlier by the fictional character Doña Perfecta, who— in the quotation at the beginning of this chapter—angrily contrasts respect for "social conventions" with "nothing but personal whim."

Whether the villagers and former villagers I interviewed welcomed or lamented the fact that young people had begun to think for themselves, almost everyone I spoke with in 1983–84 attributed the change in "mentality" to a loosening of constraints on people's freedom to act as they wanted. Those who approved of the changes celebrated their liberation. Like Antonio, they painted a happy picture of progress from repression to freedom. Those who criticized the change complained of moral decline. Like the hitchhiker, they painted a gloomy picture of people set free to act out their selfish and base desires. An older friend born before 1920, for example, sadly repeated the cliché "In Spain, we don't have liberty; we have libertinage."

As will soon become clear, I do not believe that the people I interviewed in the 1980s were significantly freer than the villagers I lived with in the early 1960s. Having read several of Foucault's works (e.g., 1973, 1975, 1977a, 1977b, 1978), I am skeptical of narratives that portray recent history as a saga of loosening constraints. Nor do I have any way of knowing whether the people I met in the 1960s were repressing their inner desires whereas those I met in the 1980s were acting them out. I claim no insight into personal motivations. But I do claim knowledge based on listening to what people said and seeing what they did. I thus believe that Antonio's implied contrast between "thinking for oneself" and "letting others think for one" captures a significant shift. But it was less a change in people's willingness or ability to act out their inner desires than a subtle difference in the concepts and practices people used for managing their presentations of self and for interpreting the actions of others. In the 1960s, people living in Los Olivos commonly talked in ways that implied a disjunction between internal desire and outward action. In the 1980s, people tended to portray actions as reflecting the actors' intentions.

When I first lived in Los Olivos, the villagers I met tended to justify and explain their actions by referring to social obligations. In the summer of 1964, for example, a young man who said he thought church was "stupid" explained his presence at Sunday Mass by observing that, in Los Olivos, "you have to go through the forms in everything, religion and politics especially, but underneath you can think what you want."[5] In the 1980s, in contrast, the villagers and emigrants I interviewed (except a few elders) commonly explained their actions by talking about what they wanted to do. Instead of implying a disjunction between thought and action, they talked about the factors they considered in deciding how to act. When Antonio, for example, explained why he did not attend church even though he thinks of himself as a religious man, he observed that he likes to participate fully in an activity or not at all. Since, in his experience, the Catholic Church in Spain is more interested in collecting money than in following Christ's teachings, he did not feel he could wholeheartedly support church programs.

During my two periods of field research, people from Los Olivos also tended to use different vocabularies for interpreting the actions of others. In the 1960s, when villagers commonly justified their own actions by referring to social conventions, it would have made little sense for someone to infer other people's inward desires from observing their outward behaviors. All that an observer could reasonably infer was whether a person was or was not "going through the forms." Indeed, I suggest that people in the 1960s deployed a complex vocabulary for describing and arguing over just what was expected of people in particular relationships.[6] In the 1980s, in contrast, it did make sense for an observer to try to infer desires from behavior—although the observer might have had to use considerable ingenuity to figure out why someone might have wanted to do what he or she did. Most of the people I interviewed in 1983–84 tended to deploy a complex vocabulary of motives to identify, and to argue over, the intentions of actors.

The contrast (and conflict) between these two ways of talking about human action is well illustrated in Benito Pérez Galdós's 1876 novel, *Doña Perfecta*, from which I draw epigraphs to introduce each chapter of this book. The novel tells the story of an ultimately tragic clash between what the novelist portrays as two incompatible systems of cultural logic. "The conflict," observes a recent commentator on the novel, "hinges upon the war to the death between those who saw in every attempt to liberalize [*sic*] thought and customs, and bring Spain abreast of other modern nations, an attack on the Catholic religion, and those who, in their enthusiasm for progress and change, overlooked all that was noble and worthy of respect in the past" (de Onís 1960,xi). Doña Perfecta, the richest landowner in a small rural city, represents the "religious" mentality of those who viewed the social hierarchy as ordained by God. The "wretched atheist" she rails against in the quotation at the beginning of this chapter is her nephew, Pepe Rey, an engineer from Madrid who has just stated his intention to marry Doña Perfecta's daughter. His reason: "She and I want it." Doña Perfecta, whom the novelist portrays as opposing the marriage because she does not want it, nevertheless does not refer to her own wishes. Rather, she contrasts "social conventions," whose observance, in her view, maintains social order, with "nothing but personal whim," which presages chaos. By contrasting social conventions and personal whim, Doña Perfecta assumes a social world in which the existence of order testifies to a disjunction between what people want to do and what they actually do.

If the novelist had allowed Pepe Rey to respond with a contrast reflecting his understanding of human action, this representative of "modern" thinking would have contrasted not social conventions and personal whim, but superstition and reason. In nineteenth-century Spain, bourgeois liberals, including Galdós, the novel's author, blamed the country's supposed backward condition on people's blind adherence to "feudal" customs. Liberals wanted men (and I do mean males) to think for themselves—to use their capacity for reason to throw off the shackles of superstition that impeded progress. But in contrasting superstition and reason, rather than social conventions and personal whim, bourgeois liberals assumed a social world in which a person's actions reflected the actor's thoughts. For liberals, adherence to feudal customs revealed a feudal mentality—a mind enslaved by ignorance and prejudice.

The distinction between Doña Perfecta's and Pepe Rey's ways of imagining the relationship between desire and action is obviously less dichotomous and more subtle than these examples suggest. Both understandings have long been available in Western thought. And both presuppose a unitary, thinking, and feeling subject who acts or refrains from acting out inner desires. The difference is thus one of degree rather than one of kind. Nevertheless, even such a subtle distinction as the one suggested by Antonio's implied contrast between thinking for oneself and letting others think for one can have profound consequences for human experience. Evidence of such consequences can be found in many domains of social life, but in this book I plan to concentrate on family relations. I trace the making of modern subjectivity in Los Olivos by exploring how people remade their families in the twenty years between my two visits.

I focus on the family for several reasons. First, the long-term distinction between public and private spheres—at least as this distinction has been imagined in the post-Enlightenment cultures of Western Europe—casts the family as a protected and autonomous space. Sheltered from the enforced laws of the state and the iron laws of the capitalist market, "home" is a place where people are supposedly free to act in accordance with their personal desires and beliefs. The family is thus a privileged site for exploring the concepts people use for managing their own actions and for interpreting the behaviors of others. Moreover, the family's composition casts it as a privileged site for exploring how people experience, enact, and enforce differences of gender and generation.

It is also true that my original research project was phrased in terms of studying family change. In one sense, families did not change. During both my periods of field research, people from Los Olivos practiced equal partible inheritance and preferred conjugal nuclear families over extended ones. In another sense, however, families changed dramatically. In the twenty years between my two visits, people remade apparently "traditional" families based on obligation into apparently "modern" families based on sentiment (see Shorter 1975). Romantic love apparently replaced status concerns in choosing a spouse; patriarchal authority seemingly gave way to partnership marriages; couples whose parents had demanded respect talked of hoping to earn their children's affection; and mourners, whose black garments once signified respect for the dead, found themselves displaying personal grief for the departed.[7]

My focus on the family also reflects the influence of people I spoke with. When I first visited Los Olivos in 1963–64, the villagers I asked to tell me about their "customs" commonly talked about kinship practices. They avidly described their long formal courtships and extended mourning periods. When I returned to Spain in the 1980s, people were eager to tell me about the demise of both customs. Many of the older people I interviewed lamented their loss, criticizing young couples for their eagerness to marry and young women for their haste to resume wearing regular clothing after the funeral of a close relative. People of Esteban's generation, in contrast, commonly condemned the courtship and mourning customs they had themselves observed in their youth. Concepción, one of Esteban's age-mates, for example, contemptuously referred to these customs as "village stupidities" [tonterías de pueblo] when gleefully describing how she threw away her black mourning clothes the day after she arrived in Madrid.

The people I interviewed also tended to discuss kinship practices when illustrating the contrast between following social conventions and thinking for oneself. Whether people approved of long courtships and extended mourning periods, everyone I spoke with during both periods of fieldwork seemed to agree that those who followed such customs were suppressing their inner desires in order to do what others expected of them. And everyone seemed to agree that young couples who married shortly after becoming engaged and women who resumed normal dress shortly after a funeral were doing what they, as individuals, wanted to do—even though by the 1980s such practices had become the expected norm for anyone under the age of forty.

Finally, I focus on kinship practices because, as suggested by Concepción's contemptuous reference to "village stupidities," kinship practices provide a key site for exploring differences between the "traditions" that became unacceptable to members of Esteban's generation and those they hoped to recover as true expressions of the Andalusian soul. Between my two visits to Los Olivos, "tradition" apparently acquired a new meaning. In 1963–64, the word was commonly opposed only to "modernity," particularly by people contrasting village courtship and mourning customs with those of urbanites (and visiting North Americans). When I returned in the 1980s, people still used a traditional/modern contrast, but they also used the word "tradition" to describe the customs of Andalusians in contrast to the "traditions" of people in other parts Spain and of the world.

In writing this book, I first tried to avoid using the words "traditional" and "modern" even though they had been used by people from Los Olivos. I did so on the advice of Spanish colleagues who pointed out to me that these value-laden terms have often been used by foreign scholars—particularly those from English-speaking countries—to characterize Spaniards (and southern Europeans in general) as "backward" or "exotic."[8] Their observation led me to realize that I did not want to participate in literatures that either blamed Spain's economic problems on Spaniards' adherence to "tradition" or celebrated Spaniards' supposed retention of "tradition" in the face of pressures to adopt international pop culture.[9] I was also troubled by the words "traditional" and "modern" because, as I noted earlier, I did not want to write the standard modernization story of progress from constraint to freedom. My reading of Foucault's works had led me to suspect that people from Los Olivos may have given up the visible chains of "traditional" society for constant, if less visible, surveillance by "modern" disciplinary apparatuses.

As I wrote, however, I found that I could not avoid using the words "traditional" and "modern," however hard I tried. My problem was not simply because people from Los Olivos had themselves used these terms when talking about the changes they experienced. I could have explored—and have indeed tried to explore—what people meant when they used the words. Rather, my problem came from the inescapable fact that I—however unwittingly—participated in making and reinforcing the contrast between "tradition" and "modernity." Even as I tried to use substitute terms, such as "then" and "now," "village" and "urban," or "agrarian" and "bourgeois," I found myself reproducing the problematic traditional/modern contrast, reinforcing the vision of tradition as modernity's devalued opposite.

When I turned to exploring why I was having such difficulties avoiding the traditional/modern opposition, I rapidly realized that I was a representative of the modern whether I liked it or not. Underlying every discussion I had with people from Los Olivos during both periods of fieldwork was the unquestioned assumption—which I shared—that my husband and I were already "modern." We stood for what we and our village friends assumed the villagers were becoming or had become. On both visits, the subtext of every conversation, whether implicit or explicit, concerned the advantages and disadvantages of villagers becoming "modern" like us. Moreover, I realized that the traditional/modern dichotomy is itself a product of modernity. Not until modernity was invented could tradition be cast as its devalued opposite (Dirks 1990). Finally, as Foucault observed, the human sciences—including anthropology—are both products and producers of modern disciplinary techniques (1973). In short, my efforts to avoid exoticizing the people I wanted to write about, and to avoid writing a progressive story of modernization, forced me to confront the fact that I was implicated in my proposed narrative in at least three ways: as a representative, however unwilling, of the "modern," as a participant in the modern discourses that produced the skewed opposition I wanted to write about, and as a user of analytic tools created by modernity.

My exploration of the traditional/modern dichotomy also led me to realize that "tradition" is not only a contested term, but also one with several meanings. As modernity's devalued opposite, it is a catchall category, lumping together the "mentality" I observed in Los Olivos in the 1960s with the very different conceptual worlds of many non-European peoples. These two types of tradition seem important to separate. The traditional mentality I encountered in Los Olivos, unlike the conceptual worlds of some non-Europeans, was, I believe, as modern and Western as the modernity that defined it as traditional. Both were created by people living in the aftermath of the European Enlightenment.

Within European modernity, the word "tradition" seems to have been used in at least three ways. The first meaning does not oppose tradition to modernity but rather casts modernity itself as a tradition. This is the meaning commonly invoked by philosophers who argue that reason can occur only within historical traditions of thought that determine what counts as rationality (Winch 1970; Williams 1977; see also Asad 1993; Tambiah 1990). I discuss this meaning of "tradition" first because, as will soon become clear, I use it to understand the other two. Not only does this interpretation allow me to understand the European Enlightenment as one philosophical tradition among many, rather than as the only tradition based on rationality, but it also enables me to portray the two "mentalities" I analyze in this book, along with the anthropological tools I use to analyze them, as products of the same historical tradition: the European Enlightenment.[10]

I realize, of course, that treating historical traditions as different mentalities raises the problem of how to translate between traditions. If rationality is inherently context-dependent, how can we understand the rationality of others? Tambiah, in an essay addressing this question, begins by observing that "many of the modern philosophers . . . share a conception of rationality that minimally identifies logical consistency and coherence as distinctive features" (1990, 117). He uses this minimal definition to suggest a middle ground in the debate between Winch (1970), who warned anthropologists against making "'category mistakes' in comparing (or reducing to a common measure) phenomena whose points or foci of interests are different as 'forms of life'" and MacIntyre (1970), who argued that it is impossible for anthropologists "to approach alien concepts except in terms of the anthropologist's own criteria" (Tambiah 1990, 121). Recognizing the truth of MacIntyre's assertion, Tambiah nevertheless emphasizes Winch's warning against "category mistakes." He endorses Winch's "preference for first understanding a people in terms of their own concepts, valuations and ideologies" as a way of avoiding too rapid an attempt to (mis)translate "their" concepts into "ours."

In this book, I approach the problem of how to understand a people's own "concepts, valuations and ideologies" by focusing on the arguments they have with one another. It might seem wrongheaded to search for a people's shared understandings by studying their disagreements. But I follow Bourdieu (1977, 168–169) in observing that it is through constant and recurring arguments that a people establish and perpetuate the shared, usually implicit assumptions that constitute their tradition and that make it possible for them to understand how they disagree with one another (J. Collier 1988).

Although historical traditions of thought are constituted and perpetuated through ongoing arguments, some disagreements involve greater differences of opinion than others. I believe that the two ways of imagining the relationship between desire and action that I observed in Los Olivos are best characterized not as separate traditions but as subtraditions within the overarching historical tradition of the European Enlightenment. They belong to the same larger tradition because European peoples since at least the seventeenth century have argued over whether individuals should follow social conventions or think for themselves. Such arguments have thus perpetuated the implicit assumption that humans are unitary, acting subjects capable of reason as well as emotion. But each subtradition has also been a field of argument. Those who shared the belief that people should follow social conventions have commonly argued over what convention requires, whereas those who agreed that people should think for themselves have struggled over assigning motives to individuals.

Because historical traditions are always fields of argument, they are constantly changing as people invent new arguments and draw on resources that were not available before. Changes vary in their significance, however. Some are far-reaching. The European Enlightenment, which constructed both anthropology and the two ways of imagining the relationship between desire and action that I encountered in Los Olivos, contrasts in historical terms with earlier, long-lasting European traditions, such as that of medieval thought. On a still broader level, all European thought since at least Roman times constitutes a single tradition when contrasted with very different historical traditions, such as that of the Chinese. Other changes are less far-reaching, particularly if considered in world historical time. Such lesser changes, however, may still seem great to those who experience them. Antonio's description of "young people" as having a different "mentality" from their elders suggests that he, at least, experienced the changes I describe in this book as profound rather than superficial.

The second meaning of "tradition" established by modernity is the one constructed by the European Enlightenment, which, through celebrating human "reason," cast all modes of thought not based on rationalism as traditional rather than modern.[11] In this second sense, tradition is also a system of thought, but it is modernity's devalued opposite. This is the meaning commonly intended by people from Los Olivos when they contrasted tradition with modernity. It is also the meaning whose implied value judgment makes it impossible for "modern" users of the term, such as me, to describe others as "traditional" without appearing condescending.

During the European Enlightenment, people who embraced reason developed the traditional/modern opposition in order to distinguish those who "thought for themselves" (to use Antonio's words) from those who supposedly let others think for them, as demonstrated by their adherence to accepted social conventions. *The American Heritage Dictionary of the English Language* reflects these meanings in its definitions of the Enlightenment and traditionalism. It defines the Enlightenment as "a philosophical movement . . . concerned with the critical examination of previously accepted doctrines and institutions from the point of view of rationalism." It defines traditionalism as "a philosophical system holding that all knowledge is derived from original divine revelation and is transmitted by . . . the passing down of elements of a culture from generation to generation." Although the dictionary defines modernism merely in terms of "modern thought, character, or practice," its definitions of Enlightenment and traditionalism clearly suggest that modern thought and practice are not simply recent but are based on the assumption that knowledge can be continuously created and discovered through human reason and scientific methods. If knowledge is always subject to revision, then nothing can be certain (Berman 1982; Giddens 1991, 21).

As a product of the European Enlightenment, anthropology is one of the human sciences that developed when people, along with their doctrines and institutions, were constituted as objects of rational, critical analysis (Foucault 1973). Anthropology participated in creating the distinction between tradition and modernity, as well as in creating such related conceptual oppositions as those between subjectivity and objectivity, and between cultural beliefs and scientific truths. Because anthropology defined itself as an objective modern science based on human reason (in contrast to the traditions, cultures, and doctrines that it constituted as its objects of study), anthropology rendered both modernity and itself invisible at the same time that it exposed the beliefs and practices of human groups to scientific scrutiny. To the degree that anthropologists accepted modernists' claims to have discarded cultural traditions in favor of reason and science, anthropologists constituted modernity as outside their purview. To the degree that anthropologists imagined themselves as objective seekers of scientific truths, they obscured the cultural assumptions and social relationships that made their practice possible.

The third meaning of tradition does not treat it as a philosophical system but rather as a set of cultural elements that have been handed down from the past, "especially by oral communication" (*American Heritage Dictionary of the English Language*). Such cultural elements are, I believe, the kinds of "traditions" sought by members of Esteban's generation and by the editors of the *Gran enciclopedia de Andalucía*. Traditions in this third sense are like possessions (Handler 1988). They are things, such as festivals, religious beliefs, collective memories, cuisines, costumes, music, dances, stories, art styles, and so forth, that individuals or peoples can "have," "use," and even market to outsiders.

I associate this third meaning of tradition with advocates of nineteenth-century European romanticism, who—in opposition to the eighteenth-century's supposed overemphasis on human reason—not only celebrated emotion but also sought to rescue or revive cultural elements that distinguished their ethnic group from other ethnic groups. European romanticism was a complex intellectual movement, with deep roots and contradictory doctrines, but I focus on its links to nationalism. In the final chapter of this book, for example, I explore the revitalization of "traditional" festivals in Los Olivos during the 1980s, as Franco's dictatorship gave way to democracy and as nationalist parties competed for votes in Spain.

Anthropology, particularly as it developed during the nineteenth century in continental Europe, participated in nationalist projects. As a self-defined objective science, it was useful not only to colonial administrators charged with managing colonized peoples but also to nationalists concerned with proving the authenticity of the beliefs and practices that established their separate ethnicity and thereby justified their demands for self-government (Herzfeld 1982). Over time, the "scientific" study of "other" cultures linked to colonialism tended to become differentiated from the "humanistic" study of folklore linked to nationalism and focused on European peasants. Both strands, however, joined in the work of Franz Boas, who remade North American cultural anthropology at the beginning of the twentieth century. As an heir of German roman-ticism, Boas respected cultural differences and argued for the right of peoples to preserve their traditions. But as a scientist, Boas also thought that people should abandon their cultural beliefs in favor of science and human reason (Stocking 1979). In fact, Boas and his students often used evidence of cultural differences to help modern peoples recognize their own harmful beliefs—such as ideas about racial inferiority—so that they could discard them.

Although Boas did urge his followers to study modern peoples like themselves, his contradictory allegiance to scientific objectivity and hu-manistic folklore encouraged his followers to confine their scrutiny to those aspects of modern behavior that could be perceived as traditional or irrational, such as people's festivals, dances, religious beliefs, racial prejudices, and so on. This tendency has had the unfortunate conse-quence, not only of maintaining the distinction between "traditional" and "modern" ways of being but also of subjecting each to different standards of analysis. Because "traditional" customs and beliefs are, by definition, not "rational," they require explanation. Anthropologists must interpret them.[12] "Modern" behaviors, in contrast, require no ex-planation. Because they reflect what any rational person would do, they are transparent.

As an anthropologist trained in North America and writing for an au-dience of educated English speakers, I inherit Boas's contradictory leg-acy. On one hand, I am condemned to misrepresent the words and ac-tions of the people I knew in the 1960s. Because I must suggest reasons why they might have wanted to talk and act as they did, I inevitably contradict their assertions that they were merely following social con-ventions. On the other hand, I am also condemned to misinterpreting the behaviors of "modern" young people in the 1980s. Because both they and I assumed that our shared behaviors reflected what any rational person would do, my efforts to explain the "normal" appear absurd.

When my friends from Los Olivos characterized me as already "mod-ern," they were right. In writing this book, I have found myself unable to avoid assuming that people's actions testify to their intentions. Con-sciously, I know that I have access only to what I could observe people saying and doing. Nevertheless, I find myself inevitably drawing on my own experiences to suggest what others might have been wanting and feeling (see Leavitt 1996). My entire analysis of change in Los Olivos rests on the premise that people want to do what they do, even if people appear to be acting contrary to their interests—and even if they them-selves claim to be denying or suppressing their desires. I deploy a vocab-ulary of motives: I try to find a reason why it might make sense for some-one to want to do what he or she did. As a result, I will portray the villagers I met in 1963–64 not only as wanting, on some level, to observe such social conventions as long courtships and extended mourning periods but also as claiming to follow social conventions because they wanted to convince themselves and others that they were virtuously suppressing personal whims.

But if I follow "modern" villagers, such as Antonio, in assuming that people's actions reflect their intentions, I do not want to suggest that people who followed social conventions either let others think for them or had minds enslaved by ignorance and prejudice. I may agree that people's observance of "traditional" customs reflects a "traditional" mentality, but I plan to argue that people who claimed to follow social conventions were just as "rational" as people who claimed to think for themselves. Instead of using "tradition" in the second sense discussed above, in which tradition is defined as lacking the rationality that constitutes modernity, I plan to use the word in the first sense in order to explore the rationality inherent in both of the Enlightenment subtraditions I encountered in Los Olivos. I follow Foucault in searching for "incitements to discourse" (1978, 18)—the institutionalized practices and techniques that required people to notice, discuss, and contest some topics rather than others. I thus argue that the villagers I knew in the 1960s had good reasons for talking and acting as they did, in the sense that any "rational" person living in their social environment would have behaved likewise.

I recognize, however, that in searching for the "rationality" inherent in the "traditional" way of life practiced by the villagers I met in the 1960s I run the risk of implying that I have discovered a truth concealed by or unknown to them. This is not my intention. If I argue that villagers who claimed to be suppressing their desires were actually enacting them, it is because I have found it impossible to do otherwise. The assumption that people's actions reflect their intentions is not only suggested by my experiences as a "modern" person but also encoded in anthropology as a discipline invented by "modernity." Tambiah was right when he agreed with MacIntyre (1970) that in order "to successfully describe the rules of use of another culture, the anthropologist (in practice a Westerner or one exposed to Western indoctrination) applies 'standards of rational criticism' as developed in the contemporary West" (1990, 121).

I can imagine trying to write within a "traditional" conceptual framework that assumes a disjunction between desire and action. But I believe the attempt would fail. On an intellectual level, I can conceive of employing a vocabulary of obligations to investigate what social conventions required of people in particular relationships. Practically, however,

I find myself continually searching for reasons why people might have wanted to talk and act as they did. In 1964, for example, María, a village woman then in her early forties, told me that she wore mourning clothes after the death of a cousin she barely knew because if she did not, other villagers would criticize her. I immediately inferred that María wore mourning dress because she wanted to avoid the neighbors' gossip. I no longer think this is what María was telling me. Rereading my field notes, I realize that she did not express either a desire to avoid her neighbors' criticisms or a desire to earn their respect. She simply stated that her neighbors would criticize her if she failed to wear expected mourning clothes. I now believe that María mentioned the neighbors' gossip not to suggest a reason why she, as an individual, had decided to conform to their expectations but rather as evidence of the fact that social conventions in Los Olivos required a woman to wear mourning clothes after the death of a cousin, however slightly she might know him. Even as I revise my understanding of María's words, however, I find that I cannot help inferring that she wore mourning clothes because she did not want the neighbors to gossip about her.

I am not alone in making such inferences. Most of the emigrants and younger villagers I interviewed in the 1980s seemed to make similar ones. Antonio, for example, contrasted his courageous willingness to think for himself with the cowardliness of villagers he knew in his youth, who, he said, let fear of malicious gossip dictate their actions. But if I, like Antonio, tend to assume that people who talked about gossiping neighbors were explaining why they, as individuals, decided to follow social conventions, I try to avoid endorsing Antonio's condemnation of such motives. Because I plan to focus on incentives for discourse, I suggest that the organization of social inequality in 1963–64, in which inherited property appeared to determine a family's income and lifestyle, incited María to talk about the neighbors' expectations, whereas a very different organization of inequality, in which an individual's personal drive and ambition appeared to determine occupation and earnings, incited Antonio to talk about his inner desires. If I were to suggest that people like María were cowards who let their actions be dictated by others' expectations, I would be as guilty of misinterpreting their words as María would have been had she taken Antonio's pride in thinking for himself as evidence that he lacked the willpower to suppress his personal whims.

My situation as a "modern" person also limits my understanding of the words and actions of the villagers and emigrants I spoke with in the 1980s. When I returned to Los Olivos after an absence of twenty years, I was struck not only by the changes that had occurred but also by the similarities between myself and the people I encountered. Like Richard Maddox, who began field research in the nearby market town of Aracena in 1981, I found that the activities, preferences, and basic convictions of people I met in the 1980s varied little from my own (1993, 172). This lack of difference affected my understanding in two ways.[13] First, I found it hard to imagine that people's words and actions required explanation. As I noted earlier, it seems absurd to wonder why people who act "normally" behave as they do. Second, the similarities between my customs and those of the people I interviewed in the 1980s made it difficult for me to recognize the differences that did exist. Because our outward behaviors and opinions tended to coincide, I seldom made the social gaffes that in the 1960s had alerted me to misunderstandings. As all anthropologists know, we derive our deepest insights into cultural differences from those painful occasions when we have said or done something that causes our hosts to burst out laughing, shrink with shame, or angrily reprove us. My failure to commit such gaffes in the 1980s, along with the politeness of Spaniards who failed to comment on the mistakes I did make, prevented me from realizing my errors and thus from asking questions that might have helped me to realize that my assumptions differed from those of the people I was interviewing. As a result, I know I have ended up attributing some of my beliefs and motives to people who did not share them.[14]

Finally, my understanding of the changes I observed in Los Olivos is limited by the circumstances of my fieldwork and by the academic environment in which I write. The story I plan to tell—linking the development of "modern" subjectivity to changes in how people enacted and experienced unequal social relations—is, like every account, necessarily partial. It is told from the viewpoint of a particular person. I, like every anthropologist, participated in creating the evidence I cite—through my interactions with villagers and emigrants, by deciding what to record in my field notes, and by choosing what to include in this book. I therefore begin by briefly describing my fieldwork experiences and the theoretical concerns that motivated the analysis I present.

I chose to study Los Olivos because it was the prettiest of the villages that my husband, George Collier, and I visted when we went to Spain in the fall of 1963. We were very young at the time—just out of college—with Fulbright fellowships to study an Andalusian village comparable to the Maya Indian hamlet of Apas in Zinacantan, Chiapas, Mexico, that we had been studying as undergraduate members of the Harvard Chiapas Project (Vogt 1994). When we arrived in Seville, we borrowed an atlas of Andalusian communities to make a list of villages that met our requirements. Because we needed a community like Apas, we looked for a settlement that had between five hundred and one thousand people, was agricultural, and was located in a mountainous region. And because we feared medical emergencies—we were the parents of a two-month-old baby—we eliminated villages that lacked a resident doctor and regular bus service. With a list of approximately ten villages in hand, we rented a car to check them out. Los Olivos not only was the prettiest one we visited but also had the friendliest people. The men who greeted us outside the bar in the central plaza assured us that we would be welcome, that there were empty houses we could rent, and that they knew a woman who would be glad to work for us as a housekeeper. Our plan to compare an Andalusian village to a Maya Indian hamlet proved misguided.[15] But I never regretted choosing Los Olivos.

Los Olivos is not a typical Andalusian village (if such a thing exists). With a population of around six hundred in 1960, it is smaller than most. Even though the village was and continues to be a separate municipality, with its own mayor and town council, it resembled a hamlet of the region more than one of its towns. The villagers I met in 1963–64 also stressed differences between Los Olivos and nearby communities. They told me that their courtships were longer and their mourning customs stricter than those of their neighbors, which I believed. But I doubted their claims that they were more virtuous than people in larger towns. I was also skeptical about their complaints that Los Olivos was poorer and sadder than other communities because it lacked employment outside agriculture.[16] When I compare Los Olivos to neighboring towns and to the Andalusian communities studied by other ethnographers (Pitt-Rivers 1954; Martínez-Alier 1971; Fraser 1973; Aguilera 1978; Gregory 1978; Gilmore 1980; Corbin and Corbin 1984, 1987; Brandes 1980; Moreno Navarro 1972, 1977; Luque Baena 1974; Pérez Díaz 1974; Mintz 1982; Frigolé Reixach 1983; Maddox 1993), I am struck by the homogeneity of its population. In the 1960s, it contained only the middle tier of the three-tier Andalusian class system. Los Olivos lacked both large landowners and landless laborers. Those who owned the most land and employed the most laborers did not live in the village. And everyone appeared to own at least a small plot of land or have hopes of inheriting one. As I later discovered, both the very rich and the very poor had left Los Olivos in the decades before my arrival.

In 1963–64, I formed my closest ties with the housekeeper and her family, the mayor who welcomed my husband and me, and the immediate neighbors. My visits with the housekeeper's and the mayor's families took me outside the neighborhood and allowed me to glimpse lifestyle differences between people at either end of the village wealth ranking. The two women who were my neighbors across the street, both of the middle wealth rank, welcomed me into their homes for long winter afternoons of knitting and talking. I had little contact with people my own age. They were still courting, whereas I was married with a baby. Instead of talking about sweethearts with women in their early twenties, I spent hours listening to older women discuss infant care, housekeeping, and the neighbors' activities.

During the nine months my husband and I spent in Los Olivos, from the beginning of September 1963 to the end of May 1964, we focused on collecting general ethnographic information comparable to information we had collected in Mexico. I interviewed the mayor, the housekeeper, and my neighbors about courtship customs and mourning requirements. I also collected some folktales. My efforts to study conflict management procedures failed because people refused to tell me about their quarrels with others. And I abandoned my planned study of medical beliefs after the women I spoke with convinced me that everyone in Los Olivos consulted the doctor. They said they knew nothing about the evil eye, and that few villagers consulted the *sabio* (wise man) who lived in a distant town. My husband, with the mayor's help, used the 1960 census and other documents in the town hall to construct a genealogical census that we continued to use in computerized, updated versions. He also constructed wealth rankings, collected systematic data on land tenure, and asked about village agriculture during long walks with the mayor.

I avoided some topics. I was too shy to ask people about their intimate relations. I also avoided discussing or studying religion because I disliked going to church. And I missed many village activities by keeping to my American schedule rather than adapting to village hours. After putting the baby to bed in the early evening, my husband and I usually relaxed at home, talking and writing field notes. I did not want to join other women in the television room above the bar, nor was my husband eager to join the men drinking below. We liked to go to bed early because our baby woke before dawn, unlike village babies who were kept awake past midnight and slept until noon.

As I prepared to leave Los Olivos in May 1964, I remember being disappointed with the results of my work. Although I had collected a great deal of information, I had not been able to explore any particular topic to the depth I had achieved in Mexico. I was never able to obtain specific courtship and mourning case histories to complement the general descriptions I had obtained. No villager seemed willing to spend long hours answering the detailed, repetitive, and often boring questions I wanted to ask.[17] Having failed to probe deeply, I thought I had little to add to the description of Andalusian village life presented by Julian Pitt-Rivers in his outstanding monograph *The People of the Sierra* (1954). I did not, in fact, write about Los Olivos until much later

(1986). I put my Spanish field notes away as I returned to Mexico for dissertation research.

Richard and Sally Price, friends from Harvard-Radcliffe who had also been undergraduate participants in the Harvard Chiapas Project, spent the summer of 1964 in Los Olivos interviewing people about courtship customs. Because they lacked children, and lived with a family whose four children were in various stages of the courting process, they were able to participate fully in the activities of courting couples. Their field notes contain rich descriptions of both private domestic life and public amusements. They were also able to collect case histories of courtship. One daughter in the family proved to be an ideal anthropological informant. As I came to know her on return visits to Spain, I was impressed by her intelligence, insight, and patience. Richard and Sally Price published two articles about courtship (1966a, 1966b) based on their summer of field research. My discussion of 1963–64 courtship customs in chapter 2 is based on their field notes and analyses.

In the summer of 1965, another friend from Harvard-Radcliffe and the Harvard Chiapas Project, Michelle Zimbalist (who became Michelle Z. Rosaldo on marriage), spent two months with her friend Sally Simmons living in Los Olivos with the family who hosted the Prices. Shelly and Sally were both undergraduates at the time, and they focused on mourning customs for their summer research project. In early July, the father in their host family died. As young women without male partners and living in a house of mourning, Shelly and Sally were excluded from the activities of courting couples. But they were welcomed by young women without fiancés or whose fiancés were away from town. Although neither published anything on their research, their joint field notes, which I draw on throughout this book, record many conversations with women about their fears of being dishonored, the stages of a woman's life, and friendships among women. My chapter on mourning customs also draws heavily on their work.[18]

Although I returned to Los Olivos for brief visits in the summers of 1972 and 1978, I did not write field notes. But the stories people told me about village happenings, combined with occasional letters and regular Christmas cards from friends, informed me that Los Olivos was becoming "sad" as emigration drained the village of people and "life."

In the summer of 1980, my husband and I returned for three months of field research, accompanied by our two teenage children and a Stanford University undergraduate who spent the summer living with a village family. Although the population of Los Olivos had dropped to fewer than three hundred year-round residents, the town filled up during July and August with vacationing former villagers and some of their friends. Our family was lucky to find an apartment in the large house we had formerly rented, which the landlady had divided into three units after our departure. Because our apartment was in the back of the house, its door opened onto a different street. I thus acquired new neighbors without having to abandon old friends. I also met village women from other neighborhoods as I did the housework that required leaving home, such as washing clothes in the public fountain and shopping for food in the local stores. (My husband did the housework that could be done behind closed doors, such as the cooking and cleaning.)

I spent the summer of 1980 interviewing neighbors and friends about the changes in courtship and mourning customs that had occurred since the 1960s. This time I had no trouble collecting stories about specific individuals. I was no longer asking questions that people found boring because everyone knew the answers but me. Instead I was asking the same questions as every returning migrant and villager. We all wanted news of friends and acquaintances we had not seen for a long time. My husband spent the summer of 1980 photocopying town hall records in preparation for analyzing the demographic causes and consequences of late marriage. He also talked with men about the decline of local agriculture.

In January 1983, I returned to Los Olivos to begin seven months of intensive field research studying the effects of emigration on kinship relations. My husband's genealogical census proved to be an invaluable interviewing tool. Before visiting each person or couple who agreed to an interview, I prepared kinship charts of their families to jog their memories about individuals and to provide a framework for collecting life histories. My husband and I often conducted interviews together. We used a tape recorder only once. It seemed to stifle spontaneity and we dreaded the thought of transcribing hours of tape. Instead we tried to take careful notes. When we conducted joint interviews, we took turns asking questions, leaving the other person free to concentrate on writing. We recorded most of our notes in Spanglish, a mixture of Spanish and English in which English predominated but crucial words and phrases remained untranslated.

During interviews, I usually played the role of polite questioner and interested listener. As a guest in people's houses, I did not feel I had the right to ask provocative questions, initiate arguments, or contest their views, however much I might have learned from forcing people to argue with me. And I had little luck playing devil's advocate during informal conversations with friends. Most people from Los Olivos have an assertive conversational style. They tend to keep talking until another person interrupts them by talking more loudly. Having been trained since childhood to talk softly and never to interrupt others, I was at a conversational disadvantage. But if I found myself tongue-tied, and unable to direct conversations toward topics that concerned me, I did learn a great deal from listening to the lively, usually witty, discussions going on around me. Furthermore, I think of this book as my opportunity to present my ideas and opinions about the changes that took place in Los Olivos.

I spent the first three months of 1983 interviewing residents in Los Olivos, followed by several weeks each in Madrid, Seville, and Barcelona interviewing former villagers who had emigrated. Although some people refused to talk with me, I found that those who welcomed me into their homes were usually as interested as I in reconstructing their own and the village's history. I particularly appreciated the opportunity to make friends with people who, like me, had been young adults in the 1960s. They were living in a very different social world from the one in which they grew up, and most of them were critical of the long courtships and extended mourning periods they had themselves observed when I first met them. Their insights on change complemented the views of older friends, many of whom lamented the loss of village customs. This book, in fact, is primarily about the experiences of people of my generation—those born between 1935 and 1950. Their participation in creating a new social world shaped the experiences of their parents and children.

As the fieldwork progressed, I focused on changes that had occurred between 1963 and 1983, collecting life histories to find out what had happened to people and to analyze the motives they attributed to themselves and others. I also collected gossip, less to learn what people had done than to hear how narrators evaluated the actions of others. My husband focused on analyzing the historical processes that shaped the village we had encountered in 1963. With the help of the people we interviewed, the census, and archival research, he reconstructed the events of the Spanish Second Republic, the civil war, and the postwar repression (G. Collier 1987). In the process of thinking about the changes that had occurred, both of us drew on the work of Richard Maddox, whose historical study of Aracena (1986, 1993), the nearby market town and administrative center, helped us to understand regional history and stratification processes.

I returned to Spain in the summer of 1984 for a final period of field research. I spent July in Barcelona and August in Los Olivos, living on yet another street and acquiring a new set of neighbors. Although I did some interviewing, I spent almost as much time analyzing data as collecting new information. During the long, hot days of August, I stayed indoors, using the census and interview notes to trace the life experiences of villagers by five-year cohorts, beginning with the birth cohort of 1900–1904 and ending with that of 1950–54. In the cool evenings, I joined friends and neighbors in the streets to talk and catch up on news. I also attended local festivals, participating in the revival of "tradition" that I discuss in this book's final chapter.

Since 1984, I have returned to Los Olivos for short visits but have not collected systematic information. I spent three days there in September 1994, catching up on news with friends and joining villagers in the annual pilgrimage to a local shrine. After its long population decline, Los Olivos seems to be growing again. Several young adults, unable to find jobs in urban areas, decided to settle in Los Olivos, where they could supplement unemployment income with food grown on family lands. Most recently, government efforts to create employment opportunities in the region seem to be paying off. A newly constructed facility for processing garbage is now employing some men from the village.

The theoretical focus of this book—the development of modern subjectivity—reflects and builds on my long-term interest in trying to understand why unequal systems of social relations persist despite the efforts of disadvantaged people (particularly women) to resist oppression and improve their lot (Collier and Rosaldo 1981; J. Collier 1974, 1986, 1988; Yanagisako and Collier 1987). Having rejected the idea of "false consciousness" as an explanation for why people act in ways that appear to prejudice their long-term interests, I have tried to explore why it might make sense for people to talk and act as they do. Drawing on the insights of practice theorists (Bourdieu 1977; Ortner 1984; Giddens 1984), I have tried to explore how wider systems of social inequality affect the experiences from which people construct their commonsense understandings of themselves and the world, and how the cumulative actions of people acting on commonsense understandings constitute the social institutions that structure their experiences (J. Collier 1988).

Although this book explores an instance of social change, rather than persistence, I continue to focus on the commonsense understandings that people construct from their experiences of living within, and resisting, unequal social relations.[19] I thus begin with a chapter analyzing the stories that people from Los Olivos told to explain why some individuals enjoyed more wealth, power, and prestige than others. Drawing on Giddens's theory of "structuration," I explore the "practical consciousness"—defined as "things which actors know tacitly about how to 'go on' in the context of social life" (1984, xiii)—required to narrate and interpret the very different success and failure stories told by people from Los Olivos during the two periods of my field research. In the 1960s, when inherited property appeared to be the major determinant of social inequality, people told stories of marriages and bequests. In the 1980s, when occupational achievement seemed more pertinent, they talked about individual desires and accomplishments. The remaining chapters of the book explore the connections between these different explanations for inequality and the subtle shift in people's techniques for monitoring and managing the self that Antonio captured in his implied contrast between "letting others think for one" and "thinking for oneself."

Antonio's implied contrast intrigued me, not only because it seemed right, but also because it echoed a distinction that Foucault discussed in a short essay on modern subjectivity (1984). Meditating on Kant's answer to the question "What is Enlightenment?" Foucault observed that Kant perceived enlightenment in "an almost entirely negative way, . . . as an 'exit,' a 'way out'" of human "immaturity." By "immaturity" Kant meant "a certain state of our will that makes us accept someone else's authority to lead us in areas where the use of reason is called for" (Foucault 1984, 34).[20] "Kant in fact describes Enlightenment as the moment when humanity is going to put its own reason to use, without subjecting itself to any authority" (Foucault 1984, 37–38).

Foucault went on to observe that putting one's own reason to use required people not only to monitor their inner thoughts and desires (rather than focusing on what others expected of them) but also to take on the task of reshaping their inner selves to become the persons they would like to be. Invoking the poet Baudelaire to illustrate the "attitude" of modernity, Foucault observed that "Modern man, for Baudelaire, is not the man who goes off to discover himself, his secrets and his hidden truth; he is the man who tries to invent himself. This modernity does not 'liberate man in his own being'; it compels him to face the task of producing himself" (1984, 42).

Giddens, too, argues that "producing oneself" is a peculiarly "modern" task (1991). He observes that all humans are reflexive, in the sense that all people monitor their actions and can produce accounts of their behavior. But only "modern" people see the self "as a reflexive project, for which the individual is responsible. . . . We are, not what we are, but what we make of ourselves" (1991, 75). Like Foucault, Giddens observes that modern reflexivity is "far more than just 'getting to know oneself' better: self-understanding is subordinated to the more inclusive and fundamental aim of building/rebuilding a coherent and rewarding sense of identity" (1991, 75). "The self," he observes, "forms a trajectory of development from the past to the anticipated future" in which "the lifespan, rather than events in the outside world, becomes the dominant 'foreground figure' in the *Gestalt* sense" (1991, 75–76). "The key reference points [in narrative trajectories of the self] are set 'from the inside', in terms of how the individual constructs/reconstructs his [*sic*] life history" (1991, 80).

Although Foucault and Giddens agree that "modern" people must "produce themselves," and both recognize the task as onerous, they disagree on the forces that require people to undertake it. Giddens stresses the loss of "traditional" certainties. He argues that "by definition, tradition or established habit orders life within relatively set channels. Modernity confronts the individual with a complex diversity of choices and, because it is non-foundational"—in the sense that all apparent certainties are subject to revision on the basis of new evidence—modernity "offers little help as to which options should be selected" (1991, 80). Foucault, in contrast, emphasized the development of new constraints. He argued that the invention and proliferation of such "disciplines" as psychiatry, psychoanalysis, criminology, and population studies forced people to produce narratives of the self that explained their present predicaments in terms of past choices and life-span events (1973, 1975, 1977a, 1977b, 1978).

My fieldwork in Los Olivos leads me to side with Foucault in this debate. I do not think that the villagers I met in the 1980s had significantly more choices open to them than those I met in the 1960s—even though they talked and acted as if they did. My disagreement with Giddens is perhaps best illustrated by his discussion of "lifestyle." Giddens recognizes that "in conditions of high modernity, we all not only follow lifestyles, but in an important sense are forced to do so" (1991, 81). Why? Because, Giddens argues, "we have no choice but to choose" (1991, 81). "Lifestyle," he observes, "is not a term which has much applicability to traditional cultures, because it implies choice within a plurality of possible options, and is 'adopted' rather than 'handed down'" (1991, 81). I find this answer inadequate. As far as I could tell, people from Los Olivos had about the same range of lifestyle choices open to them during both my visits. In neither period could poor people emulate the lifestyles of the rich, however much they might have wanted to. And during both periods, people had some choice over how to spend the money that was available to them. The question I am forced to ask, therefore, is why did people in the 1960s talk about their lifestyles as if they were "handed down" whereas those in the 1980s talked about their lifestyles as if they were personally "adopted"? Put differently, why were people in the 1980s held responsible for having chosen their lifestyles when they had as little real choice as people in the 1960s? These questions lead me to follow Foucault in searching for "incitements to discourse."

My experiences in Los Olivos also lead me to prefer Foucault's account of the development of "modern sexuality" (1978) over Giddens's critique of it. In his book *The Transformation of Intimacy*, Giddens argues that "we cannot accept Foucault's thesis that there is more or less a straightforward path of development from a Victorian 'fascination' with sexuality through to more recent times" (1992, 23). The Victorians, he claims, were sexually repressed. Not until the invention of effective methods of birth control could women join men in seeking sexual pleasure (1992, 27).[21] Giddens, in fact, portrays women as the "emotional revolutionaries of modernity" (1992, 130), taking advantage of birth control to pursue the sexual pleasure that Freud said they had always wanted. I, of course, not only have doubts about Giddens's optimistic vision of increasing choices (as well as doubts about Freud's timelessness) but am convinced by my experiences in Los Olivos that Foucault was right to stress continuities between the Victorian fascination with sexuality and the more recent transformations of intimacy discussed by Giddens. In my research, I found that the "modern" villagers and former villagers I interviewed in the 1980s talked and acted more like the American Victorians described by D'Emilio and Freedman (1988) than the villagers I met in the 1960s. Throughout this book, in fact, I use examples drawn from *Doña Perfecta*, a Spanish novel published in 1876, to illustrate "modern"—as well as "traditional"—attitudes toward marriage and family life.

But if I follow Foucault in treating modern people's search for intimacy as produced by new constraints, rather than by women set free to pursue sexual pleasure, I look to different discourses than the ones Foucault identified in his book *The History of Sexuality* (1978). I do not doubt that the invention of such disciplines as psychoanalysis, sexology, and demography created communities of people dedicated to ferreting out the sexual secrets of their contemporaries. But in studying Los Olivos, I have been more impressed by the effects of daily discourses of inequality. In this book, therefore, I plan to explore connections between how people explained inequalities in wealth, power, and prestige and how they talked about their family relationships. I suggest that when people told stories of inherited wealth, they treated property as a crucial factor affecting relationships among kin. And when people told stories of occupational achievements, they talked about making families in much the same terms as they talked about making careers.

In summary, I plan to explore the relationship between people's changing experiences of social inequality—as the growth of capitalist industry and agriculture in Spain encouraged villagers from Los Olivos to imagine that occupational achievements were more important than inherited property for determining wealth—and the self-concepts that villagers used for monitoring, interpreting, and managing their own and others' actions. Exploring the relationship between wider "techniques of domination" and intimate "techniques of the self" is, of course, the research task proposed by Foucault "if one wants to analyze the genealogy of the subject in Western societies" (1980, quoted in Burchell 1993, 268). The experiences of people in one small Andalusian village can hardly explain the development of modern subjectivity in the West. But an ethnographic account of villagers' words and actions can suggest, in telling detail, how one group of people, living in a particular time and place, went about remaking themselves and their families as they remade their social world.

The analysis I present in this book reflects not only my theoretical interest in understanding social inequality but also the questions raised by the people I encountered in Los Olivos. When I first visited the village in 1963–64, most of the people I met wondered why their courtship and mourning customs seemed to be disappearing. When I returned in the 1980s, I found people wondering why the old customs had persisted for so long. Instead of trying to understand why old customs had disappeared, "young people" in the 1980s seemed more interested in figuring out why their older relatives, and they themselves in the past, had followed customs they now regarded as "village stupidities."

Although I started out trying to answer the villagers' questions, I soon found myself asking a question they had not. The conceptual tools of anthropology, which I used to explore why villagers in the 1960s might have wanted to observe onerous social conventions, forced me to ask why people in the 1980s might have wanted to follow very different customs. Unlike most of the villagers I spoke with, I could not simply accept the idea that people in the 1980s were doing what any normal, rational person would want to do. Rather, my commitment to searching for the rationality inherent in the "traditional mentality" forced me to treat "modern" courtship and mourning customs as requiring the same kind of explanation as the "traditional" customs "modern" people rejected. I thus embarked on the analysis of modern subjectivity that is the focus of this book.

A glance at ethnographies of rural Spanish communities written by other anthropologists from English-speaking countries suggests that their analyses, too, were shaped by the questions informants were asking—as well by shifts in Anglo-North American anthropological theory. The midcentury ethnographers who produced structural-functionalist studies of values, for example, can be seen as responding to Spaniards' concern for social stability and integration in the aftermath of a devastating civil war (e.g., Pitt-Rivers 1954; Peristiany 1965; Freeman 1970; Aguilera 1978).[22] Similarly, the studies of change produced by anthropologists working in the late 1960s and 1970s, which tended to focus less on the forces responsible for maintaining social stability than on those promoting the loss of traditions, can be seen as responding to informants' questions about why "young people" seemed to be abandoning the customs of their parents and grandparents (e.g., Aceves 1971; Aceves and Douglass 1976; Aceves, Hansen, and Levitas 1976; Barrett 1974; Brandes 1975; Douglass 1975; Greenwood 1976; Gregory 1978).

By the late 1970s, informants seemed to have stopped asking why customs were changing and were asking, instead, why traditional customs had persisted as long as they had. Behar, for example, observes that when she studied a Leonese village starting in 1978, "It was not the effects of sudden, recent change that was foremost in people's thoughts; what called for explanation, mediation, was the sense that things had for so long hardly changed at all" (1986, 13). In response, anthropologists tended to write historical studies tracing the long-term development and demise of "traditional" ways of life (e.g., Behar 1986; Harding 1984).[23] More recently, anthropologists appear to be responding to informants' growing interest in discovering and reviving the "traditions" that distinguish their *país* (nation, ethnic group) from other "nations" within the Spanish state. As nationalist discourses proliferated during the 1980s, anthropologists started writing histories that traced changes and developments in "traditions" (e.g., Mitchell 1990, 1991; Maddox 1993) or that analyzed the current revitalization of "traditional" festivals (e.g., Boissevain 1992; Crain 1992; Murphy 1994).[24]

I too became interested in the proliferation of nationalist discourses. As the writing of this book dragged on through the 1980s into the 1990s, I began to wonder why people like Esteban and his wife had bought the *Gran enciclopedia de Andalucía* for their children rather than asking Esteban's lively mother to teach her grandchildren about their rich cultural heritage. As I participated in revitalized festivals on my return trips to Spain, I began to wonder about the origins of "traditional" customs, given that the most "traditional" of such "traditions" had not been part of the festivals I had observed in the 1960s. My developing analysis of modern subjectivity suggested an answer. If "modern" subjects must "think for themselves," then an analysis of the social processes responsible for defining some activities as coerced should provide insights into the social construction of other activities as freely chosen, and therefore as eligible for adoption by those who would seek traditions expressing the desires of their ethnic souls.

This book is divided into six chapters following this introduction. Because I plan to explore the nature of modern subjectivity by focusing on how the shift from a discourse of inherited status to one of occupational achievement encouraged people born in Los Olivos to "think for themselves" rather than "follow social conventions," I begin with a chapter

tracing the economic processes that changed peoples' experiences of social inequality and so encouraged them to revise the stories they told to
explain why some people enjoyed more power, privilege, and prestige
than others. The next four chapters then explore the development of
modern subjectivity by tracing changes in how people talked about and
enacted their relationships with kin. Each chapter focuses on a different
aspect of kinship, moving through the life cycle of adults from courtship
to marriage, parenting, and mourning. I decided to consider the different aspects of kinship separately, rather than contrasting kinship practices in the 1980s to those in the 1960s, in order to break up my narrative of transformation. Although the changes that occurred were all
interrelated, discussing them separately allows me to explore the particular contradictions experienced by people who passed through similar
life stages at different historical moments. In the final chapter of the
book, I use my analysis of modern subjectivity to explore the revival of
tradition that people from Los Olivos are expressing through wearing
Andalusian costumes, dancing Andalusian dances, singing Andalusian
songs, and cooking Andalusian dishes.

---

Because I introduce each chapter of this book with brief quotations
from the nineteenth-century novel *Doña Perfecta* and because I plan to
draw examples from it to illustrate the contrast between "thinking for
oneself" and "following social conventions," I will briefly describe the
novel's plot. On a superficial level, the plot is simple, and the principal
characters are easy to remember because their names are ironic. Pepe
Rey (who is not the king of Enlightenment reason he imagines himself
to be) is invited to the rural city of Orbajosa by his father's widowed
sister, Doña Perfecta (who is not the perfect exemplar of traditional
Catholic virtue she imagines herself to be), to consider marrying Doña
Perfecta's only child, her innocent daughter Rosario, heir to the largest
property in town. The story focuses on the contest between Pepe Rey
and Doña Perfecta, as he falls in love with Rosario and Doña Perfecta
turns against the marriage when she decides that Pepe Rey is an atheist.
Doña Perfecta locks Rosario in her room. Pepe Rey plots to elope with
her. Doña Perfecta orders Pepe Rey shot when he enters the garden to
fetch Rosario. Pepe Rey dies, Rosario goes insane, and Doña Perfecta is
left to spend the rest of her life alone with her pedantic bachelor
brother-in-law, Don Cayetano.

In the final chapters, the author, Benito Pérez Galdós, reveals the ulti-
mate cause of the novel's tragedy. A priest, Don Inocencio (the most
guilty character in the novel), used his position as Doña Perfecta's con-

fessor to convince the devout lady that Pepe Rey was an atheist. Don Inocencio acted at the request of his widowed niece, Doña Remedios (her remedies bring disaster), who solicited his help in preventing Pepe Rey's marriage to Rosario because she wanted her son, Jacintito the lawyer, to marry the wealthiest heiress in town. Galdós, by exposing his characters' motives rather than by focusing on conflicting social conventions, reveals his own "modern" mentality.[25]

## CHAPTER ONE

# Social Inequality:
# From Inherited Property to
# Occupational Achievement

Doña Remedios, facing the fact that her son may not
succeed in marrying the richest heiress in town, laments,

"What has my son got out of . . . making such
excellent marks, and being the pride and joy of
Orbajosa . . . ? He'll starve to death, for we know
now how much a law practice pays; or else he'll
have to go licking some Deputy's boots for a post
in Havana, where he'll die of yellow fever."
*(Pérez Galdós 1960 [1876], 202)*[1]

IN THE SUMMER OF 1983, a woman who had been born in Los Olivos
during the 1920s explained the economic situation of her natal family.
Encarnación said that her family had been one that "had something"
[tenían algo] in contrast to poorer families that had little. Her mother's
father had been rich and left "capital" in land to all his children. But
most of the properties her mother brought with her into marriage had
been gradually sold off to pay the debts of Encarnación's father, who
had been born to a wealthy commercial family but whose own commercial ventures tended to fail. By the time of the civil war in 1936, Encarnación's family was reduced to one large house, a large farm, and a
truck. But they lost these during the war. By the war's end, Encarnación's widowed mother was left with only a small house and a little
walled garden. When Encarnación contrasted her father's fate with the
fates of his brothers, she suggested that those brothers who married well
and ran successful businesses became wealthy, whereas those who failed
to marry into wealth, or who squandered the properties of wealthy
wives, sank into poverty.

That same summer, Encarnación's son Miguel, who had been born in
the 1940s, told a very different story to explain his economic situation.
He talked about the jobs he had held. When he left school at the age of
fifteen, he said, he went to work in the construction business. But he was

fired after a year because the company he worked for had a policy of dismissing workers before they became eligible for permanent positions. During that year, however, he studied at night, learning to become a plumber. So, when he was fired, he boarded a train for the north and found work immediately in his new specialty. He had to take time out to do required military service, but easily found another job when he was released. He acquired his present job after reading a newspaper announcement about openings in a government-run enterprise. More than seven hundred people took the job entrance exam. The enterprise hired only fourteen workers, one of whom was Miguel.

This shift from stories of inherited properties to stories of occupational achievements marks the change in discourses of inequality that I want to discuss in this chapter. The people of Los Olivos participated in the dramatic transformation of the Spanish countryside that occurred between 1950 and 1970 (see Brandes 1975; Aceves and Douglass 1976; Aceves, Hansen, and Levitas 1976; Pérez Díaz 1976; Gregory 1978; Cazorla 1980; Harding 1984). As the Franco regime moved from an economic policy of self-sufficiency to participation in the world market (see Carr and Fusi 1981; Herr 1971; Shubert 1990), the village system of preindustrial capitalist agriculture collapsed. Emigration, which had been occurring at a steady low rate since at least the turn of the century, doubled in the 1960s, leaving the village with only a third of its pre-1960 population. In this chapter I describe these economic and demographic changes. I also explore how the people of Los Olivos experienced them by focusing on differences in the stories people told to explain why some individuals enjoyed more wealth, prestige, and power than others.

In 1963–64, when Los Olivos farmers could still sell their produce and emigration had not yet risen from a trickle to a flood, most of the villagers I talked with told stories like that told by Encarnación. They explained inequalities in wealth by talking about the amount of property—principally land, but also stores—that a family had inherited. At that time, Los Olivos was a farming village. The size of a family's landed estate did appear to determine its members' wealth, activities, and possessions. When villagers tried to explain why families owned different amounts of land, they focused on inheritance. They traced the kinship connections through which titles to property had passed. And they talked about how individuals had managed the properties they inherited. Although a few villagers earned their living from trades rather than farming, my conversations with people about stonemasons, carpenters, or barbers also tended to focus on the kinship ties that had enabled artisans to learn their skills.

Twenty years later, the villagers and migrants I interviewed—many of whom were the same people I had spoken with in 1963–64—usually told stories like that told by Encarnación's son Miguel. They talked about the occupational achievements of family members, principally husbands, sons, and fathers. Because many former villagers were employed in cities, the positions (*colocaciones*) they held did appear to determine their incomes, activities, and possessions. When the people I interviewed tried to explain why some people earned higher wages or profits than others, they tended to tell stories about the personal characteristics, particularly intelligence, ambition, education, and hard work that—they implied—determined whether or not a person succeeded in obtaining a well-paying job or in making profitable business deals. Some villagers and migrants had, of course, used family connections to obtain their jobs or had inherited the small businesses they managed, but our conversations about these people usually focused less on their kinship ties than on the intelligence, skill, and ambition they had displayed in deploying their inherited resources.[2]

This shift from telling stories about inherited properties to telling stories about occupational achievements evokes the distinction often made between "traditional," "closed" societies in which status is ascribed at birth and "modern," "open" societies in which people achieve the statuses they enjoy. Although I stress connections between talk of inherited properties and a notion of ascribed status, and connections between talk of occupational attainments and the idea of achieved status, I do not argue that the system of social inequality in Los Olivos changed from one based on ascription to one based on achievement. Not only would it be difficult to decide if such a change occurred,[3] but I suspect that in Spain, as in other capitalist countries, status is still inherited in the sense that parental rank remains the best predictor of a person's income.

The stories told by Encarnación and Miguel also reveal that the shift in discourses of inequality was more subtle that the simple replacement of inheritance by achievement. Both criteria figure in both stories. Encarnación's family would have remained wealthy if her father had not squandered the wealth he and his wife had inherited. Miguel would not have had to take a blue-collar job at the age of fifteen if he had been born to a family wealthy enough to set him up in business or to educate him for a profession. The shift that occurred, therefore, was not the replacement of one criterion for the other but rather a reversal in the role accorded to each in explanations for inequality. Encarnación's story assumed that inherited property was the major determinant of wealth. She invoked individual accomplishments primarily to explain why some people ended up with more or less property than they had inherited from their parents. Miguel's story focused on individual achievements. He did not mention inherited wealth, but probably would have if he had been asked to compare his career to the careers of professionals and business owners.

This chapter is divided into five sections and a brief conclusion. I begin with a description of social inequality in Los Olivos as I observed it in 1963–64, followed by a discussion of the economic and political processes that created, and then transformed, the egalitarian village I encountered on my first visit. The third section considers the effect of economic changes on people's experiences of social inequality whereas the fourth explores the relationship between discourses of economic and moral worth—between "doing well" and "doing good." In the fifth and final section I discuss the stories that people told during the 1980s to explain why some individuals were doing better than others. Because these stories attribute success or failure to the personal characteristics of protagonists, they provide vivid examples of how people in the 1980s took on the "modern" task of "producing" themselves.

## LOS OLIVOS IN THE 1960s

When I arrived in Los Olivos in the fall of 1963, I was impressed by the homogeneity of its population. The village lacked the extremes of wealth and poverty visible in nearby market towns. Some village families had larger houses than others, but no one had a mansion of the kind found in the commercial and administrative center of Aracena. There were no houses with three stories, marble entry halls, and formal reception rooms with frescoed ceilings. Nor did the village have resident beggars. The first villagers I met stressed the egalitarian nature of their community. They told me that Los Olivos was a "poor" village where everyone was related to everyone else. Unlike wealthier towns, they said, Los Olivos had no rich people who refused to associate with the poor.[4]

My early field notes record my impressions of a picturesque Andalusian village. I admired its huddled-together whitewashed houses, narrow stone-paved streets, ancient church, lovely fountains, and beautiful countryside. Los Olivos was a farming community, and smelled like one. Most village houses had stables for donkeys, chickens, and goats attached to them, as well as cavelike storerooms for hanging homemade sausages and attic rooms for storing fodder, fruits, and potatoes. Chickens roamed the streets, and other animals passed through on their way to and from work or grazing. The village was surrounded by its fields. Level with the village and below it were irrigated lands, divided into small, walled gardens where people grew fruit trees and seasonal vegetables. Above the irrigation level, both on the village side of the valley and across the main stream, were unirrigated fields planted in olives and two species of useful oaks. The higher gullies were lined with chestnut trees, the lower stream banks with poplars for roof beams. I marveled at the manicured countryside; it was an ecologist's dream. Every gully was dammed to prevent erosion, every spring and stream tapped for irrigation, and every square foot of earth put to some useful purpose.

The village had two small stores that sold canned goods, staples, utensils, shoes, and even fodder. It also had two bars, one in the upper plaza and one in the lower. A baker produced wonderful bread that his sister sold from a room in the house across the street from the wood-burning oven. A butcher sold meat, mostly goat, two days a week. Two brothers delivered fresh seafood daily. They had a market stall in a larger town and brought what they had not sold—usually sardines and octo-pus, with an occasional shark—to Los Olivos, where their sisters sold it from a back room of their house. One man owned a large truck that he used for transporting produce to major cities; a few others had vans for selling Los Olivos fruit in neighboring towns; and several men had mule trains for local hauling. The village had a barbershop for men (one room on the lower plaza that doubled as a dentist's office) and a couple of hairdressers for women who specialized in teasing hair to produce the poufs then popular. There was a part-time carpenter, a man who was called "the shoemaker," and at least two stonemasons. Some women sewed for others. At least one made men's clothes, and a couple of dress-makers specialized in the latest women's fashions, which they copied from magazines.

A few villagers received regular salaries. The sheriff (*alguacil*) and the town secretary who kept the civil registry were paid by the government, as were the postman and the *peón caminero* who maintained the local highway. The bottled-gas and electric companies had village representa-tives. A young woman who collected for an insurance/burial company received a portion of her take. Other villagers undoubtedly had part-time occupations that I did not know about. Everyone in the village seemed to pursue multiple strategies for making money.[5]

In 1963, the village included a few outsiders who lived and worked there. A doctor and two schoolteachers camped out in the modern, ce-ment houses built for them on the upper side of town. They spent as little time in the village as possible, preferring their city homes in Seville and Huelva. And the village had a resident contingent of Civil Guards (Guardia Civil) who lived with their wives and children in a barracks built from renovated old houses.

Other outsiders visited the village regularly. The parish priest, who lived in the next larger town, arrived each Sunday and holy day to hold services. The regional veterinarian came each week during the winter pig-killing season. Many traveling salesmen passed through. Peddlers regularly brought yard goods, which they sold to housewives, often on credit. A tinsmith came every few weeks to repair pots and pans, and a knife sharpener brought his combination bicycle–sharpenening wheel. A van with fresh seafood, offering more variety than the two brothers, appeared irregularly, as did vans selling ready-made clothing, pastries, or fruits and vegetables from other ecological zones.

Although the people of Los Olivos emphasized the poverty of their village and the equality of its inhabitants, I noticed that they also talked about wealth differences. The woman who took care of our house, for example, regularly commented on the amount of property owned by the people we encountered when walking together. On one occasion, I asked her about social classes in the village. My field notes from November 1963 report that "She says the rich do sort of consider themselves better than others but they do not refuse to mix with them. José Antonio's daughter [whom she had once described as stuck-up] still goes to all the parties and dances with the other girls of the town. All the young people band together without distinctions." I later realized that her choice of example was not accidental. By telling me that José Antonio's daughter attended parties and dances with the other village girls, she was providing the strongest possible evidence that Los Olivos lacked class distinctions. As I discuss in the next chapter on courtship, dancing together implied the possibility of marriage.[6]

From the housekeeper, and from other villagers, I came to understand Los Olivos as containing three, loosely bounded status groups defined by the amount of property, particularly land, that a family owned. I use the term "status groups" rather than "classes" for two reasons. First, I prefer to reserve "class" for labeling an analytic category, whereas here I am concerned with villagers' perceptions of status differences. Second, I doubt that there was a class distinction in Los Olivos by 1963. During the 1930s, Los Olivos had opposed classes of capitalist landowners and proletarian wageworkers (G. Collier 1987). But the shift from autarky to consumer society that occurred in Spain during the 1950s effectively erased class differences by 1963. The capitalization and mechanization of agriculture elsewhere in Spain so devalued the marginal lands of Los Olivos that landowners were left with as little productive capital as their workers.

In 1963–64, the highest status group resident in the village was composed of *propietarios*, landowners who hired laborers and who did not have to do agricultural work themselves, although some, particularly sons of landowners who had not yet received their inheritances, often worked as wage laborers on the lands they expected to inherit. The middle status group was composed of *autónomos*, families who had enough land to feed themselves, or who were able to support themselves by pursuing an independent trade. Members of such families occasionally hired others to work for them, and occasionally did wage work for others, but they could survive without having to hire themselves out. At the bottom of the status hierarchy were the *jornaleros*, day laborers who had to work for others because their families did not control enough land to feed family members.[7]

These three loosely bounded status groups all belonged to the middle tier of the three-tier Andalusian class system. Above the wealthiest villagers was a regionally based, propertied elite. Although a few elite families had houses in Los Olivos, none lived there year-round. Their primary ties were with other elite families living in more important towns and cities. These wealthy families owned the largest agricultural properties in Los Olivos, which they managed through foremen and hired workers. Other villagers frequently mentioned elite families and speculated on their members' activities. Nevertheless, villagers recognized that the elites who owned property in Los Olivos clustered at the bottom end of the Andalusian upper class. I can recall only one man being described as a *señorito*. Otherwise, villagers reserved the term for members of aristocratic or high bourgeois households known to them through the experiences of women who had been servants in Alajar, Aracena, Moguer, and Seville.

Conceptually below the three status groups resident in Los Olivos were mobile, landless laborers. Most of these were semiskilled mine or agricultural workers who traveled with their families around the region seeking employment, but there were also artisans, such as the traveling tinsmith. Many of the poorer families in Los Olivos had relatives who moved back and forth to the mines; several families had themselves moved and might have to do so again. Just as people often talked about absent members of the regional elite, so they often discussed relatives who had gone to live in ugly mining towns, among slag heaps, where the air was gray and flowers died. At the very bottom of the status hierarchy were people who pursued degrading occupations, such as prostitutes, beggars, and traveling entertainers. Gypsies belonged to a separate caste or ethnic group. Whereas villagers sometimes talked about falling into a degraded occupation, such as prostitution, I never heard anyone talk of becoming a gypsy.

In 1964, when the mayor ranked village households by wealth, using the 1950 census, he divided one hundred seventy-seven households into five categories.[8] He put only six households into the top category. Two of these belonged to professionals temporarily stationed in Los Olivos and the remaining four to elite families who by 1963 no longer lived year-round in the village. Of the remaining one hundred seventy-one households, twenty-three (13 percent) fell into the mayor's second category. These belonged to landowners who regularly hired laborers. The mayor's third category contained thirty-four households (20 percent) belonging to families who owned enough land to support themselves. The mayor put most village households—ninety-three (54 percent)— into his fourth category. These belonged to families with some land or a trade, but whose members lacked the resources to fully support themselves. They had to work as day laborers for others in order to supplement their incomes. The mayor's lowest category, composed of landless and near landless laborers, contained only twenty-one households. The bottom two categories, composed of families whose members had to work for others in order to survive, comprised 67 percent of the one hundred seventy-one village households.

It is difficult to estimate the actual distribution of village property in the early 1960s. Men from the wealthiest families, who were responsible for recording taxable properties, had good reason to fudge the numbers, whether they did so or not. A survey of landownership conducted around 1932 revealed that one household head (whose heirs had moved away by 1963) owned one-fourth of the land in the municipality, while 70 percent of municipal land was controlled by 25 percent of household heads. At the time, "this distribution was more equitable than in other Sierra de Aracena municipalities" (G. Collier 1987, 94). By 1963, the distribution of property was probably even more equitable because emigrating villagers usually left their lands for kin to farm.

Although the villagers I met in 1963–64 preferred to stress their equality, evidence of inequality was everywhere apparent. No villager lived in a mansion with frescoed ceilings, but village houses ranged from spacious to cramped. A few were large enough to have an entry hall, separate sitting and dining rooms, and a family parlor in addition to the universal kitchen and bedrooms. The poorest houses had only a living area—for combined cooking, eating, sitting, and greeting—and some closet-sized bedrooms. In wealthier households, the principal rooms were floored with brick tiles. Poorer families had stone pavements, and the poorest lived on dirt floors. Most of the wealthier households had servants; village girls from poor families came daily to haul water from the fountain, empty the slops, wash the clothes, sweep the house, help with the cooking, watch the children, and perform other needed chores. A couple of the wealthiest landowners even had live-in house servants as well as agricultural workers who lived on their estates.

I also noticed wealth differences in clothing. Men who belonged to landowning families tended to wear hats and jackets, albeit rather shapeless ones, whereas men who worked as day laborers wore berets and shirts. Among women, age was the best predictor of dress, but the dresses, skirts, and sweaters of women from landowning families usually fit better than the clothes of poor women. In the winter, everyone wore patched clothing for working outdoors, but wealthier people wore clothes with patches whereas the poor tended to wear patches that had been made into clothes. Every village woman had at least one good black dress for funerals, and every unmarried girl had at least one fashionable outfit for dances, festivals, and visits to the city. But wealthy women and girls had several sets of nice clothing whereas poor women had only one.

Agricultural work provided the primary arena for villagers to enact unequal social relations. Within the village, on evenings and holidays, people asserted their equality by drinking together (men), chatting together (women), and dancing together (youth). But when the sun rose on a working day, they performed different roles. Landowners expressed their superiority by strolling through their estates, observing the workers and occasionally lending a hand or giving a direction. People who worked their own fields or managed their own businesses expressed their autonomy by deciding for themselves what needed to be done and when to do it. Day laborers expressed their subservience by carrying out their employers' orders, even though they often resisted domination by deciding for themselves how, and on what timetable, to carry out assigned tasks.

## THE MAKING AND UNMAKING OF
## A "TRADITIONAL" COMMUNITY

During my first stay in Los Olivos, I thought that the stratification pattern I observed had been handed down from time immemorial. Only later did I realize that the apparently timeless village I encountered in 1963 had been produced by specific historical forces. When my husband and I returned to Spain in 1983 to collect family histories from villagers and emigrants, people were finally willing to talk about what had happened to them and their relatives during the Spanish Second Republic, the civil war, and the years of postwar repression. I learned that villagers had participated in the political struggles that were occurring simultaneously elsewhere in Andalusia, and in Spain generally (see G. Collier 1987).[9]

At the beginning of the twentieth century, Los Olivos was an agricultural village based on labor-intensive capitalist farming. It was in the orbit of Aracena, where owners of large estates had "recognized that neither more intensive cultivation nor new agricultural techniques would significantly increase crop yields and that holding down the price of labor was the principal way to maintain or increase their profits" (Maddox 1993, 107). Throughout the region, the landowning elites who controlled municipal governments used state power to keep "daily wages at minimal levels, paying day workers barely enough to provide a family of four with bread alone" (G. Collier 1987, 30). Low wages forced women and children into an already crowded labor market, and the overcrowding was further exacerbated when mine workers, dismissed after the collapse of the mining boom stimulated by World War I, began seeking agricultural jobs. After 1930, when the world depression diminished the profits of landowners, the employment problem reached critical proportions.

As unemployment rose and the dictatorship of Primo de Rivera gave way to the Spanish Second Republic, the villagers of Los Olivos polarized into two opposing political factions, one of "landowners" led by the political boss who owned at least a fourth of municipal lands and whose heirs later moved away, and the other composed of socialist "workers" who had been organized by union activists from the mining region to the south.[10] Both factions agreed that the high rate of male unemployment constituted an "employment crisis" but they disagreed over how to solve the problem.

The landowners wanted to use private charity for alleviating hunger, and they wanted to use municipal funds for employing those they defined as needy—measures that put workers into the position of having to beg the rich for handouts and jobs.[11] The socialists, in contrast, wanted to establish employment as a (male) worker's right. When the socialists finally wrested control of the municipal government from landowners in 1933, they established a list of available workers whom they assigned to jobs that syndicate officials thought needed doing, regardless of a landowner's wishes. There is no record that the socialists of Los Olivos advocated land reform, but they did portray land as a community resource, to be used for providing every family with the resources needed for making a living. This vision, of course, conflicted with the landowners' concept of land as private property, to be cultivated or left fallow as the owner decided. Understandably, landowners forced to pay workers who had been assigned to them by the socialist syndicate experienced the socialist program as a direct attack on their autonomy to manage their estates in the best interests of their families (G. Collier 1987, 95–97).[12]

The struggle between Los Olivos landowners and socialist workers for control of the municipal government came to an abrupt end in mid-August 1936, when General Franco's insurgent forces swept through the region. Franco's army returned municipal offices to the landowners and, within a year, "Thirty-eight socialist men—12 percent of the town's adult males—were killed" (G. Collier 1987, 146). Several other socialist men fled, a few to be captured and die later in prison. The problem of male unemployment was thus "solved." The landowners won a decisive victory. With the aid and blessing of the victorious Franco regime, they controlled village politics for the next three decades.

The postwar years were difficult for the people of Los Olivos, as for Spaniards generally, due to Spain's economic isolation, first caused by the outbreak of World War II and later by the victorious Allies' opposition to the Franco regime. Los Olivos villagers, however, probably suffered less than many Spaniards, particularly those living in devastated cities. The people I interviewed complained of having to subsist on tomatoes and apples rather than their preferred bread, but they did not starve. By the late 1940s, village agriculture had not only revived but expanded. Previously marginal land was brought into production. Labor was cheap. Widows and single mothers, unlike married women and unmarried girls, could be hired to do a man's work, but were paid a fraction of what a man earned. Fatherless children worked in return for food. Boys herded pigs in acorn groves, while girls ran household errands and cared for younger children. In the 1980s, when I interviewed surviving members of socialist families, I found that they differed in their recollections of the period. Some spoke bitterly about the exploitation they experienced and deeply resented the fact that poor children had to forgo schooling in order to survive. Others were grateful to the landowners who had employed them and who shared food with them in a time of general scarcity.

As the years passed, many survivors of socialist families moved away from Los Olivos, first to other Sierra de Aracena towns and, after the mid-1950s, to Huelva, Seville, and other cities in Spain. By "1960 about two-thirds of the pueblo's war orphans and widows . . . had left" (G. Collier 1987, 191), along with several other poor, primarily young, villagers. Their departure, combined with the fact that the wealthiest landowners had also moved away to more important towns, created the egalitarian community I encountered in 1963.[13]

Although I experienced Los Olivos as a living, vibrant community, many of the people I met portrayed it as dying. An older man told my husband that Los Olivos "was a bad place because there was only work in the fields, and there wasn't much food. There was no industry as in the bigger towns and cities. Here one found only children and aged people, for the younger adults went off to work elsewhere. Only those who had land stayed, the rest all leave."[14] Looking back, I too can see indications that the village was "dying." During the nine months I lived there with my husband and baby, there were nine deaths, no marriages, and no births. Our baby was the youngest child in town.

Los Olivos's "history of relatively steady net outmigration dating from early in the century" (G. Collier 1987, 188) had drained it of young adults. Before my arrival, however, most of the people who left were from land-poor families. And they did not fare particularly well. Most fell into the status group of mobile, landless workers pitied by Los Olivos residents. Those who fared better, by joining the Civil Guard or finding some urban employment, seldom returned to the village. Until the mid-1960s, almost everyone who could make a living in Los Olivos tried to avoid leaving. As the old man observed, people who had land stayed.

The year after I left the village, however, those who had land started leaving as well. Nineteen sixty-five turned out to be the decisive moment when emigration changed from a strategy of the poor and downwardly mobile to a strategy of the well-off and upwardly mobile. Members of the regional elite had long been sending their children away to be educated for nonmanual professions, and a few village families with the political connections to obtain scholarships had adopted this strategy as well. But most village landowners had kept their children at home. By 1965, however, so many landless villagers had left for urban employment that landowners had difficulty hiring workers at a wage that permitted a profit. Given the impossibility of mechanizing the rugged landscape, landowners and their heirs faced the prospect of having to farm the land themselves. Young men, in particular, realizing that they might have to perform the difficult and dirty agricultural tasks their parents had hired others to do, decided to emigrate instead.[15]

According to villagers, emigration from Los Olivos changed from a trickle to a flood after one young man—who had followed his fiancée to Catalonia when her Guardia Civil father was transferred there in 1962— wrote to his parents and age-mates about the high wages and choice of jobs available around Barcelona. One migrant interviewed in 1983 said that in the early 1960s he was paid 350 pesetas for a seven-day workweek as an agricultural day laborer in Los Olivos[16] but earned 750 pesetas after moving to Catalonia. He had to work a similarly long week but earned considerably more because Barcelona employers, unlike village ones, paid overtime. Life was hard in Catalonia, however. Until housing construction began to catch up with demand in the late 1960s, families migrating from Los Olivos usually lived crowded together in decaying farmhouses without electricity or running water.

Most of the early migrants to Catalonia were young and either unmarried or just married. Those I interviewed in the 1980s told of being "called" to Catalonia by their age-mates and kin who were already resident there. In addition to the family of the youth who followed his fiancée, a socialist family, who had left Los Olivos in the 1950s and arrived in the suburbs of Barcelona by a circuitous route, also began "calling" their relatives (G. Collier 1987, 193–197). The young people who answered such calls then began calling their parents and younger siblings to join them. Migration to Catalonia snowballed until the early 1970s, when an economic recession exacerbated by the OPEC oil crisis limited the availability of jobs. But by that time, Los Olivos had been transformed.

In the early 1960s, agriculture was still thriving in Los Olivos. Villagers who owned land shipped truckloads of fruit to Seville, beginning with early spring oranges, through summer peaches, fall pears and apples, to winter chestnuts and olives. But competition from capital-intensive agriculture elsewhere in Spain slowly began to drive Los Olivos produce off the market. Urban buyers preferred the large, unblemished fruits produced with chemical fertilizers and pesticides to the tasty, but small and often wormy, fruits from Los Olivos orchards. As the market for Los Olivos produce declined and wages rose, absentee landowners changed their strategies. One fired most of his workers in 1964 and began renting out his better lands. Shortly thereafter, another converted his large holdings from food crops to a eucalyptus plantation for supplying the paper mill in Huelva. Most resident landowners, however, lacked the cash or the social contacts to convert their enterprises. They continued in the fruit business until, "one sad day in the late 1960's, two truckloads of Los Olivos fruit could not be sold at any price—the truckers had to pay to unload their fruit at the dump" (G. Collier 1987, 192).

Before the market for Los Olivos fruit collapsed, people tended to treat farming and emigration as comparable choices. In Los Olivos, as in other rural areas of Spain, high emigration and the availability of urban jobs transformed farming from a way of life into another way of making a living (see Harding 1984). But until 1970, farming was a respectable occupation. Those who compared the advantages of farming and factory labor usually noted that although factory workers received regular wages and enjoyed paid vacations, farmers did not have to submit to bosses or live in ugly cities.

Events in the 1970s, however, undermined the apparent balance between industrial and agricultural labor. After village farmers were no longer able to sell their fruit in Seville, many landowners who had decided earlier to continue working family lands with their own labor decided to seek urban employment instead. Unfortunately, the economic crisis in Spain had reduced the urban demand for "unskilled" labor.[17] As a result, most of the farmers who tried to emigrate after 1970 could not find jobs that paid enough to support their families. Several returned to Los Olivos to resume farming. But their return transformed farming from a respectable, chosen occupation to a sign of failure.

By the time I returned to Los Olivos in the 1980s, farming was a low-status occupation. The only people who praised agricultural labor were retired pensioners and salaried semiprofessionals who did not have to make a living from it. People who obtained most of their income from farming usually told me that they would prefer to be doing something else. I cannot recall anyone praising a young man or woman for taking up agricultural labor in lieu of study or an urban job. Whenever a young goatherd passed by, for example, the villagers I was with would invariably comment on how sad it was that such a promising young man had not been able to find urban employment. And the parents of a young woman who dropped out of school to work as an agricultural day laborer were horrified at her choice.

When I interviewed villagers and emigrants in 1983–84 about changes in Los Olivos, many survivors of socialist families commented on the apparent inversion of status. The former poor had become rich, they said, while the former rich had become poor. Because many villagers from socialist and poor families emigrated in the 1950s and 1960s, when urban jobs were expanding, they were able to find secure positions that paid regular salaries and offered benefits such as month-long paid vacations. Heirs of victorious landowners, in contrast, who postponed emigrating until the economic crisis of the 1970s, had to return to farming after failing to find urban employment. In the 1980s, they were condemned to working long hours for little return. Although this picture of status inversion was true in general outline, it was complicated by the fact that heirs of the regional elite and the children of municipal officials, who had been trained for nonmanual professions, continued to enjoy superior status, whereas members of poor families who had not emigrated during the 1960s remained at the bottom of the status hierarchy.[18]

## EXPLAINING CHANGE

In the introduction to this book, I noted that the people I interviewed during both my visits to Los Olivos tended to attribute the shift from "following social conventions" to "thinking for oneself" to the loosening of constraints on people's freedom to act as they pleased. "Young people," they said, "no longer wanted" to observe such village customs as long courtships and extended mourning periods once television had "opened their eyes" to new possibilities and emigration allowed them to escape from nosy village gossips. This tendency to attribute change to the "opening up" of a formerly "closed" community echoes the explanations for change collected by other ethnographers of Spanish villages. Aceves and Douglass, for example, introduced their edited volume *The Changing Faces of Rural Spain* with the observation that "Perhaps the key variable that permeates all these essays is the 'opening up' of Spanish rural society. . . . By 'opening up,' we mean a set of processes and events that allow the rural Spaniard a choice of behaviors from an expanded repertoire of behavioral alternatives. No longer need son follow father in traditional occupations and modes of thinking; new and viable alternatives have come into existence, alternatives that either never existed before or were never perceived by the rural people to exist. These alternatives are becoming ever more known as contact with the 'outside world' becomes commonplace" (1976, xi).

Although no one can doubt that television and expanded job opportunities played important roles in the dramatic changes that occurred in Los Olivos, I found myself forced to question the "opening up" hypothesis for two reasons. First, I doubted that the village had been as "closed" as the hypothesis suggests. My field notes and memories from 1963–64 reveal that villagers were not ignorant of urban ways. There may have been only four television sets in town, some trucks but no cars, and few returned migrants to tell stories of urban life, but the villagers I spoke with were aware of how urbanites thought and acted. Many of them watched nightly television in the local bars. Several women had been servants in urban areas before returning to marry in the village. And village women regularly perused glossy magazines depicting the clothes, lives, and loves of film stars and royalty. I also recall many conversations with villagers in which they contrasted their courtship and mourning customs with urban ones. When the villagers I knew in 1963–64 observed long formal courtships and extended mourning periods, they did so with full knowledge that people in urban areas not only thought and behaved differently but also disparaged such village customs as "rural" and "backward." Second, I doubted that the availability of urban jobs had allowed people to escape from the surveillance of gossiping neighbors. I actually heard more gossip in 1983–84 than I had in 1963–64, although this may have occurred because I knew more people and was therefore more fun to gossip with. Nevertheless, the ease with which I collected stories about absent others led me to realize that travelers and migrants to large, anonymous cities had not succeeded in evading the scrutiny of people whose good opinion they valued. People who moved among strangers may have escaped daily surveillance, but they had not escaped having their activities endlessly discussed and evaluated by kin and former neighbors. I did, however, notice a change in how people talked about gossip. In the 1960s, villagers frequently mentioned the neighbors' propensity to gossip. In the 1980s, people gossiped but rarely talked about gossiping neighbors.[19]

Finally, my theoretical framework forced me to question the unstated assumption underlying the "opening up" hypothesis: the idea that once people have been exposed to "modern" ways, they "naturally" want to adopt them. Because I assume that people always want to do what they do (at least on some level), I must explain why people who wanted to follow social conventions in the 1960s wanted to think for themselves by the 1980s. I thus suggest that television and opportunities for urban employment did not simply offer villagers exposure to different ways of behaving and an expanded range of occupational choices. Rather, I argue that people taking advantage of new opportunities changed the wider socioeconomic context for everyone, transforming the consequences of individual action.

Spanish sociologist Victor Pérez Díaz also explored the wider socioeconomic effects of television and emigration on rural villages. Adopting a historical view in his study of a Castilian peasant community (1974, 1976), he observed that rural Spanish villages were never as isolated from wider social processes as some observers portrayed them. Rather, rural communities "have submitted throughout their history to a continuous process of change as a result of external pressures as well as internal tensions" (Pérez Díaz 1976, 123). " 'Traditional' rural society had emerged in the second half of the nineteenth century as a result of population growth, expansion of cultivation, and disentailment, and it had been continuously but slowly undermined by urban and industrial development. Finally, during the [nineteen] sixties, it collapsed" (Pérez Díaz 1976, 126). Emigration was a major factor in the collapse of "traditional" rural society, "not only by bringing back to the countryside 'elements' of urban and industrial culture, but in the sense of undermining technological and economic arrangements on which rural economies were based" (Pérez Díaz 1976, 126).

In Los Olivos, as I have observed, the agricultural economy collapsed after day laborers emigrated to industrial jobs and competition from capital intensive agriculture elsewhere in Spain destroyed the market for Los Olivos produce. Rising labor costs and disappearing markets undermined the profitability of farming in a region where mechanization was impractical. The immediate causes of change, emigration and the opening up of the village to outside ideas, did not simply alter the hierarchy of people's occupational choices, replacing a preference for

local farming with one for emigration to an industrial job. Rather, emigration, along with the loss of markets for village produce, transformed
people's experiences of social mobility and their understandings of
work.

When I first visited Los Olivos, downward mobility was the primary
experience, and fear, of the people I met. One of the first things a friend
told me was that her father had a farm large enough to support his family, but because he had eight children, none of the children inherited
enough land to be able to make a living without having to work for
others. In Los Olivos, parents divided their property equally among all
children. Those who had more than one child, therefore, did have to
worry about how to provide each child with enough land to replicate the
parents' lifestyle (see Friedl 1962).

But land was difficult to acquire and hard to keep. All the land in the
municipality was already owned. One family could acquire more of it
only if another family—usually a neighboring and well-known one—lost
property. In the past, a couple of village families had traded lands, and
one man sold his Los Olivos property in order to purchase land elsewhere, but such egalitarian transfers were rare. More frequently, those
who acquired land did so at the expense of others. In the period during
and after the Spanish civil war, several socialist families had to sell or give
up land in order to ransom imprisoned relatives or solicit support from
political leaders. But no one involved in such land transactions—either
buyers or sellers—benefited from publicly recalling past tragedies, particularly during the years of General Franco's dictatorship.

At the same time, sources of income apart from land ownership
seemed of doubtful worth and required capital or skills difficult to obtain except through inheritance or help from kin. Local commercial enterprises were in decline, suffering from external competition. The flour
mills and olive press that operated after the civil war closed in the 1950s,
as did some of the larger village stores. The only artisanal skill that remained lucrative in 1963—stonemasonry—was passed down within
families and it was not clear that the village could, in fact, support more
stonemasons. People could make money by growing fruit and by truck-
ing village produce to urban markets, but fruit-growing required good
land and aspiring truckers needed both driver's licenses and cash for
down payment on a vehicle. There was also the possibility of emigration.
During my first visit to Los Olivos, a few villagers were away working in
Germany and Switzerland. None, however, was expected to return in
the near future and most of the stories I heard about them concerned
their homesickness and problems with Germans. Moreover, no emigrant
had returned wealthy since the 1930s. Three of the largest landowners
in the village earned the money they used to buy their estates by emi-

grating to America in the 1920s. But, as I noted above, few people wanted to discuss their successes because talking about their land purchases inevitably revived painful memories of the tragedies suffered by families who had been forced to sell land.

In contrast to the 1960s, when most of the villagers I met feared downward mobility, most of the people I met in the 1980s seemed to expect and hope for upward mobility. The growth of industry and commercial agriculture during the 1950s and 1960s had created jobs paying very different amounts. By the 1980s, people born in Los Olivos were participating in the national labor market, where employers justified hiring, promotion, and wage decisions as reflecting the market value of a worker's labor, determined through competition with other job seekers. Although the economic crisis of the 1970s had led to rising unemployment, the fact that employers claimed to pay workers for the "value" of their work encouraged people to imagine that individuals who could increase the value of their labor could acquire better jobs and earn higher wages. Seven hundred people might take a job entrance exam, but each applicant could hope to replicate Miguel's achievement and be among the fourteen hired for the job. Men and women born in Los Olivos may have remained, by and large, in the lower echelons of Spain's economic pyramid, but all paid workers could hope to make more money than they were presently earning.[20]

The shift from an agricultural economy to participation in the national labor market also changed villagers' experience of the relationship between work and social status. During both of my visits to Los Olivos, most families depended on wage work to survive. As I noted earlier, the mayor in 1963 estimated that 67 percent of village families were supported wholly or in part by the wages family members earned. That percentage had probably increased by the 1980s. But between 1960 and 1980, the role of wage work in determining a family's status relative to other families changed dramatically.

In the 1960s, wages were less important than property ownership in determining a family's income and lifestyle, even among the majority of families who had to work for wages. At that time, almost all the jobs available were in agriculture and domestic service, neither of which required special skills. Almost every village man knew how to do male agricultural tasks and almost every woman knew how to keep house and do the agricultural tasks commonly performed by women. Moreover, the low minimum wage earned by day laborers was set by law rather than by market forces. It varied with a worker's sex, age, and marital status rather than with a worker's abilities or the nature of the task performed. As a result, land ownership remained the most important determinant of family's status relative to other families. Just as owners of large properties enjoyed more wealth than owners of small ones, so workers who had been fortunate enough to inherit houses and small plots of land enjoyed a better lifestyle than workers whose lack of property forced them to spend most of their meager earnings on rent and food.

Moreover, villagers in the 1960s lived in a social world where the wealthiest landowners appeared not to "work" at all. They hired others to perform needed agricultural and domestic tasks. As a result, the people I met on my first visit to Los Olivos experienced "working" as a sign of low status. It signified that someone was too poor to hire others. Working for wages signified the lowest status. Members of families who owned enough land to support themselves could at least care for their own properties while they performed needed agricultural and domestic tasks. But people who had to work for wages were forced to leave home to work on the lands and houses of others.

By the 1980s, in contrast, "work"—particularly for wages—had become not only the major determinant of a family's wealth relative to others but also a source of prestige. Families in which wage earners received good salaries enjoyed considerably better lifestyles than families in which adults earned only the minimum wage, were underemployed, or were unemployed. Although most workers from Los Olivos held positions in the blue- and pink-collar sectors of a labor market segmented by sex, age, and class (as well as by region, ethnicity, and race), the hiring practices of employers—combined with fact that many workers from Los Olivos held jobs that paid considerably more than the minimum wage set by law—created a social environment in which the size of workers' paychecks did appear to depend on the market value of their labor, as determined through competition with other workers. Even among those who were self-employed, a person's "productivity" appeared more influential than inherited property in determining income. Farmers and shopkeepers who had improved their properties through hard work and creative investments earned higher profits than those who, for one reason or another, had failed to expand their enterprises. By the time I returned to Los Olivos in the 1980s, people no longer lived in a social world where the wealthiest adults did not "work." Quite the contrary. The richest people not only worked but credited their work with making them wealthy.

## DISCOURSES OF ECONOMIC AND MORAL INEQUALITY

These dramatic shifts in people's experiences of social mobility and work required them to develop different explanations for why some people might enjoy more wealth, prestige, and power than others. Encarnación's and Miguel's stories reveal, in a particularly dramatic way, the shift from stories of inherited properties to stories of occupational achievements that is the focus of this chapter. Before industrialization offered agricultural workers access to better jobs and Los Olivos farmers lost markets for their produce, the amount of land a family owned did appear to determine the income and lifestyle of its members. It made sense for people like Encarnación to explain their economic situations by telling stories about the properties they had—or had not—inherited. After the changes, when many villagers held jobs in factories and offices, it made sense for them to explain their economic situations by recounting the job histories of family wage earners.

But if such stories appeared factually true, they also contained moral overtones. Doing well and doing good are inevitably connected. Whatever storytellers might intend, their explanations of why people succeeded or failed necessarily convey information about the speaker's answer to the question of whether the protagonists deserved their fates. All explanations for inequalities in wealth, prestige, and power have to draw connections between economic and moral worth. But the actual relationship they posit between doing well and doing good tends to vary according to the nature of the inequalities being explained.

I never heard friends from Los Olivos repeat the clichés "tanto tienes, tanto vales" [what you own or have is what you are worth] and "tanto cobras, tanto vales" [what you earn or charge is what you are worth]. But these sayings were popular in Spain at the time of my fieldwork and the difference between owning and earning captures the subtle shift in linkages between economic and moral discourses that I want to explore.[21] Both clichés are ironic. They purport to express a literal truth while reflecting the speaker's outrage at the situation. A person's moral worth should reflect his or her virtue, not wealth. Nevertheless, wealth and virtue tend to coincide, even if the coincidence is never perfect.[22] Because rich people usually enjoy both the influence to publicize their virtues and the power to distribute social rewards, the relationship that elites draw between doing good and doing well tends to enjoy wide currency.[23]

I focus on the relationship between doing well and doing good because such discourses of inequality expose the "techniques of the self" enjoined on those who would gain the respect of their fellows—or who would at least try to avoid their condemnation and contempt. Owning and earning, I suggest, implied very different "attitudes" toward the self and the world. Owning encouraged an attitude of trying to "hang on" to what one had inherited from the past. Earning encouraged people to evaluate their inner capacities and take on the task of "producing themselves."

In the 1960s, when landownership appeared to be the major determinant of social inequality, village and regional elites who wanted to justify their privileges had to explain why they owned more land than other people. They commonly referred to inheritance. Even though many of the wealthiest families had in fact bought their estates, or acquired land from desperate socialist families after the civil war, inheritance—as I noted earlier—was the most acceptable explanation for privilege. When elites tried to explain why their families had provided larger inheritances than other families, they commonly credited their ancestors with having successfully protected the family's property and made advantageous marriages. As suggested by Encarnación's story of her father's failures, elites did not portray owning as a passive condition. Rather, they described it as an activity that involved not only defending the family's property and reputation from current threats but also forestalling downward mobility by pursuing such family-based strategies as marrying well, limiting the number of heirs, and maintaining ties with distant kin who might die childless or provide assistance in times of need.

Such family strategies were, of course, more easily pursued by the rich than the poor. Wealthy people enjoyed more power to protect their properties and reputations than poor ones. And young people who expected large inheritances had an easier time finding a wealthy spouse than those who expected to inherit little or nothing. But even poor people could try to protect their properties and reputations, and to marry as well as they were able. If the children of poor people tended to end up with smaller inheritances and less desirable spouses than the children of rich ones, such outcomes merely confirmed the efficacy of elite strategies for avoiding downward mobility.

In the 1980s, when I returned to Los Olivos, the wealthiest villagers and emigrants no longer claimed to have inherited their privileges. Rather, they justified making higher salaries and larger profits than others by claiming to have earned them in open competition with other sellers of labor and commodities. Everyone knew, of course, that competition was not really open. They realized that the distribution of wealth in Spain reflected class advantages rather than differences in individual merit. After all, even the richest people from Los Olivos belonged to Spain's working class. They all knew—at least on some level—that market processes systematically disadvantaged people like them. Nevertheless, they lived in a social world where national and international elites—whose class advantages ensured their own success on the market[24]—organized and enforced the vision that earnings reflected merit. The banking and commercial elites who regulated Spain's commodity markets justified prices as reflecting supply and demand. Farmers who could produce more valued goods earned more money. And the urban employers who hired people from Los Olivos commonly justified the salaries they paid as reflecting the market value of a worker's labor. Even emigrants who had obtained their jobs through kin and who worked for small contractors reported that they kept their jobs because their bosses admired the quality of their labor. One construction worker proudly reported that his boss kept rehiring him because, his boss had told him, he laid tiles better and faster than anyone in the boss's acquaintance. People born in Los Olivos thus lived in a social world where they were continually being told not only that their earnings reflected the value of their individual labor but also that they could improve their earnings by increasing their productivity. Miguel's story of how he studied at night to become a plumber reflects this strategy for success.

The different relationships between economic and moral worth posited by the discourses of owning and earning are nicely captured in the nineteenth-century novel *Doña Perfecta*. In the quotation that introduces this chapter, Doña Remedios, the widowed niece of Doña Perfecta's priest, Don Inocencio, reproaches her uncle for failing to break the engagement of Pepe Rey, the engineer from Madrid, to Doña Perfecta's daughter Rosario. Doña Remedios wants her son, Jacintito the lawyer, to marry the richest heiress in town. In lamenting that "my beloved son is to remain forever a beggar" (Pérez Galdós 1960, 201), Doña Remedios reveals her assumption that inherited property—rather than individual achievement—determines a person's wealth. "What's the use of having talent? What's the use of so much studying and beating out his brains?" Doña Remedios cries (Pérez Galdós 1960, 201). Unless Jacintito marries an heiress, he will "starve to death, for we know now how much a law practice pays" (Pérez Galdós 1960, 202).

Because Doña Remedios is a poor person who expects to remain poor (albeit unwillingly), she tries to deny a relationship between moral and economic worth. "My poor, darling little boy!" she moans, "To be so good, and to have to spend his life condemned to poverty" (Pérez Galdós 1960, 202). Nevertheless, she suggests a strong link between economic failure and moral deficiency when she laments that unless her son marries an heiress, "He'll have to beg for a paltry job; . . . he'll have to go licking some Deputy's boots for a post in Havana" (Pérez Galdós 1960, 202). By suggesting that the poor have to beg and lick boots, she implies, however unwittingly, that poverty corrupts. People who are "starving" must put their need for food above their moral obligations to family and society. Doña Remedios thus endorses the vision of virtue advanced by landed elites who credit their high status to their own and their ancestors' faithful enactment of social conventions. For Doña

Remedios, as for the landed elites she aspires to join, riches enable rectitude.[25]

Pepe Rey, the engineer from Madrid, belongs to a different social world from the one inhabited by Doña Remedios and other residents of the rural city of Orbajosa. Although he comes from a respectable, professional family, Pepe Rey expects to rely on his own abilities, rather than on any inheritance he or his wife might receive, to determine his wealth and lifestyle. He plans to spend his time in Orbajosa exploring the local river bed for mining possibilities and surveying his inherited properties for their productive potential. He participates in an expanding market economy. In his view, wealth can be created by those with the vision and ambition to mine the earth, practice scientific farming, construct highways, build dams and railroads, and so forth. For Pepe Rey, what individuals "earn" through their work rather than what they "own" determines their wealth and lifestyles.

As a result, Pepe Rey draws a different connection between moral and economic worth than the one posited by Doña Remedios. In a scene near the beginning of the novel, Don Inocencio asks Pepe Rey about his first impressions of the rural city. Pepe Rey replies that "from the little I have seen, it seems to me that Orbajosa could do with half a dozen fortunes to spend on it, a couple of intelligent minds willing to direct its renovation, and a few thousand willing hands" (Pérez Galdós 1960, 31–32). By blaming Orbajosa's appearance of "ruin and death" (1960, 15) on the stinginess, idleness, and lack of ambition of its citizens, Pepe Rey suggests that moral failure breeds poverty. Like Doña Remedios, Pepe Rey assumes a correlation between moral and economic worth, but he reverses the causal arrow. Instead of treating wealth as a prerequisite for virtue, he regards rectitude as a requirement for riches.

In the novel, neither Doña Remedios nor Pepe Rey discusses wage work, but their imputations of moral failure suggest that they had different understandings of its ethical implications. Doña Remedios's reference to bootlicking suggests that she perceived selling one's labor as equivalent to selling one's soul. A person who received wages had to do whatever his or her employer required, however shameful or degrading. For Pepe Rey, in contrast, workers earned their just rewards. Instead of denying their moral being, workers realized themselves through their labor.

*Doña Perfecta* illustrates not only how contrasting visions of moral and economic worth can coexist and clash with one another but also how the encoding of such visions in social institutions shapes the consequences of people's actions, despite their desires or intentions. Pepe Rey, the engineer from Madrid, pays with his life for misunderstanding the moral vision of landed elites in his aunt's rural city. But if the novel provides apt examples for illustrating the competing ideologies of owning and earning, my use of it is misleading in the sense that Galdós was less interested in exploring how organizations of social inequality required elites to advance different justifications for their privileges than in contrasting the moral visions of the two elites who were contesting state power in Spain at the time he was writing. Galdós thus portrays the conflict as one between religious conservatives and liberal advocates of science and progress, rather than as one between landed elites justifying the unequal distribution of property and industrial elites justifying the unequal distribution of wages and profits.

Richard Maddox, in his history of the Sierra de Aracena (1993), reveals how the religious and scientific visions contrasted by Galdós were, in fact, easily reconciled. He reports that by the end of the nineteenth century, liberals and conservatives in the region around Aracena, which includes the village of Los Olivos, had joined forces and combined their competing ideologies into a consolidated justification for rule. "Class hegemony and political domination were simultaneously 'sacralized' and naturalized through a rhetorical confluence of progressive scientific and traditional religious discourses channeled to communicate the notion that the possession of 'knowledge and wisdom' created an unquestionable right to social power" (Maddox 1993, 128).

But if liberals in Aracena cooperated with conservatives in developing a consolidated justification for rule, the social institutions they jointly established reflected and enforced the moral vision of landed elites rather than that of industrial entrepreneurs. Together they created a social world in which owning was more important than earning. As I noted earlier, landowning elites in the region used their political power to enforce a very unequal distribution of property and to hold down the wages of agricultural day laborers. As a result, both rich and poor tended to share Doña Remedios's understanding of the relationship between wealth and virtue. They all lived in a social world where people who were already wealthy enjoyed greater leisure to cultivate the "knowledge and wisdom" that conferred social power. The poor were forced by lack of land to beg for the daily wage work that allowed them to survive, even as the lack of employment opportunities outside agriculture condemned them to participating in a job market where wages were determined by law rather than by market competition.

By 1980, however, people taking advantage of the employment and investment opportunities opened up by industrialization and the development of commercial agriculture elsewhere in Spain had transformed social institutions in the Sierra de Aracena. As men and women born in

Los Olivos participated in the wider national market, they created a world in which earning was more important than owning for determining a person's income and lifestyle. Pepe Rey's faith in science and progress may have been easily co-opted by conservative landed elites at the end of the nineteenth century, but his vision that riches awaited anyone with the intelligence and ambition to pursue them rang true in the 1980s. Once people were participating in job and commodities markets where buyers and employers justified pricing, hiring, and wage decisions as reflecting the market value of a worker's products or labor, virtue—in the form of an individual's ambition, hard work, and skilled deployment of resources—did appear to determine wealth.

Although people from Los Olivos tended to accept the moral visions of regional and national elites, they also contested them. Given their relatively low position on Spain's social ladder, villagers recognized that however hard they tried to realize elite values, they were unlikely to achieve elite status. But the oppositional discourses that people developed to question elite linkings of wealth and virtue nevertheless tended to reproduce crucial aspects of elite moral visions. When landed elites dominated the region, for example, people who contested the unequal distribution of property commonly wanted everyone to have enough land to support themselves without having to beg. They thus affirmed the elite vision that ownership enabled virtue. Similarly, when people contested this linkage between ownership and virtue, they commonly did so by affirming the elite vision that morality consisted of acting on moral principles rather than succumbing to bodily urges. Some young women, for example, wrote "El Camino de Todos" [The Road Everyone Travels] on a wall lining the road to the cemetery, suggesting that God judged people not by how much they owned but by how well they fulfilled the obligations associated with the station in life to which He had assigned them. For these young women, God might endow people with unequal wealth on Earth, but they were all equal as souls before God in Heaven.

In the 1980s, in contrast, people who wanted to contest elite equations of economic and moral worth no longer tended to equate virtue with self-denial. Rather, they commonly argued that people who earned little or nothing, such as homemakers, did useful and important work. But in affirming the value of low-paying and upaid labor, such critics endorsed the moral vision of elites that virtue consisted in realizing one's productive potential, whatever that might be. Similarly, when people in the 1980s proposed solutions to high unemployment, they no longer advocated giving each family the land it needed to produce its subsistence. Instead, most people favored job-creation programs and the passage of laws designed to prevent rich people and nations from monopolizing the most lucrative and interesting jobs. In short, people wanted the labor market to work as elite ideologists claimed it should. They wanted earnings to reflect merit rather than inherited advantage. For these people, nature endowed humans with unequal abilities, but laws should ensure them an equal chance to realize their productive potentials on Earth.

## EMPLOYMENT HISTORIES IN THE 1980s

In the previous two sections, I explored the relationship between people's experiences of social inequality and the moral visions contained in their explanations for why wealth, prestige, and power were unevenly distributed. I did so in order to uncover the "techniques of the self" associated with the different discourses of owning and earning, arguing that owning encouraged people to avoid downward mobility by hanging on to their family inheritances and reputations whereas a discourse of earning encouraged them to seek upward mobility by actively taking charge of producing themselves.

Because the attitude of "hanging on" is amply illustrated in the sections of the next several chapters dealing with "traditional" kinship practices, I plan to devote this section to exploring the stories of occupational achievement told by people in the 1980s. On the surface, employment histories appear to have little to do with how people imagine and manage their relationships with kin. But I plan to argue in the sections on "modern" kinship practices in the subsequent chapters that people in the 1980s took on the task of "producing" their families in much the same way they took on the task of "producing" themselves. If the villagers I met in the 1960s tried to ensure that they and others fulfilled social and family obligations, "young people" in the 1980s tried to ensure that they, and those they cared about, made the most of their capacities and opportunities. When occupational achievement became a more important determinant of social status than inherited property, people who once had to worry about what people did started having to worry about what people, including themselves, thought and felt. They had to monitor people's intentions, emotions, and abilities in order to assess and to enhance personal capacities.

The employment histories I tell are drawn from those George Collier and I collected from the villagers and emigrants we interviewed in 1983–84. I begin with three male "success" stories: one provided by an emigrant who would have inherited enough land to become a *propietario*, another by an emigrant who would have had to supplement his meager landholdings with wage labor had he remained in the village, and the third by a man who emigrated but later returned to the village to develop a small business. I also relate a couple of male "failure" stories, contrasting the protagonist's version with versions told by others. I have invented names for the characters and combined events from several narratives to mask people's identities. But I have tried to keep the flavor of the stories as recorded in field notes.[26]

Gumersindo recounted his employment and migration history as if it were a saga. Although he was born into a family that farmed its own land and often hired workers, he nevertheless portrayed himself as a poor country boy. He attended the village school until the usual age of fourteen, he said, and then went to work in his father's fields. But he was always restless and adventurous. So one day, in 1965, he decided to emigrate. Carrying an old suitcase and seventy-five pesetas, he hitchhiked alone to a northern city. Arriving on a holiday afternoon, he first found a place to stay, and then began hunting for work the next morning. He found a job in a small factory that paid him by the hour. He received no benefits and had no job security, but he was allowed to work as many hours as he wished, until late in the evenings and on the weekends. In this job he learned how to drive trucks. After three years, he switched jobs and went to work for a larger company that taught him to repair trucks and that sent him to various cities around the country. Two years later, he switched jobs again, going into construction work to earn more money. In the years that followed, he switched jobs several more times, each time to a position that offered more pay and better benefits, and that allowed him to learn new skills. He proudly reported that he was never fired from a job. "I have always been a hard worker," he said, "and I have always behaved well." Even though he had been steadily employed in one factory for the past four years, he proudly reported that his old employers still called on him when they needed extra workers or someone they could trust.

A similar success story was told by José, a young man who did very well in school but who was unable to obtain scholarships for further study because he came from a poor family with socialist connections. José considered a career in the military, volunteering for service even though he could have avoided it. But he did not like military life. So he followed his brothers to a northern city, moving there in the late 1960s. At that time, he reported, "You could choose among many jobs." "You might not find exactly what you desired doing, but you could surely find something of the general kind of work you wanted to do." José tried four different jobs before going to work for the Spanish subsidiary of a German company, a job he obtained with help from a relative who worked there. He entered the company "as a *péon*, but learned the work quickly." After six months, he "took and passed exams to get promoted." But he later quit the company over their payment policies. By this time it was 1974, and José noticed that "the job situation was worsening and that he had better get a secure job." So he took entrance exams for civil service positions in two separate government agencies. He passed both exams and chose the job that required the least commuting.

Buenaventura was a cousin and age-mate of Gumersindo. As a young man, he migrated to an industrial city, but he did not like urban living. When the plastics factory where he worked went bankrupt in 1973, he took the severance pay he received and invested it in modernizing the small village store his wife had inherited after the death of her father. Through the 1970s, Buenaventura continued to expand his business, buying a truck for transporting goods and animals, setting up a chicken farm, marketing fertilizers, and building a processing plant for sausages and hams. When telling his story, Buenaventura emphasized the obstacles he had to overcome. He had never run a store, so he apprenticed himself to store owners in a nearby town to learn the business. He also faced competition from other store owners in Los Olivos. So he began to seek markets outside the village, using his truck to transport his products to other communities. He also took and passed the job entrance exam for a part-time government position, thus supplementing his income.

Male success stories tended to come in only one version. Other villagers usually echoed the accounts told by protagonists, emphasizing the ambitions and personal qualities of men who succeeded. Several people, for example, told me that José had always been an outstanding student and was the smartest child in his generation. Buenaventura was universally praised for his intelligence, ambition, and hard work. Even those who emphasized the special advantages enjoyed by successful men, such as inheriting small businesses or having well-placed relatives, talked about the protagonists' personal qualities, thus suggesting that it was not protagonists' special advantages but their personal abilities that enabled them to make the most of their opportunities.

In contrast to male success stories, male failure stories tended to come in several versions. The men whose circumstances condemned them to telling stories of failure usually provided short, factual accounts of their work histories. They either did not provide reasons for their failures or stressed structural and historical factors over which they had no control. Other villagers, in contrast, usually mentioned personal, as well as structural and historical, factors when explaining why some men earned little or nothing. Other narrators thus tended to suggest that failed men lacked the personal qualifications that had enabled successful men to get ahead. Here I tell two "failure" stories, followed by accounts I heard from other villagers.

When asked about his life, Andrés simply listed the jobs he had held. Born about ten years before Gumersindo, José, and Buenaventura, Andrés came from a poor family with socialist connections (his father had been executed during the civil war). From a young age, he had to work in the fields to help support his widowed mother and younger siblings. As a young man, he obtained a steady job working for one of the absentee landowners, but he was fired in 1965, when the landowner converted his holdings from food crops to a eucalyptus plantation. By that time, Andrés was married, with small children and an aging mother to support. He continued to look for agricultural work in Los Olivos, supplementing the money he earned as a day laborer with crops grown on his own small holdings and with money his wife earned doing occasional jobs for other villagers. In 1975, Andrés finally decided to seek urban employment. "I worked like a slave in the country," he reported, "but I was never able to save any money." Andrés left his family in Los Olivos and went to seek employment in Huelva, where one of his younger brothers was living. With his brother's help, he obtained a job as a night watchman at the factory where his brother worked. A year later, he took over some janitorial duties to earn more money. Andrés ended his story here. He did not report that even after combining his night watchman job with a janitorial job he still did not earn enough to move his wife and children to the city. They remained in Los Olivos, where Andrés's visited them on weekends and holidays.

Even though everyone I spoke with recognized that urban jobs were hard to find at the time Andrés left Los Olivos in 1975, they nevertheless mentioned his personal failings. Manuel, a distant cousin through Andrés' mother, who had migrated to Barcelona as a young man, told me that Andrés should not have put up with the low salary and poor working conditions his boss imposed. If only Andrés had more gumption, Manuel said, he would have faced his employer and demanded a raise. Another, even less sympathetic, distant relative of Andrés blamed him for failing to find a job that would pay enough to support his wife and children in the city. "Andrés is a hard worker," she told me, "but his head is made of wood. It was always made of wood."

Ildefonso, a cousin of Gumersindo, also told a matter-of-fact story, attributing his unemployment to the economic crisis. Like Gumersindo, Ildefonso was born into a family wealthy enough to hire laborers. And he, too, left Los Olivos as a young man to seek employment in the city. At first Ildefonso was successful. He easily found urban employment. But by 1983–84, he was unemployed. He explained that he lost his job because the factory where he worked had closed down. The owners, he said, had borrowed heavily to expand production during the boom years of the 1960s. When the market for their products declined in the economic crisis of the 1970s, the owners could not repay their debts and the factory went bankrupt. Ildefonso was still hoping to collect severance pay and back wages from officials supervising the bankruptcy proceedings. He was also looking for another job. But, he explained, jobs were scarce due to the ongoing economic crisis, and his search was hampered by the fact that he had to spend a lot of time filing petitions against his former employers.

Gumersindo recognized that his cousin Ildefonso was unemployed because of the economic recession and the factory owners' miscalculations. But Gumersindo nevertheless blamed Ildefonso for his failure. If only Ildefonso had mastered several job skills, Gumersindo said, or if he had earned the respect of his former employers, as Gumersindo had, then Ildefonso would have been able to find another job when his factory closed. And if only Ildefonso were as daring as Gumersindo, he would not be waiting around to see what he could obtain from the bankruptcy settlement. He would be moving to another area with better job opportunities.

As these stories reveal, the villagers and emigrants I interviewed in the 1980s tended to explain success and failure in terms of what kind of person a protagonist was. Was he (less often she) intelligent? Ambitious? Hardworking? Energetic? Persevering? Adventurous? Flexible? Enthusiastic? Loyal? The causal role storytellers attributed to such personal characteristics suggests, of course, that people who wanted to get ahead—or who at least wanted to avoid being condemned, pitied, or insulted by those they cared about—had to examine their inner selves in order to assess their capacities and desires. But individuals could never rest content with what they found inside themselves. Knowing oneself was only a prelude to making oneself better. In a world of unlimited opportunities, there was always room for improvement. It was not enough simply to police and monitor one's inner thoughts and feelings to make sure they were appropriate. Rather, people had to take on the task of remaking their inner thoughts and feelings in order to eradicate those that bred failure and to encourage those that promised success.

At the same time, storytellers' focus on personal characteristics suggests that those who wanted to interpret and respond appropriately to others' actions had to ask themselves what those actions revealed about the actor's inner abilities and intentions. It was not enough to know what someone had done. Rather, anyone who wanted to understand what people's actions meant for future relationships had to figure out why people behaved as they did. They had to assign motives to actions.

These stories of employment successes and failures also reveal that narrators were concerned about structural factors as well as about the personal characteristics of protagonists. Everyone I spoke with in the

1980s commented on the ongoing economic crisis and they all lamented the high rate of unemployment, particularly for young people. Not only did people's past experiences with socialism provide them a language for understanding the booms and busts of capitalism but Spanish newspapers in the 1980s constantly published unemployment statistics and structural analyses of Spain's disadvantaged position in the world economy.

I, too, was impressed by the effects of structural factors on people's fates. In fact, my research convinced me that structural factors were far more important than personal characteristics in shaping the fortunes of people born in Los Olivos. I have already noted the correlation between time of emigration and likelihood of success. Men who moved to urban areas before the economic crisis of the 1970s tended to find good jobs. By the 1980s, most of these early migrants enjoyed secure employment with good wages. Men who emigrated after the economic crisis, in contrast, had difficulty finding urban jobs that paid enough to support their families.

Structural factors also played a role in shaping who emigrated before the economic crisis of the 1970s. Until 1965, family wealth was the most important factor determining who went and who stayed. As the old man reported, those who had land stayed in Los Olivos, whereas those without land left. After 1965, when people who had land began emigrating as well, age was the most important factor determining who sought urban employment before the 1970s. Men who had recently established families, and who therefore had wives, young children, and aging parents to care for, tended to remain in the village. By the 1980s, most of these men appeared to have failed. Slightly younger men, in contrast, tended to be successful. Lacking wives, small children, and dependent parents in the 1960s, they found it easier to emigrate when news of plentiful urban jobs reached the village. Many of these migrants later called their younger siblings and still active parents to join them in cities. Although some of these younger migrants, such as Ildefonso, later lost their jobs when factories closed in the 1970s, most were doing well in 1983–84, either because they still had secure employment or because they had saved enough money to invest in productive resources, such as trucks, or in modernizing the small Los Olivos businesses they, or their wives, had inherited. The next cohort of men, however, who reached working age just as the OPEC oil crisis of 1973 disrupted the world economy, seemed to be faring less well. Although they were still near the beginning of their careers in 1983, when I learned of their achievements, most seemed to be struggling. Having entered the labor market at a time of rising unemployment, few had found secure jobs with prospects for future advancement.

I was also more impressed by the effects of job success on personality than the reverse. When interviewing villagers and emigrants in 1983–84, I noticed that men who held good jobs were full of pride and self-confidence. They seemed glad to tell their stories. Men who were unemployed or held menial jobs, in contrast, were usually reluctant to talk about their lives. They appeared discouraged and sad. Some had sought solace in drink. I was particularly saddened by the fate of one man I had known in the 1960s. When I first met him, Manuel was a poor wage laborer, but everyone respected him as a hard worker, good husband, responsible father, and caring son. No one blamed him for his poverty. It was not his fault that he and his wife had been born into families that lacked land. By the 1980s, however, everyone blamed Manuel for his, and his family's, miserable condition. It was his own fault that he had not been able to find a good job. Understandably, Manuel's self-esteem had plummeted. (Fortunately, his self-esteem seemed to be rising again in 1994, since he had retired from his demeaning job and returned to the village where his farming skills earned him the respect of his neighbors.)

Given that the villagers and emigrants I interviewed in 1983–84 were as aware as I of how important structural factors had been in determining people's fates, why did they focus on people's personalities when explaining individual successes and failures? The answer, I think, lies in people's daily experiences as these were shaped by the practices of employers and the organization of commodities markets. People recounting employment histories understandably focused on the factors that employers claimed to take into account when making decisions about hiring and wages, such as a worker's intelligence, education, willingness to work hard, ambition, and so on. People explaining the successes of small businessmen and shopkeepers understandably focused on factors that market analysts claimed enabled some sellers to be more responsive than others to variations in market demand, such as a seller's intelligence, salesmanship, adaptability, productivity, and willingness to work hard.

In short, people negotiating the ongoing process of daily living had to take notice of the factors that employers and markets privileged. Because employers claimed to pay workers for the "value" of their labor, workers and would-be workers had to assess their personal qualifications. Adult wage earners had to consider their desires and abilities if they wanted to ask for a job, a pay raise, or a promotion. Everyone who earned wages or a salary received regular reminders of how much their work was "worth" every time they collected a paycheck. Even among self-employed villagers and former villagers, the amount a farmer, storekeeper, or bar owner earned appeared to depend on the share of the market he or she could command, which in turn appeared to depend on the self-employed person's intelligence, hard work, and business sense relative to competitors. Moreover, parents of growing children had good reason to worry about whether their children had the intelligence and perseverance to acquire the diplomas and skills they needed to qualify for desirable jobs. In several of the families I interviewed, children were studying to take entrance exams for positions with the military, police, banks, hospitals, or other employing institutions. Those who were successful—such as one young woman who was among nine people to pass a banking exam taken by three hundred applicants—understandably attributed their success to their individual intelligence and hard work.

It is also true that although people knew structural factors were more important than personality characteristics in accounting for general success and failure rates, such structural factors could not explain why one person succeeded when similarly placed others had failed. The lack of good jobs for young people might explain why seven hundred applicants showed up to take a job entrance exam for fourteen positions, but it could not explain why the fourteen people who actually got the jobs were picked over the six hundred eighty-six applicants who were turned away. Test scores, purporting to reflect the applicants' personal intelligence and abilities, were the key.

Because structural factors could never by themselves explain the successes and failures of particular individuals, people who mentioned economic and historical forces inevitably sounded as if they were offering apologies for failure. Whatever a speaker's intentions, observations about structural factors were inescapably interpreted against a background, however implicit, of personality traits. When Ildefonso, for example, described the closing of his factory, he must have known that I had heard, or would be likely to hear, other stories from his kin and former neighbors. And when people admitted that it was hard for older, displaced agricultural workers like Andrés to find urban jobs in 1975, the observation almost invariably prefaced a discussion of the personality traits that explained why Andrés (or some other unlucky person) had not managed to obtain one of the few good jobs that were still available.

## CONCLUSION

Some colleagues who read this chapter in draft form questioned whether the shift from stories of inherited property to stories of occupational achievement was as dramatic and complete as I have portrayed it. They suggest that people during both my visits must have told both kinds of stories, even if they tended to tell one kind of story more frequently than another. I think these colleagues are wrong. Although people during both my visits talked about inheritance and achievement, achievement did replace inheritance as the major explanatory variable.

But I can understand why colleagues might think that people from Los Olivos must have told at least some achievement stories in the 1960s and some inheritance stories in the 1980s. When I compare Los Olivos to other Andalusian communities, I am struck by its small size. Most Andalusian communities in the 1960s were larger than Los Olivos and contained at least some resident professionals—such as doctors, lawyers, bank managers, and teachers—for whom stories of occupational achievement would have made sense. Los Olivos, however, lacked members of the professional class. The only people who were on career ladders during my first visit were the doctor and the schoolteachers who were not born in Los Olivos and who tried to spend as little time there as they could manage. As a result, there was no one in Los Olivos in the 1960s for whom a story of occupational achievement would have had much explanatory power.

Similarly, Los Olivos in the 1980s lacked a class of wealthy landowners. In contrast to nearby larger towns, such as Aracena, whose landed elites continued to play an important role in town politics (Maddox 1993), no one from Los Olivos owned a farm large enough or productive enough to provide even a middle-class standard of living. Those who did own the largest and most modernized farms in the 1980s earned their incomes primarily from the semiprofessional positions they held. People who made their livings from running small stores, bars, and factories had good reasons to explain success in terms of their business acumen rather than attributing it to the dilapidated enterprises they had inherited. As a result, there was no one from Los Olivos in the 1980s for whom a story of inherited property would have had much explanatory power. No wonder people tended to mention inheritances primarily as a prelude to focusing on the personal achievements of heirs.

Although I think that stories of occupational achievements really did replace earlier stories of inherited properties, the shift may have occurred more slowly and less dramatically than my account implies. I missed the years between the time when land was still the major determinant of a family's wealth and the time when a person's wages or profits determined income. My first visit to Los Olivos occurred just before emigration changed from a strategy of the poor and downwardly mobile to a strategy of the upwardly mobile. I returned to Los Olivos just as those who had emigrated before 1970 were reaching their peak earning years.

Letters from friends in the village written between 1964 and 1983, combined with impressions during my brief visits and the memories of those I spoke with in the 1980s, suggest that villagers from the late 1960s through the 1970s were uncertain how to account for wealth differences. Land in Los Olivos was becoming increasingly worthless, but it was not yet clear that emigrants would do well. Most were still young and at the bottom of urban job ladders. The letters I received from village friends at this time convey primarily a sense of loss—of how "sad" Los Olivos had become as emigration drained it of people and life. But these letters also contain a sense of hope for emigrants' occupational success in a new environment.

# Courtship: From Honor to Romantic Love

Doña Perfecta to Pepe Rey, after he has declared his
intention to marry her daughter Rosario as soon as
possible:

> "No one marries in the haste you want. It might
> give rise to unfavorable judgements on my
> daughter's honor."
> *(Pérez Galdós 1960 [1876], 80)*[1]

IN 1983, WHEN I was reminiscing with an older woman from Los Olivos about village courtship customs, her adult daughter, Conchi, walked into the room. Conchi joined us at the table and listened with increasing horror as her mother and I talked about the twelve-year courtships that had been common in the past. Finally Conchi could not contain herself. "Those earlier customs were not normal!" [¡Lo de antes no era normal!] she burst out.[2] She was right. Between my two visits to Los Olivos, people had revised both their courtship norms and their assumptions about the "normal" (i.e., natural) proclivities of women and men.

When I first arrived in Los Olivos in the fall of 1963, people were eager to tell me about their courtship customs. Their long, formal courtships, they implied, distinguished them from neighboring towns, and particularly from "modern youth," "urban dwellers," and "foreigners" like me. Indeed, my husband and I felt the distinction. We were the youngest married couple in the village.[3] Our age-mates, people in their early twenties, were just beginning formal courtships. Fiancés spent their days apart, working for their parents, and their evenings together, sitting under the watchful eye of the girl's mother or attending well-chaperoned dances and public walks. They did not expect to plan their weddings until the bride approached the age of thirty (see Price and Price 1966a, 313).

When I returned to Los Olivos in 1983, people were once again eager to talk about courtship. Courtship customs, they said, had "changed from night to day." Young men and women now went out alone together, they reported, unlike in the 1960s when courting couples never escaped from "the mother's skirts." And couples no longer postponed marriage. One woman who had married in the late 1940s told me that "today, young people want to get married as soon as they become engaged," unlike couples in her youth, she said, who had enjoyed long courtships. The people I interviewed in the 1980s also told me that suitors had stopped asking a girl's father for formal permission to enter her house. Several older women complained that "men no longer respect women."[4]

In this chapter, I plan to argue that these changes in courtship practices reflect the shift from following social conventions to thinking for oneself that occurred as people from Los Olivos replaced a discourse of inherited property with one of occupational achievement. Conchi's mother and other members of her generation would have agreed with Conchi that their courtship customs were not "normal." They were not meant to be. At that time, socially accepted norms required young people to suppress, rather than to express, what everyone assumed were their "natural" sexual desires—although young people could continue to think what they wanted underneath. For Conchi and members of her generation, in contrast, courting couples were supposed to express, rather than repress, their "naturally" evolving desire for one another. Young people who courted after the shift to a market economy did not portray themselves as following "customs." Rather, socially accepted norms required them to do what their hearts told them—which meant, of course, that they had to figure out what their hearts were saying, and to police their hearts for any signs of inappropriate or "abnormal" desires that required correction or repression.

In broad terms, I suggest that the shift from "honor" to "romantic love" reflects a transformation in what it made sense for people to notice, comment on, and try to influence about the process of choosing a spouse. As people born in Los Olivos moved into the national labor market, transforming the socioeconomic context in which they lived, they changed the consequences of marriage, shifting the qualities that were desirable in a future spouse. During my first visit to Los Olivos, when inherited property appeared to be the most important determinant of a family's income, occupation, and lifestyle, people monitored the choices and actions of courting couples for evidence of a family's wealth and reputation. As Doña Perfecta said in the quotation at the beginning of this chapter, undue haste to marry might call into question a woman's honor. When I returned to Los Olivos twenty years later, villagers and emigrants monitored the activities of courting couples to assess the strength and quality of their love for one another. When a family's income and lifestyle appeared to depend on the occupational preferences and achievements of its members, a young couple's actions testified to their intentions and emotions. Undue delay in marrying could call into question the depth of their commitment.

Although I argue that romantic love replaced honor as the major concern of people contemplating courtship, I do not want to suggest that villagers in the 1960s chose marriage partners on the basis of "lineage and status" whereas those in the 1980s were looking for "personal happiness and individual self-development," as some historians of the family have characterized similar shifts (e.g., Shorter 1975, 5). Not only are people's motives always complex but, as I plan to show, people's conceptions of status and personal happiness also changed. Instead of suggesting that people from Los Olivos substituted one criterion for another, I argue that transformations in the wider social context shifted the consequences—and so the meanings—of both "honor" and "romantic love."

Nor do I want to suggest that romantic love eclipsed status concerns. Rather, both concerns were present during both time periods. The villagers I met in the 1960s, who focused on prospective inheritances and family reputations, also wanted fiancés to love one another, as have all Spaniards studied by ethnographers (e.g., Pitt-Rivers 1954; Brandes 1975; Lison-Tolosana 1966; Gilmore 1980). Similarly, the villagers and emigrants I interviewed in the 1980s, who wanted couples to develop an enduring love, also worried about their earning capacities.

This chapter is divided into four sections and a brief conclusion. I begin by comparing two discourses of gender, using examples from the novel *Doña Perfecta* to explore connections between discourses of inequality and people's understandings of masculinity and femininity. In the second section, I describe the "traditional" courtship customs I encountered on my first visit to Los Olivos, paying particular attention to ethnographic evidence suggesting how young men and women experienced the process of courting. This section is quite long because I use it to explore the self-monitoring techniques required of those who would convince themselves and others that they understood and observed social conventions. The third section is much shorter. It discusses the development and later demise of the elaborate courting customs I encountered in the 1960s. In the final section, I focus on "modern" courtship. This section is much shorter than the earlier section on "traditional" courtship in the 1960s because people had much less to say about the topic. After all, what is there to say about the "normal"? But if Conchi and other members of her generation thought they were behaving as any "normal" young man or woman would, I use my interview notes to explore the self-management techniques enjoined on those who would convince themselves and others that they experienced "normal" desires.

## DISCOURSES OF GENDER

In an article I coauthored with Michelle Zimbalist Rosaldo (1981), we argued that gender conceptions cannot be understood as direct representations of what women and men are or do. Rather, gender conceptions must be seen as aspects of cultural systems through which people understand, manipulate, rationalize, resist, and reproduce relations of inequality within complex social wholes. Reversing Freud's dictum, we suggested that destiny is anatomy—in the sense that people notice those aspects of anatomical sex differences that affect the nature and quality of their relationships with others. If destiny is anatomy, then different conceptions of destiny should encourage people to develop different understandings of human bodies.[5] In this section, I follow this line of reasoning to suggest some logical connections between discourses of inequality (both monetary and moral) and images of sexual difference.

Galdós, author of the nineteenth-century novel *Doña Perfecta*, does not explain why his title character should worry that a hasty marriage between Pepe Rey and Rosario "might give rise to unfavorable judgements on my daughter's honor" (Pérez Galdós 1960, 80). But it is easy to guess the nature of her concern. She is worried about Rosario's reputation for chastity. A hasty marriage might lead the neighbors to speculate that Rosario had to marry quickly because she was having sexual relations with Pepe Rey and was already pregnant or about to become so.

In a later scene, Doña Perfecta's confessor, the priest Don Inocencio, discusses Rosario's chastity with his niece Doña Remedios. Because they have discovered that Rosario met Pepe Rey alone in the garden of her mother's house at midnight, Don Inocencio tells his niece that she must forget her plan of marrying her son Jacintito to the richest heiress in town. "Get this through your head, and don't be stubborn: Rosarito can't be the wife of our idolized Jacintillo. . . . Serious obstacles, the evil of one man [Pepe Rey], [and] the unquestionable passion of the girl, [Rosario] . . . have knocked the bottom out of everything" (Pérez Galdós 1960, 197). When Doña Remedios continues to suggest ways of preventing a marriage between Pepe Rey and Rosario, Don Inocencio declares, "twist and turn it as you will, Don Pepe gets the girl. It can't be avoided now . . . if Rosario didn't love [Pepe Rey] . . . well . . . everything could be arranged. But, alas, . . . she fell, my dear niece, she fell into his devilish and lustful trap" (Pérez Galdós 1960, 198).

Doña Remedios, however, refuses to give up. She tells her uncle that "this business about Rosarito is nothing but one of those whims that pass, one of those that can be cured by a couple of good scoldings or half a dozen whacks." Don Inocencio disagrees; "when serious things have happened, little whims are not called little whims but something else again." At this, Doña Remedios's "face suddenly flamed." She cries out, "are you capable of thinking that Rosarito . . . ? How awful! I'll defend her, yes, I defend her. . . . She's pure as an angel" (Pérez Galdós 1960, 198).

Several unstated assumptions lie behind this interchange. Don Inocencio assumes that if Pepe Rey and Rosario met alone at midnight, they probably had sexual intercourse—after all, men are "lustful" and women are "passionate." More important, he assumes that once a woman has been in a situation where she may have had sexual relations with one man, no other man can marry her. Doña Remedios shares this assumption. As a result, her only hope of salvaging her plan to acquire Rosario's inheritance for her son is to argue that Rosario did not have sexual relations with Pepe Rey. When she declares that Rosario is "pure as an angel," she is equating purity with sexual innocence. "Angel" is a complex metaphor, linking Heaven, spirituality, and renunciation, in contrast to Hell, carnal desire, and indulgence.

Several ethnographers have described and analyzed these assumptions as part of the complex "values of honor and shame" found in many communities around the Mediterranean Sea (see particularly Peristiany 1965; Pitt-Rivers 1954, 1965, 1977; Schneider 1971; Schneider and Schneider 1976; Gilmore, ed., 1987). Such assumptions, however, are also found in other areas of the world and they should be familiar to readers of Shakespeare. As a result, I want to use a "destiny is anatomy" line of argument to suggest why people who use a discourse of inherited rights (to property or to political privileges) when negotiating relations of social inequality might independently arrive at similar ideas about the importance of female chastity for family honor and the maintenance of social order (see also Ortner 1976).

When people trace lines of inheritance in order to justify, claim, or contest legally enforced status rights, they must find themselves frequently discussing the sexual chastity of women. Because women give birth to children, maternal lines are usually obvious. But because a woman may acquire sperm from various men, people who want to trace paternal lines of inheritance must speculate on a mother's sexual history. It is little wonder, therefore, that people who base their claims to status on inherited rights often conclude that the best way to establish paternity, and thus to determine a child's paternal inheritance, is to ensure that a child's mother has sexual relations with only one man.

It is also easy to understand why people who trace inheritance lines might conclude that a man's honor depends on the chastity of his close female relatives. A man whose mother's chastity is open to question is at a disadvantage if someone challenges his right to the property or political privileges he claims to have inherited from his father. Similarly, a man whose wife is unfaithful may find himself ridiculed for working to enhance or preserve property that another man's children will inherit. Moreover, when people talk about their status relative to that of others as determined by inheritance, they must experience a deep sense of disorientation if their ancestry is questioned. "Bastards" who cannot trace their paternal ancestors suffer not only from a lack of property but also from a lack of social identity. No one knows who they "are." It is thus easy to understand how people who base their claims to status on inherited rights might conclude that women must remain chaste if social order is to prevail. Were women to mate promiscuously, chaos would result. No one would know who anyone was. Social life would cease. Women as well as men would suffer.

If destiny determines anatomy, then a woman's "openness" and "penetrability" must appear to be the most significant anatomical quality affecting her role in a world where inherited property organizes social inequality.[6] A woman has the physical capacity to bring bastards into the family and the world. This fact requires her, and those whose honor depends upon her chastity, not only to prevent unauthorized men from penetrating her but also to prevent even the appearance of unchaste behavior on her part. Were Rosario to marry Pepe Rey with such haste that the neighbors imagined her pregnant, Rosario's (and her family's) honor would be destroyed because Rosario and her kin would have allowed people to suspect that they had been unable (and therefore would be unable in the future) to prevent Rosario from having sexual relations with a man to whom she was not married.

Given that conceptions of masculinity and femininity tend to be defined in relation to one another, people who characterize women's bodies as open and penetrable are likely to imagine male bodies as closed and impenetrable. The most socially significant thing about a man's body is that he cannot bring bastards into his own family. Men's ability to beget bastards on other men's families, however, commonly leads people to extend the metaphor of impenetrability to assess a man's capacities for preventing other men from penetrating what he claims as his (his women and property).[7] When people use a discourse of inherited status, they are likely to conclude that lechers pose less of a threat to social order than cuckolds. A lecher does not cast doubt on the legitimacy of his wife's children and he threatens social order only if other men are too weak to prevent him. But a man who allows other men to penetrate his women not only destroys his own family but tolerates the female promiscuity that threatens to destroy the social order on which everyone depends. When Don Inocencio argues that Jacintito cannot marry Rosario after she "fell" into Pepe Rey's "lustful trap," he is observing that if Jacintito were to marry Rosario he would become a cuckold.[8]

In Pepe Rey's very different world, Rosario is not the passionate fallen woman of Don Inocencio's imagining. Rather, Galdós, the liberal bourgeois author, depicts her as "a girl of delicate and fragile appearance." Her "real beauty . . . lay in a type of translucency, . . . through which all the depths of her soul could be plainly seen; depths not bottomless and forbidding like those of the sea, but like those of a clear and gentle river" (Pérez Galdós 1960, 26). Rosario is emotional, but her emotions are not strong ones, such as lust or anger. Rather, Rosario's eyes are continually filling with tears, and she is forever sinking down weakly. At her first meeting with Pepe Rey, "she blushed crimson and was barely able to murmur a few commonplaces" (1960, 26). Rosario is "innocent" and "pure," but these qualities are more akin to the ignorance of an inexperienced child than to an angel's principled renunciation of earthly pleasures.

Pepe Rey falls in love with Rosario because, he tells her, "You have the marvelous quality of being able constantly to project the lovely light of your spirit over everything around you" (Pérez Galdós 1960, 51). Indeed, Galdós writes that when Pepe Rey first stepped into the room Rosario had prepared for him, "Pepe recognized the diligent and loving hand of a woman in all the details of the house. Everything was arranged with great taste, and the neatness and freshness of everything invited rest in such a charming nest" (1960, 27).

Rosario, the emotional nest builder, and Pepe Rey, the rational engineer, exemplify the gender stereotypes associated with industrial society, particularly as found among urban middle classes in the nineteenth century.[9] In a social world where people justify inequality by telling stories about individuals' successes (or failures) in the market for jobs and commodities, people continually find themselves having to suggest reasons why one person succeeded (or failed) in obtaining the job or market share that others also wanted. They have to speculate about the productive capacities of bodies and minds. Not surprisingly, people tend to discover (and continually rediscover) that female bodies are "designed" for producing babies, whereas male bodies are designed for producing things. Socially, the most significant anatomical difference between the sexes is not that women's bodies are penetrable whereas men's are not, but that women's bodies can make babies whereas men's bodies cannot—leaving men free to use their bodies for making marketable goods and services.

At first glance, the ability to produce babies and the ability to produce goods might seem equally necessary for human survival. But markets (whether "free" or state-controlled) do not reward them equally. Laws allow goods and services to be traded on the market, but laws prohibit selling humans, including babies.[10] As a result, women cannot earn money—at least not legally—for bearing and rearing their own children. Nor are capitalist employers eager to hire women (or men) who bring their young children to work with them. This inability of women to earn money for performing their anatomically destined role tends to cast women as men's opposites, rather than as men's inferiors on a single scale.[11] In the social world inhabited by Doña Perfecta and her allies, both men and women appeared to want the same things: both desired earthly pleasures and both were capable of renouncing them in favor of observing God's commandments (although women's "open" anatomy left them more vulnerable to the Devil's temptations than men's "closed" bodies). In Pepe Rey's world, in contrast, women and men were required to want different things. As producers of goods and services for the market, men were required to want money. They were supposed to use their brains for calculating the expected costs and benefits of their actions. Women, as homemakers for children and husbands, were required to want love. They were expected to follow their hearts (and hormones) without calculating the advantages or disadvantages of spending their time serving others.

Although market processes tend to cast men as rational and women as emotional, men are actually required to want both money and love—both homes and careers—whereas women are forever suspected of wanting the money they are supposed to disdain.[12] Humans, as I just observed, have to produce both goods and babies if the species is to survive. Adults have to make homes where unconditional love prevails, even as the inevitable "scarcity" of goods and time requires them to calculate the costs and benefits of pursuing particular activities. But if both men and women need both love and money, only men can pursue both goals without incurring social sanctions.

Because men can pursue both love and money, their actions set the standard for distinguishing between, and therefore for defining, whether an act is performed for love or for money. Men and women both participate in the "marriage market" where young people choose mates with whom they will sign "marriage contracts." But only men can appear to choose brides based on pure emotion, because only men are expected to achieve their own incomes through market participation. Cynics may portray men as motivated by lust to pick the sexiest babe. But romantics tend to portray men as searching for the unique woman of their dreams. Pepe Rey, for example, wants to marry Rosario because, as he tells her, "you're the woman my heart has long promised me, telling me night and day . . . 'she's coming now; she's near; you're warm, you're warm'" (Pérez Galdós 1960, 51). Unlike men in Doña Perfecta's world, who always married for money as well as for love because a wife's inheritance—along with her husband's—determined the amount of property a new family would own, Pepe Rey imagines that he is marrying Rosario solely because, as he tells her, "I love you madly" (Pérez Galdós 1960, 51).

Women in market societies, however, find it difficult (if not impossible) to attain the standard of pure love set by men. Because a mother's income and lifestyle are determined less by her own achievements than by the money she receives from her husband, a woman's choice of husband always appears tainted by greed. Rosario, for example, hints at mercenary motives when she tells Pepe Rey that "The woman who catches him can consider herself lucky" (Pérez Galdós 1960, 52). As a result, women can appear to be acting out of pure love only when their actions are impossible to construe as leading to monetary gain. No wonder people in market societies so often claim to be confused about what women want. Rosario, the romantic nineteenth-century heroine, aptly illustrates the stupidity that market societies require of women who would demonstrate emotion untainted by reason. Not only does she weep and wilt at the slightest provocation, but she meets Pepe Rey alone in the garden at midnight. By surrendering her body to him before he has incurred the legal obligation to support her and the children she bears, she decisively proves that she is acting on her emotions rather than rationally calculating how best to catch a rich engineer. Ironically, this act of emotional surrender, which demonstrates Rosario's pure love for Pepe Rey, is the very act that makes her ineligible to become the mother of Jacintito's heirs.[13]

The contrast between silly, emotional Rosario and her smart, calculating mother provides a good illustration of the different ideals of womanhood associated with the discourses of inherited property and occupational achievement. In Doña Perfecta's world, women were admired for intelligence and ambition, as long as they used these gifts to protect and enhance the inheritances of their children. Silly women like Rosario were feared, for they could destroy themselves and their families by acting on their emotions. In Pepe Rey's world, in contrast, smart women like Doña Perfecta were feared, for if women, like men, were to rationally calculate the market costs and benefits of their actions, no one would provide the selfless, unconditional love that babies need and husbands want.

Given the stupidity required of women in market societies, it is little wonder that people who use a discourse of occupational achievement seldom portray women as posing a threat to social order. Women are too weak and silly to do much harm. In fact, they hardly qualify as persons. When describing Rosario, for example, Galdós observed that "the material to make a complete person was missing" (Pérez Galdós 1960, 26).[14] In contrast to people who use a discourse of inherited property, who commonly fear women's ability to destroy society by mating promiscuously, people who live in market societies are more likely to worry that men might destroy society by failing to provide helpless, childlike women with the food and shelter women need to successfully bear and rear future generations.[15]

Finally, people participating in social worlds dominated by landed elites and market entrepreneurs tend to draw opposite conclusions about the similarities between human marriages and animal matings.[16] Because people who tell stories about inherited properties tend to imagine that people (particularly women) must suppress their sexual desires in order to contract marriages that will ensure the legitimacy of heirs, they are likely to stress the differences between human marriages and animal matings. People who live in market societies, in contrast, are likely to stress the similarities. Not only do people who tell stories about individual achievements tend to conclude that marriage requires people (particularly men) to give in to their emotional desires for sexual intimacy, but their stories about human productivity must lead them to conclude that humans are differentiated from animals less by humans' ability to abstain from sexual activity than by humans' ability to produce goods and governments. If humans rise above animals by producing goods and services, then humans must appear to resemble animals in mating and reproducing their own kind.[17] No wonder Conchi and other members of her generation thought it was "abnormal" for lovers to wait twelve years before consummating their union.

The conceptual gulf that separates Doña Perfecta's imagined world from that of Pepe Rey is suggested by a dialogue Galdós wrote for his main characters, which occurs just after Pepe Rey has announced his intention to marry Rosario because "She and I want it." "You fool! [screams Doña Perfecta] Perchance there's no one in the world but she and you? Aren't there parents? Isn't there society? Isn't there a conscience? Isn't there a God?" Pepe Rey responds gravely, "Just because there is society, because there is conscience, because there is a God" (Pérez Galdós 1960, 143–144). But if I, like Galdós, have stressed differences between the imagined worlds of Doña Perfecta and Pepe Rey, I do not want to suggest that real people are restricted to only one set of gender conceptions at a time. Because people living in the aftermath of the European Enlightenment inevitably tell stories about both family inheritances and individual achievements, even if they tend to tell one type of narrative more often, they have a wealth of contradictory images to draw upon in the process of negotiating their relations with others.

Moreover, the differences I have emphasized occur against a background of similarities. Doña Perfecta and her allies might have focused on women's penetrability while Pepe Rey's allies might have stressed women's ability to make babies, but both imagined that women's bodies doomed them to be men's dependents and inferiors. Similarly, both cast the opposition between male and female as one between reason and emotion, although they defined reason differently. For Doña Perfecta, people exhibited reason by understanding, and adhering to, God's plan for the world. For Pepe Rey, people exhibited reason by rationally calculating the (market) costs and benefits of their actions. Doña Perfecta and Pepe Rey also agreed in casting men as active and women as passive, but differed in how they imagined men creating the society that women needed. For Doña Perfecta, men created social order by ensuring the proper transmission of inheritances through constructing impenetrable barriers around their properties and women. For Pepe Rey, in contrast, men created society by producing the goods and governments that allowed women to get on with their specialized task of bearing and rearing the children.

## COURTSHIP IN LOS OLIVOS IN THE EARLY 1960s

Shortly after I arrived in Los Olivos, in November 1963, I interviewed the mayor and his recently married niece about village courtship customs. The notes I wrote up the next day, including parenthetical comments added at the time, report that

> On Sunday afternoons the girls dress up and walk out along the paved road that leads from town to the main highway. The boys also walk then, and the two sexes get a chance to look each other over. The girls are generally around fifteen years old. Then there are the Sunday dances when the boys and girls get to meet each other. On fiestas and Sundays in the summer they dance in the plaza. In the winter, they dance in the town hall. Also the boys can plan a dance by going to the mayor's house to ask permission. If he grants it, the boys obtain a record player or they form a band. Two or three of the girls' mothers attend the dance as chaperones. There are no dances in November, however, as the entire month is devoted to the dead.

Young people also hold winter gatherings (*reuniones*) in private houses. The boys get a bottle of anise or cognac and the girls bring chestnuts for roasting. If it is not November, these gatherings often turn into dances.

Once a boy has chosen a girl, he has plenty of chances to accompany her places. He can wait for her to come out of church after the evening Rosary and walk her almost home, stopping to talk for a few minutes on her street corner and then leaving. He does not walk up to her door with her. Of course, everyone knows who is talking on the corner with whom, but the parents and neighbors pretend not to notice. (This system gives the parents of both the boy and the girl fair warning of what is going on before it becomes serious. At this early stage, the parents can probably discourage a child from forming a relationship of which they do not approve.) A boy can also accompany a girl when she goes to the fountain to get water. Young people can also arrange to meet at fiestas given in other towns, such as the *feria* in Aracena. The girl then goes with her family, or with some family friends. The boy goes too and the couple take this opportunity to spend some time together. Again, if the girl's parents accompany her, they pretend not to notice the boy's presence or to know what he is there for.

After about a year of informal courtship, the boy asks for entrance into the girl's house. He and the girl may have been known to be *novios* (fiancés) before, but after the boy enters the girl's house, it is *ya formal* (formalized). The boy's asking to enter the house is a relatively informal thing between the boy and the girl's father. The boy may ask when he meets the girl's father at a convenient time in the bar or the fields. But usually the boy goes to the girl's house. That is what happened in the case of the mayor's niece. The boy always tells the girl beforehand that he is planning to speak to her father. The girl then tells her mother who tells her father what is about to happen. When the boy shows up, both the girl and her mother leave, so that the father will be there alone to receive the *novio* (suitor). The boy comes dressed in his good clothes, enters the house, and asks the girl's father if he may come to visit his daughter. He says that he loves her, or that they are in love, and that he eventually wants to marry her. The girl's father always says yes. (He has had his chance to stop the courtship if he disapproved. Refusal can cause a public scandal, for if the couple continue meeting in the street, the girl's father's only recourse is to kill the boy.) The whole interview is probably quite short, and after that the boy is allowed in the girl's house. If the girl's father is dead, then the novio asks permission of her mother. If both parents are dead, he asks an elder brother.

Once a novio has entered his novia's house, he has to come and visit her for around two hours every evening he is in town. In the summer, he comes from 10 P.M. to midnight and talks to her at the door of her house. In the winter, he comes a little earlier and sits with the family around the *mesa camilla* (a round table with a brazier under it) or sits in another part of the living room with the family. The couple are never allowed to be alone in the house. Someone always has to be there. (When I asked the mayor and his niece if visiting every evening got boring—what, after all, could the novios have to talk about night after night—they both laughed as if that were inconceivable. Finally, the mayor said that novios were always whispering together. It was the poor girl's parents who suffered because they could not go out until the boy had left.) Other than these evening visits, the novios continue their former activities. They still go to dances and parties. When the novio is away, the novia can go to dances, but she can only dance with other girls. She cannot dance with another boy. But the novio can dance with other girls when his novia is not there.

After several years of courtship, the novios begin to think about getting married. The novio may suggest marriage to his novia. If she seems agreeable, they inform their parents and begin planning the wedding. [The mayor's niece and her husband courted for eleven years before getting married.]

Richard and Sally Price, who studied courtship in Los Olivos during the summer of 1964, wrote an article about the process that parallels the account I obtained from the mayor and reflects the stories and explanations recorded in their field notes. Their "general description of *noviazgo* (courtship), from its inception to marriage" (1966a, 302) reproduces, as accurately as is now possible, the standard courtship narrative recounted by villagers—a story beginning with teenagers' awakening interest in the opposite sex, their pairing off, and their passage through set stages of courtship, and finally culminating in a wedding.

Because the Prices focused on courtship, and because they lived with a family whose four children were courting, their published description of noviazgo in Los Olivos provides far more details about the courtship process than I was able to obtain by interviewing married people. They report, for example, that although only unmarried youth participated in the *paseo* (the Sunday walks to the highway), as many as one hundred people could attend, from "6-year old children to 30-year old *novios*" (1966a, 304). Younger teenagers usually walked in large, single-sex groups, the girls linking arms. Occasionally a girl broke away to walk with one boy, but only couples who were recognized novios spent the paseo walking together.

Like the mayor, the Prices focused on parental reactions to incipient relationships. They reported that when young people of fifteen and sixteen began pairing off informally in what villagers called *noviazgos de calle* (street courtships), unions are extremely fragile, involving few obligations and creating no stigma if broken. Furthermore, these unions, in striking contrast to later ones, are based purely on personal whim [*sic*]. However, though formal considerations do not enter into the formation of *noviazgos de calle*, they often presage their end. For it is precisely at this informal stage that parents—ostensibly oblivious to their children's passing attachments—attempt to cut short unions of which they disapprove. The public nature of *paseos* and an effective system of community gossip keep parents well informed of their children's activities, and should the wealth or family reputation of a potential son-in-law or daughter-in-law be undesirable, a number of sanctions are brought to bear; a boy's spending money may be cut off, and a girl may be kept in on Sundays until she thinks better of favoring her current pretender. (Price and Price 1966a, 306)

The Prices also describe two transitional stages between informal street courtships and the boy's formal entrance into the girl's house. When a youth began arriving at the corner of the girl's street every evening, and she joined him there for a couple of hours of talking until darkness fell, they were

no longer *novios de calle*, but *a la esquina* (at the corner), and no longer are they *hablando* (talking), but *pelando la pava* (plucking the turkey)—the local euphemism for the more serious turn which their conversations have suddenly taken. For the first time they are publicly referred to as *novios*, and they see each other nightly instead of weekly. Friends offer standard congratulatory phrases: "*Me alegro mucho*" (It makes me very happy), "*Me alegro de tu contento*" (Your joy makes me happy), but parents pretend to be oblivious of the rapidly developing situation. (Price and Price 1966a, 307)

After two or three weeks of meeting at the corner, couples were supposed to move to the door of the girl's house. It was considered less "shameless" to meet in full sight of the girl's mother (Price and Price 1966a, 307). Once they arrived *a la puerta* (at the door), the novios began to use affinal terms for their future in-laws, although contact between the novio and his future wife's parents remained minimal. The novio avoided his father-in-law, but might "banter a bit from time to time" with the girl's mother as she sat inside the house keeping a close watch on her daughter (Price and Price 1966a, 308).

The Prices also provide a vivid description of the nightly visits a novio was expected to pay after he had been granted formal permission to enter to his novia's house and the couple had started the third and longest stage of courtship. The Prices sat through many such visits during their summer of living in a house with four young people. They write that

"The boy, hair plastered and shoes polished, enters the kitchen and accepts a chair. *Suegro* (father-in-law) and *novio* discuss crops or the weather until the girl's father, uncomfortable in this social situation, retires to the café for some coffee and male companionship. The mother, however, must sit close by her daughter, *haciendo la cesta* (literally, 'basket weaving') while the *novios* 'pluck the turkey.' Physical contact is forbidden at any time, and the rule is generally respected" (1966a, 309). After a novio had entered his novia's house, he was required to "appear after dinner every night, and the girl's father traditionally barred the door if he skipped a visit, for this act of disrespect insults not only the *novia* but her whole family" (Price and Price 1966a, 310).

When the Prices observed that parents in Los Olivos cut short their children's budding attachments if "the wealth or family reputation" of the child's choice was "undesirable" (1966a, 306), they accurately reflected the reasoning of the villagers they interviewed. At that time, the wealth of a child's spouse did appear to be the most important factor determining the child's future income and lifestyle. As I noted in the previous chapter, villagers in the 1960s commonly used a discourse of inherited property to explain why some families enjoyed more wealth, prestige, and power than others. Because Los Olivos parents expected to divide their property equally among all their children, regardless of sex, parents had good reason to worry about whether their children would obtain enough property to replicate the parents' lifestyle. No wonder village parents tried to discourage their children from marrying spouses who expected to inherit little or nothing.

The Prices' field notes record many stories of budding attachments cut short by parental intervention. I reproduce three of the more detailed accounts here, modifying them slightly to disguise the identities of protagonists. Although stories of failed courtships may seem quite different from the stories of occupational successes and failures that I reproduced in the previous chapter, the stories are similar in that both purport to explain the economic fates of individuals. Such stories thus reveal people's assumptions about the factors that matter most in determining someone's social status.

Bartolomé and Ana loved each other very much. In fact, she was the only girl from Los Olivos he ever cared for. He is quite rich; she very poor. She has only a mother living. They were novio'd formally for four years, including three or four periods apart (one lasted six months). He was able to gain entrance to her house again, after splitting each time, because he only had to ask her mother—and mothers are always more lenient in such matters than fathers. The splits were all caused by his family, who put constant pressure on him to leave her, because of money. Finally, with many regrets, he broke with her for good. She has since married an outsider. He is still looking—but not in Los Olivos because there is no one here of sufficient financial status that is the right age. Thus, he spends Sundays in nearby towns. [A few years after the Prices left, Bartolomé married a village girl from a wealthy family who was several years younger than he.][18]

Guillermo tried for six months to begin a serious relationship with Loli, but his mother eventually was successful in forcing a split. She would ask other people whether they had been walking together in the paseo, seen together, etc., and if yes, she would not give him any money the next Sunday. Thus, he found himself cut off from his mother, without money for fun, and decided to leave the girl. Two reasons combined for the mother's hostility to Loli—neither of which had to do with the girl herself. First, both her grandmother and aunt were illegitimate, and as if that weren't enough, the family had no money at all. That clinched it for the mother. Guillermo then began walking with Magdalena, but she went into mourning soon after, and he left her since she couldn't leave the house, and he was not about to ask entrance yet.

Belen was the most attractive, nicest girl of her generation in Los Olivos. But she had bad luck. First, a novio from Sevilla split with her after only three months of noviazgo—which naturally knocked down her stock as far as Los Olivos was concerned. Then Santiago seemed to win out over two other pretenders—all walking with her during the summer. But his relationship with her was short-lived—one month—because his family absolutely vetoed a union with such a poor girl. (His family is rich.) This split finished her for Los Olivos, thus she had to search elsewhere. At the fiesta in Aracena, she met a boy from Huelva with whom she corresponded for the next couple of months. Then, at Christmas, he visited her in Los Olivos, asked entrance to the house, and they married before long. Thus, one of the most eligible Los Olivos girls, by various circumstances, found herself completely blocked from achieving a Los Olivos spouse, and had to live her life elsewhere.

After collecting detailed "courtship histories . . . for more than 300 people in Los Olivos" from 1890 to 1964, and correlating the permanence of pairings with the wealth ranking of individuals, Richard and Sally Price concluded that

> relative wealth influences to a great extent both the choice of a marriage partner and the pattern of progression through the courtship stages. Within Los Olivos people tend to marry partners whose wealth is similar to their own. Parents never attempt to arrange marriages, and as long as the partner is of suitable wealth feign ignorance of their children's courtships.

But they are quick to intercede and impose sanctions if they feel there is a "mismatch." This is reflected in the combination of a very high incidence of informal courtships between a rich and a poor partner, with few such formal courtships or marriages. (1966b, 527–529)

Strikingly, none of the courtship histories collected by the Prices mentioned the intelligence, ambition, or willingness to work of the young people themselves. In the summer of 1965, however, Shelly Zimbalist reported in her field notes that "Concepción broke up with Rafael [her novio of the summer before] because her parents thought he was too poor. Rafael, though, according to Estebana, is worth more than Marcelino [Concepción's current novio], who is uneducated, coarse, and lacks ambition. Rafael is handsome, educated, and studying for a profession in Seville." Although young people in the 1960s apparently valued a potential partner's good looks, education, and professional prospects, their parents—who controlled the purse strings—did not. Parents assessed children's potential spouses by calculating prospective inheritances. However promising Rafael's professional future might have appeared to his contemporaries, Concepción's parents succeeded in blocking her marriage to a youth from a poor family.[19]

In the 1960s, when I interviewed villagers about inheritance norms, they invariably repeated the rule that all children, regardless of sex, should inherit equally. Several people told me that they achieved the ideal of equal inheritance—and thus avoided conflicts among heirs—by drawing lots.[20] One woman said that after the death of her widowed father, his six children met with a respected uncle to divide the property in equal shares. When everyone agreed the shares were equal, they recorded them on slips of paper, put the slips into a vase, and each child drew in turn, beginning with the eldest. This procedure, although equalizing shares, could disrupt people's lives. The woman who told me this story had to move from the house where she had lived for several years because it fell to her brother. To avoid such disruptive moves, many heirs tried to reach an agreement without having to resort to chance.

Given this norm of equal partible inheritance, the most direct way for someone to assess a young person's wealth was to sum the wealth of his or her parents and divide by the number of children in the family. Richard and Sally Price report that "this computation was used consistently by informants in assessing the economic aspect of marriageability" (1966b, 533n.5). It was also used by the Prices to assess the wealth of individuals for their analysis of courtship and stratification. Other considerations could complicate this simple computation, however. I found that villagers regularly considered a person's childless aunts and uncles, or even more distant relatives, when assessing inheritance possibilities. The Prices report that informants also considered the timing of bequests. "For example, it is clear that a potential *novio* of given wealth who has lost both parents and has therefore already received his inheritance is in a somewhat different position from one of identical wealth with young parents and a probable long wait until inheritance" (Price and Price 1966b, 533n.5).

Although the stories of broken courtships collected by Richard and Sally Price focus on parental attempts to discourage children from marrying people who expected lesser inheritances, the stories also show that villagers cared about romantic love. They wanted fiancés—and married couples—to love one another. Indeed, both the Prices' and the mayor's accounts of courtship begin by describing the paseo as an opportunity for young people "to look each other over." Had love not been important, parents could have locked their daughters up and arranged appropriate marriages through intermediaries. But they did not. Parents sent girls out, dressed in their best clothes, to walk and dance with prospective suitors. And they allowed girls in mourning—who would otherwise have had to remain indoors—to attend nightly rosary services at the church, where young men could observe them and walk them home. Unlike rich families in nearby, larger towns, who sponsored private dances and parties for their children (Maddox 1993, 124–125), the wealthiest parents in Los Olivos did not prevent their children from attending public events. This lack of separate dances for the children of rich and poor families provides the most powerful evidence possible that Los Olivos in the 1960s was an egalitarian village without significant wealth differences.

Love, however, was always interpreted against a background of property considerations and concern for family reputation. The Prices' field notes reveal that as long as a couple continued to see each other, villagers assumed they were in love. But if a couple separated, people speculated on the strength of their attachment. Those who were not sorry about a breakup commonly portrayed a couple's affection for one another as merely a passing "whim." The Prices' description of "street courtships" as "based purely on personal whim" (1966a, 306) reflects the villagers' commonsense assumption that if parents were able to break up their children's early attachments, they could not be very strong. In his field notes, Richard Price reported a friend's observation that a young man who "wanted to split, under pressure from his parents about the desirability of the girl, would never tell her the truth. Rather, he would wait a few nights until he found some other trifling excuse. All this because if he did tell the truth, that his parents had forced the split, the girl would say 'then you do not really love me. If you did you would not obey your parents.' And, in effect, the girl would have a point."[21]

Villagers who lamented the termination of a courtship, in contrast, often cast the victims of failed relationships as brokenhearted heroes and heroines of romantic stories. The description of Bartolomé and Ana as "lov[ing] each other very much" reflects this interpretation. Women, in particular, relished tales of thwarted love. They followed radio soap operas, read love comics and magazines, and talked of love. Many villagers told me that an elderly spinster (who appeared perfectly content to me) was still pining for her wealthy lover, whose parents had forced him to marry a rich woman (with whom, my gossiping friends reported, he constantly fought).

Because both "passing whim" and "enduring love" stories were equally available to villagers, opposing accounts could circulate about the same failed courtship. In the 1980s, for example, I heard two versions of what happened during the 1960s when a couple I knew separated. Some people told me that the woman broke up with her Los Olivos novio because on a visit to Madrid she fell in love with the man she eventually married. These narrators portrayed the woman's first attachment as a passing whim that was easily forgotten when she met her true love. Other people, however, told me that the woman's Los Olivos novio had left her because his parents thought her family was too poor. Brokenhearted, the abandoned novia married an outsider to escape from the scene of her tragedy.

By portraying love against a background of property considerations, these courtship stories reveal the sense in which villagers during the 1960s experienced a disjunction between what people wanted to do and what they actually did. Marriages, according to storytellers, reflected the economic and status concerns of a young couple's parents more than the feelings of the young people themselves. Love might play an important role in the initial stages of courtship, but expected inheritances and family reputations determined whether or not an initial attraction resulted in marriage. Bartolomé and Ana might have "loved each other very much," but they ended up married to other people.

The courtship histories collected by Richard and Sally Price also reveal that parents considered family reputation when assessing children's potential marriage partners. Guillermo's mother, for example, reportedly disapproved of Loli not just because she came from a poor family but also because "both her grandmother and aunt were illegitimate." "Reputation," however, differed from wealth in two crucial respects. First, it was not as easy to calculate as the amount of property a young person was expected to inherit. Second, villagers commonly held individuals responsible for the reputations they acquired, in contrast to inheritances over which individuals were assumed to have little control. In the rest of this section, therefore, I plan to focus on "reputation" in order to explore the techniques of self-management enjoined on young people in the 1960s. In particular, I examine how young people talked about their experiences of courtship, because the hopes and fears they expressed shed light on the gender-linked norms that they invoked to monitor their own and others' actions.

In the early 1960s, neither the Prices nor I thought that the courtship customs we encountered in Los Olivos were "normal." Like Conchi in the 1980s, we could not understand how young couples could bear to sit together, night after night, under the watchful eye of an ever present chaperone, unable to do anything more than touch hands and steal a quick kiss when the chaperone was not looking. We expressed our curiosity in the questions we put to the villagers we interviewed. I asked the mayor and his niece if visiting every night got boring. And Richard Price asked the young men he knew if it was not "a chore to have a novia."

The villagers' most common response to our questions was the one expressed by the mayor and his niece. People laughed. They pointed out that courtship was the happiest and most exciting time in a person's life. To emphasize how enjoyable courting was, they commonly told the story of a legendary (but apparently real) novio who visited his novia faithfully every night for fifty-four years until he finally became too debilitated by age to totter across the street to her house.[22]

I was never able to get beyond this surface reaction. But Richard Price, who hung out with young men, obtained a complex—and contradictory—account of their experiences of courtship. On one hand, men said they did perceive nightly visits as a chore.

> Courting men treat *noviazgo* as but one aspect of their rather full lives. Evening visits are generally pleasant, sometimes boring, and occasionally—should their *novia* upbraid them for something—an ordeal. But men's lives still center on work and recreation with male friends, and this pattern continues into married life. They seem to tolerate *noviazgo* with a smile, as if aware that it is not an institution designed primarily for their needs or pleasures. During courtship men learn to live for the first time, as they say, "with resignation," which continues to serve as a main orientation toward life until the end of their days. (Price and Price 1966a, 310)

In actuality, of course, most of the "resigned" young men Richard Price interviewed emigrated from Los Olivos shortly afterward. By the 1980s, they were telling stories of occupational achievements.

On the other hand, young men had good reasons for preferring formal courtships over both playing the field and marriage. When Richard Price asked one young man if it it was not a "lark to be free to go after the pack of unmarried girls at will," he answered that having a formal novia "gives a guy something to do every night besides drink, it provides amusement Sunday afternoons, and it doesn't prevent escapades [with prostitutes] elsewhere." In his field notes, Richard Price ruminates that "this makes sense here. Within the confines of the pueblo, a boy without a novia can never be with girls—and as Mariano said, most normal boys enjoy female company, even if it is only talk."[23] Most young men, in fact, entered formal courtships around the age of nineteen, before leaving town for compulsory military service (Price and Price 1966a, 311).

Young men also gave positive reasons for prolonging the stage of formal courtship once they had entered a novia's house. Two young men "carefully explained" to Richard Price that "noviazgo is far easier than the early years of married life. It is very pleasant; no economic problems. As Antonio said '*no tenemos preocupaciones*' (we have no worries). They claimed that the lack of responsibilities during noviazgo was one of the main reasons for late marriage."[24] Later in his field notes Richard Price observes again that "from the point of view of the novio, life is much more pleasant before than after marriage. There are fewer responsibilities, no need for initiative."[25]

An examination of inheritance practices suggests a reason why young men might have perceived formal courting, with its required evening visits, as preferable both to informal courtships and to marriage. Because the system of equal partible inheritance in Los Olivos ensured that family properties were not preserved intact through time, but rather constituted anew each generation with the birth of children who united the separate inheritances of their parents, marriage—which created the possibility of legitimate heirs—marked the point at which men and women passed from being dependents of their parents to assuming responsibility for the properties their children would inherit. Unmarried adults had few responsibilities. Married adults had to worry about preserving, and hopefully enlarging, the estate their children would inherit. Villagers commonly expressed this distinction between free youth and burdened adulthood through a conceptual opposition between *diversión* (entertainment) and *obligación* (obligation). Unmarried youths were encouraged to seek amusement. Married adults were expected to sacrifice pleasure for duty.

Although pleasure might seem preferable to duty, pleasure had its drawbacks, as I explain in this chapter and the next. For a man, lacking obligations condemned him to inconsequence—without responsibilities no one would take him seriously. As someone who had nothing to lose, he could not be trusted. This, I think, explains why young men in Los Olivos were eager to enter formal courtships—even if they did not expect to marry for many years. By entering his novia's house, a youth assumed—at least symbolically—responsibility for the property he expected to manage for his heirs. Until a man chose his bride, it was idle for people to speculate on his future property. But once the choice was made, people could imagine, often in very concrete terms, which fields and houses he was committed to protecting. Choosing a bride also revealed which woman a man was committed to defending from slights on her reputation.

In fact, the Prices describe a dramatic shift in young men's behavior when they initiated the formal stage of courtship by asking a novia's father for permission to enter his house. "*Novios* at the door are more openly affectionate with each other than at any other time; the relationship is budding and the tone is distinctly romantic. Couples do not hesitate to hold hands or pet if no one is watching for a moment. It is only after asking entrance that boys take seriously their responsibilities to respect the girl's family, and it is only with greater experience that they realize the futility of 'shameless' behavior" (1966a, 308). Once formalized, "*noviazgo* becomes extremely staid. Boys join adults as defenders of morality, actively chastening younger boys when they go on drinking sprees and sing abusive rhymes about the pueblo's girls" (1966a, 310).

In his field notes, Richard Price expresses his surprise at how "staid" formal courtships became. He asked his friend Juan "how much novios really get to be alone" and received the answer that novios have to "buscar la oportunidad" [search for the opportunity]: "Look, remember when María [Juan's novia], you and Sally, and I were talking by the door before? Well, when you and Sally went inside, María and I were alone for about 15 minutes. That is one of the longest times we have ever had alone together." And they had been formal novios for seven years! Richard Price adds that "during this rare occasion together, Juan and María were standing outside her house, in the sight of passersby, should there have been any in the falling darkness."[26]

On another occasion, two young men explained to Richard Price why suitors in Los Olivos generally respected the prohibition on physical contact with their novias.

> In a town of this size, [they said], the risks were too great to try anything secret with one's novia. They told how a couple which on the *paseo* strayed even slightly off the road immediately became the focus of intensive gossip and ridicule. The consequences of being found out are simply too great for

someone who wants to live the rest of his life in Los Olivos. So, they said, a man must have *mucha resignación* [much resignation]. Of course, they emphasized, there is often desire—Felipe says he's wanted many times to take [his novia] out into the fields to *aprovecharse* [take advantage], but he is always able to master himself, to think better of it in time. Besides, there are many opportunities to be with women [i.e., prostitutes] in other towns.[27]

This excerpt from Richard Price's field notes provides a dramatic illustration of how young men in the early 1960s talked about the relationship between internal desire and outward behavior. These two novios claimed to experience sexual desire for their novias but to suppress such desires in favor of following social conventions. Through their way of talking about what they did, these young men imagined—even as they reproduced—a social world in which people's actions testified to their respect for social conventions (or at least to their concern for what gossips would say) rather than to what a person might be thinking or wanting "underneath." Moreover, their way of talking ensured the continued salience—and thus existence—of the "internal desires" men said they were suppressing. Through claiming to repress their sexual desires for novias, and to express desire with prostitutes in appropriate contexts (i.e., where men's actions would not disrupt the orderly transmission of paternal inheritances), young men imagined, even as they reproduced, a social world in which men experienced sexual desires that they could either express or repress.

Fear of pregnancy was another reason why it did not make sense for young men to "take advantage" of their novias. Miguel, for example, explained to Richard Price that "few novios would risk sex with their girls, in spite of strong desire. For . . . one such experience could not but lead to a desire for more, and before they knew it, the girl would be pregnant."[28] Miguel and his fellow villagers had good reason to worry about pregnancy. Should a novia became pregnant, her novio faced two unpleasant options. He could abandon her, but would probably have to leave Los Olivos as well. No man who had so betrayed the trust of a village family could remain in town.[29] More likely, the novio would marry his novia before the child was born. Although couples whose first child arrived soon after the wedding were not openly stigmatized (indeed, George Collier and I found out about such couples only by looking up marriage and birth dates in the civil registries), the premarital pregnancy was never forgotten and could be recalled by villagers whenever they wanted to deflate the pretensions of either husband or wife. For example, one of my friends who criticized another woman not only told me that the woman was a shrew, gossip, and bad housekeeper who caused endless trouble for her long-suffering husband but added, as a final blow, that she had been pregnant when she married.

If young men in Los Olivos portrayed themselves as "resigned" to avoiding sexual intimacy with their novias, courtship was still preferable to marriage in some ways. A youth might have to give up "shameless" behavior with his novia, but he could still visit prostitutes in nearby towns. And even though he assumed responsibility for protecting his novia's reputation, he could abandon her if she misbehaved. It was not easy for a youth to abandon his novia. José told Richard Price that if a boy left a girl after having entered her house, "the boy's good name is . . . somewhat tainted. José said that the increased difficulty of finding a desirable novia here [in Los Olivos] after having had an earlier relationship here dissuades some boys from becoming involved in [a formal] noviazgo merely to pass the time."[30] Nevertheless, a novio could renounce a novia who had lost her public reputation for chastity—unlike a husband who lost his own honor if his wife lost hers.

Finally, the Prices report an advantage of courtship that was not mentioned by the young men they interviewed—the power that a formal novio acquired over his novia. The Prices observe that "As soon as boys have secured entrance to the house, they try to dictate their *novia*'s behavior, insisting on longer skirts, higher necklines, or longer sleeves, and often forbidding lipstick and makeup or prohibiting cutting and tinting the hair" (1966a, 311). Most novias obeyed. One woman, for example, told me that after she became engaged, she wore long sleeves all the time, even though the summer heat in Los Olivos can be oppressive. The power that a novio enjoyed over his novia derived from her insecurity—from the fact that a woman whose novio abandoned her had a hard time finding a suitable husband.

The Prices' observations and my experiences with older women suggest that for women in Los Olivos courtship was the high point of life. Whereas young men treated "*noviazgo* as but one aspect of their rather full lives," the Prices report that "*noviazgo* is the focus of a girl's life for more than a decade. Days are spent preparing for the evening visit, fantasying about marriage, and busily accumulating a hope chest. *Novias* spend countless hours sewing everything from embroidered underwear to linen napkins for their husband's lunches in the fields, all the while imagining what marriage will someday be like" (1966a, 310–311).

It is easy to understand why women experienced courtship as the high point of life. It appeared to be the time when they enjoyed the most power. Courting customs, after all, seemed designed to meet their needs and pleasures rather than those of men. Boys had to seek girls out at paseos and dances, flirt with them to gain their attention, walk with them to their street corners, flatter them, beg for favors, ask permission to enter their houses, and finally visit them every evening until the wedding.

Older women also reminded girls that they should enjoy themselves while they could. My neighbors with teenage daughters returned to this theme endlessly as we spent long winter afternoons sewing and knitting together. For women, the *obligación/diversión* (obligation/pleasure) conceptual opposition combined with a *casa/calle* (home/street) contrast to cast courtship as the one time in a woman's life when she would be able to pursue public pleasures. After she married, a woman was expected to stay home and sacrifice herself for the sake of her children. The villagers I met in the early 1960s were too polite to openly pity me for having cut short my time of pleasure by marrying so young. But women could not contain their expressions of dismay at Sally Price's youth (she was twenty). For several weeks after Richard and Sally Price's visit to Los Olivos in April 1964, women who met me in the streets kept recalling the scene of Sally washing her husband's trousers in the public fountain. Their allusions to the event invariably provoked choruses of "Ay, ¡que pena!" [What a tragedy!] from nearby listeners. Even though unmarried young women in Los Olivos regularly washed the soiled work pants of their brothers and fathers, the image of Sally washing her husband's pants seemed to evoke, more than any other incident, the sense of what a woman sacrificed by taking on the heavy obligations of marriage.

But if young women experienced courtship as a time for pleasure, the pleasure was spiced with danger. I picked up a sense of this danger from listening to mothers warn their teenage daughters. Shelly Zimbalist, who hung out with young women in the summer of 1965, captured in her field notes the heady mixture of power and fear that courting girls experienced. Because Shelly and her friend Sally Simmons focused most of their interviews on mourning customs, however, the fears of courting girls emerge primarily in short interchanges.

The women and girls Shelly interviewed consistently characterized the male/female conceptual opposition as one between women who were *amarradas* (tied down) and men who were *libres* (free).[31] One woman responded to Shelly's question about why girls had to worry about shame (*verguenza*) more than boys with the statement that "girls have to look out, because men are not the same as women; men are free, they are not tied down, they don't pay attention to any of that [gossip]; women are the ones who have something to lose."[32] What a woman had to lose, of course, was her honor. She could lose her reputation for chastity, as one woman explained when telling Shelly and Sally why men could show sexual desire whereas women could not. "Here a man cannot dishonor himself, but a woman can."[33]

In the early 1960s, the penalties suffered by a girl who was "dishon-ored" were immediate and far-reaching. Richard Price reported a con-versation with a young man who claimed "that virginity is an absolute necessity to Los Olivos males. . . . A *novio* who finds out that his *novia* has the slightest taint of another man upon her—even complete hearsay that she has fooled with other men in the past—leaves her immedi-ately."[34] The slightest suspicion could doom a girl's chances of finding a husband in the village, condemning her to spinsterhood, marriage with an undesirable man (such as a widower or drunkard), or marriage with an outsider who would take her away from her kin.[35]

People did recognize that it was unfair to condemn women for what men were allowed to do, especially if a woman was condemned on hear-say alone. Men, in particular, could be very sympathetic to women's plight. Both George Collier and Richard Price were told by male friends that many prostitutes and calendar pinup girls were actually "good" women. One man, for example, said that he had talked to several girls about how they became prostitutes, and found that "except for those that are born that way, most are girls who lost their virginity on a fling at some fiesta or other, and the word got around, thus forcing the girl to leave town and try to find work elsewhere, which often turns into prostitution."[36] Similarly, village men could talk movingly of the plight of servant girls raped by their masters who were dismissed when they became pregnant. Village women, who neither patronized prostitutes nor bought nude calendars, were less sympathetic. They tended to ob-serve that since women knew the consequences of their actions it was their own fault if they incurred them.

For women, innocence was not a virtue. When Shelly and Sally were pestered to dance, drink, or take a walk by youths from a nearby town, Angeles, one of the village girls, told them that "the boys wanted to take advantage of our innocence, and *reírse*, to laugh at us." Angeles went on to observe that young women "in Los Olivos aren't vulnerable to this kind of approach,"[37] implying that although boys from other towns might regard any Los Olivos woman as fair game (unlike local boys who knew the girls' families), foreign boys did not bother to pester local girls because they knew that village girls, unlike visiting North Americans, understood the consequences of dancing, drinking, or walking with a boy.

What local girls understood, of course, was that women who re-mained publicly "tied down" enjoyed more freedom of action than women who apparently escaped the bonds. As suggested by the man who said "the word got around," a woman suspected of having lost her virginity became the prey of any man. Angeles, after telling Shelly that local girls were not vulnerable to the kind of pestering inflicted on "innocent" foreigners, went on to say that Los Olivos girls could become vulnerable to such abuse if "they have hugged and kissed their *novios* in public."[38] In Los Olivos, a girl who avoided any situation where she could be suspected of acting out her sexual desires could dance, flirt, and choose her novio because she retained the power to say no. A woman who had once let down her guard, however, was likely to find her refusals ignored.

The fate that awaited women who lost the power to say no was visibly enacted by the few unmarried mothers in Los Olivos. All five had been more than thirty, and thus recognized spinsters, before giving birth (Price and Price 1966a, 317). But after bearing a child they were far more tied down than their age-mates. Single mothers had to be extremely careful about their movements in order to avoid provoking physical attacks by men and verbal attacks by women who would blame them for seducing men. As one said, "having a child as I do, that is something that you have to carry inside you always."[39] The permanent vulnerability of an unwed mother was dramatically demonstrated in the summer of 1965, when a village man was murdered and a woman was jailed for the crime. The accused murderess tried to offer the one defense available to a woman: she killed to protect her honor. No one listened. She had an illegitimate child. She had no honor to defend.[40]

When the women Shelly and Sally interviewed portrayed themselves as "tied down," they implied, of course, that women, like men, experienced sexual desire. Had women not experienced desire, there would have been no need to restrain them. As a result, women in Los Olivos, like men of the village, implied disjunction between what a person wanted to do and what a person actually did. They, too, imagined—even as they reproduced—a social world in which people's actions testified to their respect for social conventions, rather than to what a person might be thinking or feeling underneath. Felisa, for example, explained to Shelly that a woman who openly looked at men would feel shame, not for having looked, but at the fact that men would talk about her. When Shelly asked why a woman would not want men to talk about her, Felisa responded that it was because men would interpret the woman's looking as a sign that she "wanted something" (i.e., sex).[41]

Women, like men, also ensured the reproduction of repressed desires by enacting them in appropriate contexts. In the summer of 1965, for example, Shelly heard several jokes about women's sexual desire when she accompanied village girls on an all-female expedition to collect *brevas* (figs—but also a metaphor for testicles). Her field notes report that the girls "laughed a lot and said that for *brevas* they'd even miss lunch."

They also joked that "the *breva* you eat today '*se cria mañana*' (grows [like a baby] tomorrow)," and claimed to be ill with *pancho de breva* (fig stomach) when they had eaten their fill.[42]

Given women's portrayal of themselves as feeling sexual desire while fearing dishonor, it is easy to understand why girls in Los Olivos experienced courtship as an intoxicating mixture of pleasure and anxiety. Simultaneously flattered and endangered by their novios, they were invited to enjoy public entertainments while scrutinized to assess their "shame." But if women relished courtship, its pleasures tended to pale over time as its dangers increased. When first initiated, formal courtship represented security. Richard Price observed that a girl in the transitional stages of courtship "knows that she must be charming in order to hold onto her man, in order to get the security of [formal courtship] where splits would be much more difficult."[43]

As time passed, however, a novia's vulnerability increased, because the longer a formal courtship lasted, the less likely a novia would be able to find a suitable marriage partner if her novio should leave her. Richard Price observes in his field notes that after the boy enters the girl's house, "The girl is far more emotionally concerned than the boy—and with good reason. She must hold on to him hard, because once he leaves her, she will have the greatest difficulty finding another partner, and if she gets one at all, he is bound to be less desirable. The boy, meanwhile, takes advantage of the situation and tries to dominate her, telling her what to wear, that she should not go to Aracena alone for shopping, etc."[44]

In later field notes, Richard Price concludes that if a girl broke up with a novio she had been seeing for several years, she was "pretty much finished as far as future Los Olivos relationships are concerned."[45] Men in Los Olivos could happily "resign themselves" to prolonging worry-free courtships, but women could not. When Shelly suggested to Angeles, a young woman who had been a novia for several years, that she "didn't have to worry about [the] kind of abuse" boys inflicted on innocent foreign girls and "dishonored" local ones, Angeles replied "that as she wasn't married yet, she still couldn't be sure."[46]

Women's comments also suggest that novias were more eager for sexual intimacy than their suitors.[47] Both Juan and his novia María may have told Richard and Sally Price separately that novios "have to be on the lookout always for opportunities" to be alone together.[48] But María, unlike Juan, did not go on to observe that novios had to practice restraint in taking advantage of the opportunities that presented themselves. Another woman, talking with Shelly about a novia who became pregnant, said that she thought the novia got pregnant on purpose: because the novia "wanted a family so much . . . she 'got married before she was married.'"[49] No woman talked with us about the advantages of premarital pregnancy, but it must have been obvious to anyone who bothered to think about it that the social consequences suffered by a pregnant bride were slight compared to those inflicted on a novia whose long-term suitor left her.[50]

Finally, women had good reason to hasten the wedding because marriage lightened their workloads. Richard Price observes in his field notes that "women, in contrast to men, work less and have an easier life in the years following marriage than before. There is little to do in the house [a woman acquires at marriage], and girls spend a large part of their time at their mother's home, but they do only as much work as they wish. They no longer have the same responsibilities there. María thus looks forward to the time when she will be married and have the easy life as far as household tasks go."[51]

Although a woman's tasks did lighten because the house she moved to upon marriage was likely to have fewer people residing in it than the house she shared with her natal family, this was not the only reason a wife's workload diminished. A married woman had far less work than a single one because—finally—she could claim to have adult "obligations."

In Los Olivos, women, unlike men, could not symbolically acquire adult obligations by simply choosing a spouse. Women had to wait until after they were married and had their own houses to manage. Moreover, having obligations had a greater impact on a woman's life than on a man's. For men, marriage brought increased responsibilities and worries, but not an increased workload. Both before and after marriage, adult men did the work required of them by the properties they expected to inherit. Women's workload, in contrast, diminished drastically, at least at first. Marriage not only put a bride in charge of a small household, consisting of only herself and her husband, but also provided her with *the* culturally valid excuse for refusing other women's requests for household help. In Los Olivos, a woman who lacked obligations had no control over her life—as I discovered after observing one spinster whose married relatives never allowed her a moment's peace.[52] A woman with her own house to manage, in contrast, could refuse other women's requests for aid with the excuse that she had to attend to her obligations. A married woman could also ask her unmarried sisters, daughters, and nieces for help in performing chores she would rather avoid. Older girls, in particular, were usually asked to perform the heaviest and dirtiest household tasks. No wonder burdened novias were more eager to marry than their carefree novios. The fiancée of the legendary suitor who so enjoyed courtship that he visited her every evening for fifty-four years was apparently less enthusiastic about their relationship than he. She reportedly hoped that "he would start talking 'marriage,' but he never did."[53]

Courting girls were caught in a classic example of what Betty Friedan, writing about the plight of North American housewives in the 1950s, called "a problem without a name" (1963, 11–27). Enjoying what everyone told them was the time of greatest pleasure and freedom in their lives, novias in Los Olivos understandably found it difficult to talk about the fears and misgivings they experienced. When Shelly asked Josefa "why people wait so long to marry and who is most anxious, boys or girls, she said 'boys' and then said, 'girls too, but they can't say so' . . . the decision to marry is always up to the boy, and though the girl may be anxious, she can only confess this to a friend, never a novio."[54]

Not only did women fear appearing "shameless," but their anxieties must have seemed insignificant compared to the pleasures they were supposed to be enjoying. How could a woman claim to be vulnerable and powerless when her novio's nightly visits visibly displayed her power over him? How could she express her sexual frustrations when her novio's refusal to take advantage of their few opportunities alone demonstrated his "respect" for her reputation? And how could she complain about her workload when her mother and all her older relatives constantly told her that she had nothing to do but seek her own pleasure? Forced to live such contradictions, novias in Los Olivos understandably appeared emotionally unstable. In contrast to novios, who "resigned" themselves to "tolerating *noviazgo* with a smile," novias apparently cried at the slightest provocation. After attending a dance at which three novias burst into tears, Richard Price observes that "everyone thought this behavior fairly ordinary, and no one thought much of it. It still seems a bit strange to us, when the motives for the outbursts [some insignificant remarks] are investigated and the ages of the girls are considered [two were well into their twenties]."[55]

## THE MAKING AND UNMAKING OF "TRADITIONAL" COURTSHIPS

The villagers who described their courtship customs in the early 1960s reported that "no village for miles around [had] such formal courting procedures" (Price and Price 1966a, 315). Morals were looser in other communities, they said, particularly in Aracena, the major market town in the region. Indeed, Richard Price, who accompanied young men on trips to sell fruit in regional markets, observes that "The difference between Los Olivos girls and those from Aracena and Galaroza is striking, with the latter being much more worldly and ready to flirt."[56]

Villagers also reported that courtship customs had changed over time. "Fifty years ago," an older woman told the Prices, "*noviazgo* was considerably less formal than it is today." She and other members of her generation reported that before the civil war, "Several years of active 'playing the field,' replete with rivalries and male fisticuffs, preceded entrance into formal unions" (Price and Price 1966a, 314).[57] "In some less formal families,[58] apparently a minority, a pretender entered the girl's house without any formal *pedida* [petition]. Coming at first on the pretext of visiting with the girl's father or brothers, the pretender would gradually shift his attention and conversation toward the girl. . . . Marriages hastened by knowledge of a novia's pregnancy were [also] more common. In spite of the steadfast protectiveness of parents and the careful chaperonage, people were apparently quicker to profit from those rare moments when parents' guards were dropped" (Price 1964).

George Collier, in his analysis of political conflict in Los Olivos before the Spanish civil war, suggests that differences between more and less formal families might reflect the class difference between workers and property owners. "Poor people experienced marriage differently from the rich, often marrying with only wages to support themselves, whereas richer couples married with established household properties" (1987, 181). His examination of the civil registries revealed that women born to poor families in the 1870s and 1880s married "up to five years younger" than women from propertied families, most of whom postponed marriage until after the age of thirty (1987, 181). Rich and poor men born in these decades "did not differ significantly in the age at which they married before the war [around thirty-one or thirty-two]. . . . But Socialists had been twice as likely as rightists to enter marriage with a pregnant wife near term, possibly thus heralding the ideology of free love of leftists of the era" (1987, 182). Leftist workers may also have felt freer than rightist property owners to enter the homes of fellow socialists to court eligible sisters and daughters. And the "rivalries and male fisticuffs" reported to the Prices may have reflected political as well as sexual rivalries among unmarried young men.

Most of the villagers born before 1905 were married by 1936, but most of those born between 1905 and 1915, who were courting when the war broke out in 1936, had to postpone their weddings. Many poor women, particularly those with socialist suitors, lost novios in the massacres of 1936 and 1937 or had to wait for their novios to be released from prison. The postwar famine also affected rich and poor differently. Wealthy couples, and those from rightist families who benefited from Franco's victory, were able to marry in the early 1940s. Couples from poor families, unable to accumulate the resources necessary for setting up independent households, had to postpone marriage until economic conditions improved. Among women who married between 1939 and 1949, poor brides tended to be older than rich ones.

By the 1950s, variations in courting customs by economic class and political ideology had disappeared (G. Collier 1987, 183). Villagers born between 1915 and 1924, most of whom reached courting age after the massacres of 1936 and 1937, tended to reminisce about how unified they were as teenagers and young adults. When I interviewed women of this cohort in the 1980s, many reported that all the girls in their age group had attended dances together and had formed close friendships without distinctions between rich and poor. Indeed, several cross-class friendships endured into the 1980s.

Class and political distinctions did not disappear, however. They actually sharpened in some ways. Several women born between 1915 and 1924 remained functionally illiterate because poverty forced them to forgo schooling, whereas others became avid readers as servants freed them from household tasks. Many women from socialist families lost fathers and brothers in the massacres of 1936 and 1937. Although no member of the 1915–24 birth cohort suggested—at least to me—that the unity they remember might have been a reaction to prewar political and economic conflict, it seems obvious that in the years immediately following the war no villager benefited from calling attention to class or political differences. Any young person who expressed socialist views or resentment of economic inequalities risked imprisonment, while young people from wealthy families had reason to remain silent about the massacres their senior kin had failed to prevent.

The disappearance of variations in courting patterns must also have been fostered by poor women's need to emulate the behavior of rich people if they hoped to marry within the village.[59] The Prices, who calculated a 15 percent celibacy rate for the 80 percent of village adolescents they defined as poor,[60] concluded that poor *solteros* (spinsters, bachelors), in contrast to rich ones, were "the products of a more fluid system, in which idiosyncratic shortcomings—the main determinant of rich *solteros*—combine with the stigma of previous courtships to count against them. While for a rich person the chances of remaining single are largely determined from the start, poor people have many opportunities to 'acquire' undesirability as they move through the courtship system" (Price and Price 1966b, 531).[61]

Among poor women's "many opportunities to 'acquire' undesirability" were the activities that poverty forced upon them. Girls who had to work for employers outside their families, either as domestic servants or as agricultural wage laborers, were vulnerable to sexual advances from masters or overseers. Because girls from poor families could not expect to marry rich men even if they remained chaste, many villagers assumed that poor girls had less reason to guard their virginity than rich ones. Poor girls thus had to demonstrate their chastity through stricter adherence to village norms than rich women, who were usually presumed chaste unless proved otherwise.

In the years following the civil war, courtships also became more "formal," and they became longer. Villagers told the Prices that "It was only during the late 30's and 40's that the *paseo* and the 'corner' and 'door' stages of *noviazgo* were gradually institutionalized. And the average age at entrance into first formal *noviazgo* . . . dropped a full 3 years" between the civil war and the 1960s (Price and Price 1966a, 314). These changes were carried out primarily by villagers who were born between 1925 and 1934, who reached courting age as economic conditions were improving after the civil war and postwar famine. Their long, formal courtships thus reflect the effects of living in a community dominated by the victorious landlords, where expected inheritances were the major factor determining whether an initial attachment would lead to marriage.[62] Unfortunately, the number of people from this cohort whose marriages I could trace is very small. Nevertheless, the data on age of marriage are revealing. The average age at marriage for the eighteen men born between 1925 and 1929 was thirty-one years. For the seventeen men born between 1930 and 1934, it was thirty-two years. The average age at marriage for the eleven women born between 1925 and 1929 was thirty years. And for the nine women born between 1930 and 1934, it was thirty-one years. Almost all of these people were married by the time I arrived in Los Olivos.

The couples who were courting during my visit, and who welcomed Richard and Sally Price in the summer of 1964, were primarily those born between 1935 and 1944. Of the eleven men born between 1935 and 1939, three were already married by 1964. They married young by village standards: at ages twenty-four, twenty-six, and twenty-seven. The remaining eight men were still courting and expected to postpone their weddings until the bride approached the age of thirty. But their plans, along with the plans of villagers born between 1940 and 1944, were disrupted by rising emigration and the collapse of village agriculture. Many courting couples married shortly after the Prices left the village. Suitors who emigrated to urban jobs needed wives to perform domestic services—a traditional reason given for hastening marriage by village men who lacked unmarried sisters or an active mother. At the same time, courting became less amusing for those who remained in Los Olivos. Paseos and dances became *tristes* (sad) as emigration reduced attendance and as *viudas* (girls with absent novios, literally "widows") had to dance with each other. For the eleven men and sixteen women in the 1935–39 birth cohort, the average age at marriage for both sexes fell to twenty-eight years. For the five men born between 1940 and 1944, the average age at marriage dropped to twenty-seven years, whereas for the sixteen women born between 1940 and 1944, it dropped to twenty-five.

The courting couples interviewed by the Prices were, in fact, the last villagers to observe "traditional" courtship customs. The adolescents who were just beginning to "look each other over" in the early 1960s married after relatively short courtships. For the nineteen men born between 1945 and 1949, the average age at marriage fell to twenty-six,[63] whereas for the seventeen women born between 1945 and 1949, the average age at marriage remained at twenty-five years.[64] Most of the people born after 1945 adopted "modern," "urban" ways of courting. Many courted in cities. They emigrated as teenagers or young adults to accompany parents or to join older siblings in Seville, Huelva, Barcelona, and Madrid. Others spent extended periods living with urban relatives who could help them find factory jobs. Even young people who remained in Los Olivos began abandoning "traditional" courtship customs as young men's search for urban jobs made it difficult for them to visit their novias every night, and as more teenagers began to spend their days together in classes at the secondary school in Aracena.[65]

### "MODERN" COURTSHIP

Even though the people I interviewed in the 1980s characterized the changes in courtship customs as "from night to day," they tended to emphasize the "loss" of traditional practices rather than their replacement by modern ones. They talked, for example, about the disappearance of constant chaperoning, the demise of long courtships, the decline of formal petitions, and men's loss of respect for women. On the surface, it is easy to understand why people experienced the changes primarily as "losses." The customs of the 1960s did seem to fade away as their requirements became harder for young people and their parents to meet.

On a deeper level, however, the changes represented losses because the practices that replaced them were hard to think of as "customs." "Modern" young people seemed to be doing what earlier couples had wanted to do but had been constrained by custom from enacting. The four most frequently mentioned "new" practices, for example, all involved activities that courting couples in the early 1960s claimed to crave but had refused to enact out of respect for social conventions. Novios who went out alone together appeared to be acting on couples' frequently expressed—but suppressed—desire to steal moments alone. Novios who began making wedding plans shortly after becoming engaged appeared to be realizing couples' previously suppressed desire to initiate sexual intimacy as soon as possible. Young men who gained entrance to a girl's house without asking formal permission appeared to be avoiding an encounter dreaded by earlier novios. And "men who no longer respected women" appeared to be indulging masculine appetites that youths expressed when visiting other towns but suppressed in their home communities out of respect for local families.

Finally, courting customs seemed to disappear because "modern" young people claimed to be doing what they wanted, rather than what was expected of them by others. In contrast to villagers I met in the 1960s, who had a well-developed vocabulary for talking about how young people should behave and who could regale visiting anthropologists with vivid descriptions of their courtship customs, the people I interviewed in the 1980s seemed to have a hard time explaining the behavior of young people. They could describe some of the things that courting couples did, such as going out alone in the evenings and starting to make wedding plans as soon as they became engaged, but these practices were hard to think of as "customs." They were not activities that young people were required to do by convention, tradition, or fear of gossip. Rather, they seemed to represent what any "normal" young person would do if left free to decide how to act.

Because I, like members of Conchi's generation, also thought that "modern" courtship customs were normal, I too had difficulty thinking of them as activities that young people might be required to do. In this section, however, I want to suggest that "modern" courtship customs were as culturally constructed, and socially enforced, as "traditional" ones. New courtship practices did not represent either a loss of custom or people's release from previous constraints. Rather, they represented people's adoption of new customs in response to a new set of constraints and incentives. In particular, I use a contrast between "traditional" and "modern" courtship practices to suggest that villagers and emigrants who adopted "new" courting practices did so as their experiences of participating in the wider market economy encouraged them to change their gender conceptions and associated understandings of gender-appropriate behaviors. "Modern" customs did not simply reflect what any normal person would do if freed from "traditional" constraints. Rather, they reflected a particular understanding of the "normal" encouraged by a discourse of occupational achievement.

I begin by reproducing some stories of courtship from my notes on interviews with married couples in the 1980s. These stories are not directly comparable to the courtship histories collected by the Prices in

1964. For one thing, my stories are not about broken relationships but about courtships that ended in marriage. And I collected these stories from protagonists rather than from people describing the courtships of others. Nevertheless, the stories I obtained in interviews do capture the flavor of how people talked about courtships that occurred after emigration and the collapse of markets for village produce had changed villagers' experiences of social inequality.

> Miguela and Evaristo said they had been novios, at least informally, from childhood. Miguela, who was several years younger than Evaristo, explained that she had gotten to like him when she was still in primary school and he was attending secondary school. She "had never liked any other man the same way." But the formal noviazgo began later. When Evaristo left the village for military service, he began writing to Miguela. They continued corresponding after he left the army and took an office job in Madrid. Evaristo took advantage of his first vacation to return to Los Olivos and do the *protocolo* of entering the house and formalizing the noviazgo with Miguela's parents. When I asked Miguela and Evaristo how they conducted their courtship after he returned to Madrid, leaving her in the village, Evaristo chuckled and said they "spent hours on the phone planning the wedding."
>
> Urbano and Isabel laughingly described their first impressions of each other. She had noticed his hairy legs at a village soccer game, and he first noticed her on the Sunday paseo. Even though Urbano was going out with another girl at the time, he said that he walked behind Isabel and already wanted her.[66] Isabel observed that even though they were not novios that summer, Urbano watched her and refused to let her go out with anyone else. A couple of years later, after both Urbano and Isabel had emigrated with their families to Barcelona, they met again. At this time, they began seeing one another regularly. When I asked how they conducted their courtship in the city, Isabel laughed and said they did it just as if they were in Los Olivos. Urbano is "very traditional," she said. "He even asked my father for permission to enter the house." Urbano disagreed. He said that "One day Isabel was sick. When I went to inquire after her, Isabel's mother invited me in."

The most striking thing about these stories is that they are about how the couple came to choose one another. Miguela had "never liked any other man the same way." And Urbano knew that he "wanted" Isabel even though he was going out with another girl at the time. Some of the married couples I interviewed even told stories of instantly recognizing the unique other destined for them. One woman, for example, reported that the first time she saw her future husband she knew that "this one's for me."[67] And a man reported that after he saw his future wife walk by the store where he worked, he turned to his coworker and announced that he was going to marry that woman.

Commentators also talked about love when discussing the courtships of others. In the summer of 1983, for example, some emigrant parents stressed a suitor's faithfulness when telling their Los Olivos relatives about their daughter's courtship with a young man from Barcelona. "He came to inquire after her every day when she was sick," they said. And whenever I heard people discussing the problems of a young couple who held jobs in different cities, I noticed that they regaled each other with stories of how the novios constantly wrote and telephoned one another, and of how they used all their vacations to spend time together.

In contrast to villagers in the 1960s, who were apparently able to assume that novios loved one another if they stayed together, the people I spoke with in the 1980s seemed to feel that they had to document love's progress with stories about lovers' feelings and actions. This is the subtle shift from honor to romantic love that I believe occurred between my two visits to Los Olivos. In the early 1960s, people who wanted to understand whether or not a particular couple would marry had to focus on the properties and reputations of their respective families and on the couple's respect for social conventions. Villagers' experience of living in a social world where inherited property was the most important determinant of family wealth taught them that parents usually intervened to prevent marriages between status unequals, and that girls who acquired bad reputations were unlikely to find village husbands. After people from Los Olivos began participating in the wider market economy, however, those who wanted to assess the likelihood of a wedding, or to explain why one had occurred, had to focus on the couple's love for one another. People's experience of living in a social world where individuals appeared to achieve the statuses they enjoyed encouraged them to imagine that individual intention was the best predictor of eventual outcomes.

Although the villagers and former villagers I interviewed in the 1980s commonly implied that young people were doing what they wanted when they observed "modern" courtship customs, I plan to suggest that the techniques of self-management required to demonstrate "love" for one's future spouse were not significantly less onerous than those required to demonstrate respect for social conventions. Couples in the 1980s were not free to do what they wanted. Just as a young man in the 1960s had to visit his novia every night or her father would bar the door, so a novio in the 1980s had to inquire after his sick novia if he did not want her and her family to assume that his affection was waning. Similarly, couples separated by distance had to enact their love by constantly telephoning and writing one another.

In fact, courtship customs in the 1980s may have been even more onerous than those in the 1960s, because young people in the 1960s could at least think what they wanted underneath. They could admit to feeling anger, hostility, and doubt without endangering a future marriage. A young man who was having a fight with his novia, for example, could take a pocket novel along to read during his required nightly visits (Price and Price 1966a, 311). A suitor in the 1980s could not have done such a thing without calling into question his love for his novia. If couples were mad at each other in the 1980s, they had to confront their quarrel and assess its effect on their relationship. Once young people had to think for themselves, they could no longer refer to social conventions or to the neighbors' gossip to explain their actions. Instead, they had to come up with reasons why they, as unique individuals, had decided to do what they did. They had to produce the kind of narrative trajectories of the self that Giddens (1991) characterizes as peculiarly modern.

Although I have no way of knowing what the people I spoke with were actually thinking and feeling inside, my own experiences as a "modern" person lead me to imagine that they, like I, must have felt pressure to ensure that that their inward desires matched their outward actions. During my own courtship, I remember feeling that I had to monitor my emotions constantly to be sure I really loved my fiancé, even as I also felt compelled to suppress or to counteract any emotions deemed inappropriate for those who truly loved one another. As someone who was supposed to do what she wanted, I felt constant pressure to produce myself as the kind of person who would want to do what I did.

In order to explore the self-management techniques required of young people who would "think for themselves," I plan to focus on the four most frequently mentioned changes in courtship customs. I discuss each in turn, beginning with an explanation of why it made sense for people to talk about the change as a loss of custom rather than as the invention of a new one. Then I consider the constraints and incentives that encouraged young people to imagine—and to ensure—that they wanted to behave as they thought they should.

The first change people invariably mentioned was that "young couples now go out alone together." On one level, going out alone reflects an obvious change in people's real circumstances. Novios from Los Olivos had always "gone out together," in the sense of attending paseos, dances, and chestnut roasts, but couples in the early 1960s were never "alone" because they were always surrounded by villagers who knew who they were and who watched their every move. Urban novios, in contrast, usually went out alone in the sense that they frequently moved among strangers who neither recognized them nor cared how they behaved.

"Modern" novios, however, went out alone in another sense. After all, parents in urban areas could have insisted that novios take a chaperone along if they had wanted to ensure that couples were never without supervision. But parents did not. This fact, I believe, reflects the importance of love. Once love became the crucial factor determining marriage (and it could no longer simply be assumed to exist), love had to be nurtured. Couples had to be left alone to explore and develop their feelings for one another. The presence of a watchful mother—which in the 1960s had ensured that novios restrained the sexual desire for each other that everyone assumed they felt—must have seemed in the 1980s to prevent young people from discovering and communicating their feelings. No wonder Conchi thought that the courting customs of her parents' generation were not "normal." How could young people decide they truly loved one another if girls were never allowed "out from underneath the mother's skirts"? When I interviewed parents who courted before 1965, I noticed that their teenage and young adult children invariably reacted with surprise and horror at their parents' descriptions of nightly visits in the novia's kitchen. For these young people, as for Richard Price and myself in the 1960s, the idea of having to court under the watchful eye of the girl's mother seemed appalling. Couples had to be able to hold hands, kiss, and embrace in private if they were to find out whether their initial attraction could develop into lasting affection.

Not only did young couples have to go out alone together, they also had to want to do the activities they pursued. Young women, in particular, had to convince themselves that they really wanted to do what their novios proposed. The emotion work involved is suggested by one woman from Los Olivos who married a man from Barcelona. Chari laughingly reported that when she and her husband were courting, he took her to soccer matches every weekend even though she disliked the game. He was a passionate fan of the local team; she spent her time watching the people around her rather than the players. "I had to endure it," Chari reported, and then laughingly added that her fiancé could have had a worse passion. She also teased her husband for seldom taking her dancing—her preferred activity.

Chari's effort to rationalize her "endurance" contrasts with the "resignation" expressed by young men in the 1960s. Unlike Chari, the young men interviewed by Richard Price did not offer spontaneous explanations for why they—as individuals—had decided to observe courting customs they perceived as designed to meet women's needs rather than their own. They simply took it for granted that young people in Los Olivos had to follow social conventions, even as they remained free to think what they wanted underneath. Chari, in contrast, had to reconcile her thoughts and actions. Instead of accepting the fact that she hated soccer (and thus recognizing that socially enforced gender in-equalities allowed her novio to dictate their joint activities), she went through a cost-benefit analysis to convince herself and her listeners that, as an individual who thought for herself, she really wanted to attend soccer matches.

The second most frequently mentioned change in courtship practices concerned young people's haste to marry. Instead of prolonging court-ship, as novios had before 1965, young couples "wanted to get married the day they became engaged." This shift from long to short courtships also reflects a change in people's circumstances. There was less reason to prolong courtship as paseos, chestnut roasts, and dances became less amusing; urban youths "needed" wives to take care of them; and—as I explain in the next chapter—couples were no longer required to furnish a house before marrying.

But novios' reported "haste" also reflects, I think, a change in the concepts people used to interpret and assess the behaviors of courting couples. Once love became the most important factor for predicting whether or not an initial attraction would lead to marriage, a couple's reluctance to set the wedding date must have testified to their lack of commitment to one another. No wonder Miguela and Evaristo "spent hours on the phone planning the wedding." They had to. When review-ing my interview notes from the 1980s, I noticed that among couples who married before 1960, those who had courted less than four years usually offered an explanation for why they had married so soon. Among couples who married after 1970, in contrast, couples who had courted for more than four years usually tried to explain why they had been forced to postpone the wedding.

Novios' haste to marry also reflects, I believe, a shift in the concepts people used to interpret "work" and its opposites. During my first visit to Los Olivos, courtship and marriage fell on opposite sides of a concep-tual opposition between amusements and obligations. Courting couples could amuse themselves because, unlike married couples, they did not have to worry about preserving and enhancing the property their chil-dren would inherit. After people from Los Olivos began to participate in the wider market economy, however, courtship and marriage fell to-gether on the leisure side of a work/leisure opposition. Neither court-ship nor marriage was undertaken to earn money. Rather, people did them for their own benefit and enjoyment. As a result, marriage no longer signified the end of novios' freedom to pursue pleasure. Rather it represented the culmination of courtship's delights. No wonder couples had to begin planning their weddings as soon as they became engaged.

The third most commonly mentioned change in courtship practices does, I think, represent the loss of a "traditional" custom without its replacement by a "modern" one. Young men now "enter a girl's house without asking," people told me, implying that young men no longer asked a girl's father for formal permission to court her. Like other changes, this one also reflected a transformation in people's circumstances. In the early 1960s, a young man who had not asked entrance to his novia's house had few opportunities to be with women. But in the 1980s, young people had many opportunities to spend time together—attending classes, working in factories and offices, and going out in the evenings with friends. In fact, young people could be well on the way to deciding they were meant for each other before they met one another's families. Such meetings could be very informal, as indicated by Urbano's statement that his mother-in-law invited him inside when he went to Isabel's house to inquire after her health.

Ironically, I believe that the failure to replace this custom with a new one was what allowed it to assume the status of a "tradition" that "modern" people could want to follow. In contrast to going out alone together and wanting to marry as soon possible, both of which "modern" novios were required to want on pain of not appearing to be in love, no novio in the 1980s had to want an "informal" meeting with his future parents-in-law. As a result, a young man could ask formal permission without casting doubt on his feelings for his novia, even as his act testified to his desire to observe "traditions." Evaristo, a self-proclaimed Andalusian nationalist, proudly described how he took advantage of his first vacation to ask Miguela's parents for formal permission to enter her house. And Isabel jokingly described Urbano as "very traditional" for having asked her father's permission—even though Urbano disagreed with her account.

The fourth and final change in courtship customs, which was mentioned to me only by older women, concerns men's alleged "loss of respect for women." This is a more subtle shift than the others and my explanation for it is more subjective. I think it reflects a deep, albeit undiscussed, change in the gender conceptions people used to understand and assess the behavior of women and men. When older women implied that men in the past showed "respect," they were referring to men's concern for women's chastity. Village boys "respected" local girls by not pestering them for walks, dances, kisses, and so forth. And novios "respected" their novias by refusing to take advantage of rare opportunities alone. Men, in particular, had to separate the "love" they felt for future wives from their desires for sexual intimacy, which they satisfied with prostitutes. As people from Los Olivos began actively participating in the wider market economy, however, this separation between love and sex broke down. Men had to seek sexual favors and women had to grant them if couples were to explore—and develop—their feelings for one another.[68]

In the earlier section on gender conceptions, I suggested that participating in a social world where status is achieved encourages people to imagine that women's bodies are designed to produce babies whereas men's bodies are designed to produce goods and governments. Not only do these gender conceptions encourage people to envision marriage as a contract between persons with different abilities and needs who agree to share their lives because they love one another; these gender conceptions also pose a particular problem for women who—because the market discourages attempts to combine motherhood with making money—have difficulty demonstrating love untainted by greed. When I was interviewing Resurre, a woman from Los Olivos who reached courting age around 1936, she observed—somewhat ironically—that in her day "the men used to come looking for us" whereas "now the women go out to look for the men." I do not think that her statement was literally true. During both my visits, young people used public occasions to "look each other over," as the mayor stated in 1963. But Resurre's observation does capture the crux of women's dilemma in a market economy. When I first visited Los Olivos, both boys and girls needed to marry if they were to assume adult roles. Marriage was a prerequisite for acquiring the legitimate heirs that allowed both men and women to claim adult obligations. When I returned to Spain in the 1980s, in contrast, women "needed" husbands more than men needed wives. A man did not have to marry in order to fulfill his adult role as a producer of income-earning goods and services. The amount of money a man earned appeared to depend on his own skills and abilities. But a woman had to marry in order to fulfill her adult role of bearing and rearing children. The amount and quality of care a mother could provide for her children depended less on her own abilities as a nurturer than on her success in finding a husband (or husband-substitute) who loved her enough to share his income with her.

Although no one told me in bald terms that women needed husbands, I did notice a shift in how friends characterized the source of constraints on women. In the 1960s, as I discussed earlier, people tended to observe that women, unlike men, had "something to lose" (i.e, their honor). In the 1980s, in contrast, people talking about the constraints on women commonly observed that women "have children."[69] This observation came up most frequently during discussions of women's paid employment. Friends talking about the upcoming marriage of a well-paid office worker, for example, invariably discussed whether or not she should give up her job after she became a mother. In contrast, no one I spoke with talked about men having to give up their jobs if they became fathers. When I sat in on discussions about a young couple who both held factory jobs while sending their two small children to a local nursery, I noticed that people who argued heatedly over whether or not it was right for the mother to "work" never—not once—considered the question of whether the father should give up his job in order to stay home with the children. On the rare occasions when people did talk about men "having children," they commonly implied that men with children had a greater incentive to seek paid employment than childless men.

In the earlier section on gender conceptions, I observed that women's need for husbands made it difficult for women to attain the standard of pure love set by men. Because wives obtained both money and love from husbands, women always appeared mercenary, in contrast to men, whose ability to earn their own incomes allowed them to separate the pursuit of money from the pursuit of emotional goals, such as love or lust. Women's most obvious strategy for demonstrating love untainted by greed, however, was also problematic. By acting in ways that were impossible for others to construe as leading to monetary gain (such as succumbing to overwhelming emotion without calculating the costs), a woman might prove her love. But such a strategy could leave her vulnerable to exploitation by men who were seeking sexual pleasure rather than lifelong mates. Women were thus faced with the problem of having to hold out for Mr. Right but succumb when he came along.

Women's need to simultaneously resist men's advances while remaining ever ready to explore possibilities for true love constitutes, I think, the reason why men in the 1980s could not show "respect" for women. During my first visit to Los Olivos, young people could indulge initial attractions secure in the knowledge that smart girls—as well as smart boys and a girl's parents—would not risk a woman's reputation for chastity. Youngsters who participated in the wider market economy, however, could never be sure if a woman's no really meant maybe. Girls had to be coy and boys had to pester them. For example, a woman who married a man from Los Olivos reported that she refused to go out with her future husband the first three times he invited her. Even though she was attracted to him, she said, her friends warned her that she should not appear too eager to begin a relationship. She thus made him ask several times before finally agreeing. Clearly this couple—who each claimed to have fallen in love with the other on first sight—would never have married had the man respected the woman's refusals and stopped asking her out.

Although people during both periods of fieldwork told me that couples should postpone sexual intercourse until after the wedding, those I met in the 1980s seemed more disturbed than those I met in the 1960s by the question of whether or not an unmarried woman should have sex with a man she loved. On my first visit to Los Olivos, the answer was clear. Under no circumstances should a woman have sexual intercourse with a man who was not her husband. She would lose her honor. In the 1980s, in contrast, people were not sure what to think about premarital intercourse. On one hand, they disapproved of the widely reported increase in unmarried Spanish couples living together. Sexual intimacy might be the "normal" culmination of a couple's growing love for one another, but couples whose relationship had deepened to the point where they knew they were meant for each other should hasten the wedding rather than simply moving in together. On the other hand, people were uneasy with the idea that a woman should withhold sexual favors until she had obtained a wedding ring. Such withholding implied either a lack of proper feeling or mercenary motives on her part.

Villagers' ambivalence on this question came to the surface in February 1983, when Spanish television aired a program titled "Amor a la española" [Love, Spanish Style]. On the program, a panel of six "experts" discussed whether such a thing existed and, if so, whether it was "in crisis." My sketchy field notes record that the panel agreed on its existence: Spaniards, they concluded, are passionate lovers in contrast to cold northern Europeans, particularly Swedes, who are like "calculators." Panel members also agreed that Spanish love was in crisis. Most of them blamed women's "new demands." But one psychiatrist argued that the real problem lay in women's upbringing. Spanish women, she said, had difficulty realizing their passionate nature because they were brought up to be careful, frigid virgins. According to this psychiatrist, women who guarded their virginity posed a greater threat to the Spanish family than women who gave in to passion.

The day after the program aired, the village buzzed with heated arguments. A friend who discussed the program with me expressed the ambivalence that many villagers seemed to feel. On one hand, she reported that her favorite panel member was a popular woman singer who spoke of love as an enduring passion that existed outside and even in opposition to, such social conventions as marriage. My friend praised the singer for arguing that love is absolute and forever. On the other hand, my friend said that the singer should not have lived with her husband before marrying him. That was wrong. But my friend could not explain why it was wrong. It just was. In contrast to villagers in the 1960s, who could give practical reasons to explain why it did not make sense for a courting couple to have sexual intercourse before the wedding, the villagers and emigrants I met in the 1980s seemed tongue-tied. They "knew" it was wrong for couples to have sex before marriage. But when they tried to suggest practical reasons for restraint, they found themselves making cold calculations that appeared antithetical to the unconditional love required of lifelong mates.

## CONCLUSION

The difference in standards used by people in the 1960s and the 1980s to assess the behaviors of courting couples was poignantly expressed in an interview I had in March 1983 with a lively widow who had married just before the civil war and her equally lively daughter who was born shortly after it. Our conversation gradually drifted into a discussion of two village girls who had given birth to illegitimate children. Neither the widow nor her daughter overtly blamed the women for their disgrace. But they differed radically in their opinions of the men who fathered the illegitimate children.

The widow exclaimed that Spanish men are the "worst" in the world for taking advantage of innocent women. She was enraged by the actions of a young man who had abandoned his pregnant novia in order to marry a woman from a different town. And when the widow talked about a master who had impregnated his servant, she said the man should never have seduced the poor girl, knowing that he had no possibility of marrying her, or even of supporting her, since he was dependent on his wife's wealth.

The daughter presented an entirely different picture of the men involved. As a close friend of the first unwed mother, she said she had many opportunities to observe the girl and her novio. They were so deeply in love, she said, that they were like "two bodies with one soul" [dos cuerpos y un alma]. The reason the couple never married, she explained, was because the brothers of a pregnant girl in another town threatened to kill the novio if he did not marry their sister. (The abandoned pregnant novia had no brothers and her father was dead.) Similarly, the daughter stressed the master's love for his servant. If divorce had been legal at the time, she said, he would have divorced his wife immediately in order to marry his beloved. By stressing how much each man loved the woman he impregnated but did not marry, the daughter painted a picture of lovers who had found their unique mates, but who had been prevented by adverse circumstances from meeting society's conventions.[70]

Although both the widow and her daughter focused on the men who failed to marry the women they had impregnated, their accounts also implied different attitudes toward the unwed mothers. The widow may have overtly blamed the men, but she covertly blamed the women. If Spanish men are the "worst" in the world, then it is up to women to know the score and to carefully guard their virginity. And although the daughter did not overtly praise the unwed mothers for succumbing to passion, her metaphor of two bodies with one soul certainly implied that only a woman who lacked a soul could resist uniting her body with the body of her soul mate.

The village of Los Olivos.

A street in Los Olivos.

The church of Los Olivos in the 1980s. Notice the cars parked near it.

The lower plaza in the 1960s. Jane Collier, holding her baby, watches women washing clothes. The spring water flows out of four spouts at the square upper fountain, where people collect drinking water. It passes through the trough for animals where the horses are drinking, and down into the circular basin where women are washing clothes. It then flows through small channels to irrigate walled gardens below the town.

The lower plaza in the 1980s. The horses have been replaced by cars, and many women have washing machines. But some women still wash clothes in the public fountain.

The patron saint is carried through the narrow streets of Los Olivos in 1980.

The road leading from town to the cemetery. It is "El Camino de Todos," the road everyone travels.

The pilgrimage to the chapel of San Bartolomé in the summer of 1992. The line of pilgrims approaches the church.

The decorated farm carts that brought ritual objects from nearby towns to the isolated chapel of San Bartolomé.

The bull that did not get away. Pilgrims in 1992 watch the beginning of the "bullfight."

## CHAPTER THREE

# Marriage: From Co-owners to Coworkers

Doña Perfecta's late husband was a man whose

"property matched his extravagance. Gambling
and women so captivated the heart of Manuel
María José that if death had not carried him off
before he could squander it, he would have
dissipated his entire fortune."
*(Pérez Galdós 1960 [1876]:18)*[1]

WHEN GEORGE COLLIER and I arrived in Los Olivos in September 1963, the villagers we met were amazed and disturbed by our lack of worldly possessions. We had only three suitcases and the remains of a large box of disposable diapers. They expected young couples to acquire and furnish a complete house before marrying. Twenty years later, when we returned to Los Olivos, friends laughingly recalled their earlier horror and pity. One woman told us, "Now, we have become like you. We too marry with nothing." This was an exaggeration. Couples who married after 1965 still tried to acquire at least an apartment and some furniture before the wedding. But such possessions had become "nothing." Unlike couples marrying before 1965, who expected their house, furniture, and linens to last a lifetime, couples marrying later expected to replace their small apartments and cheap furniture with better items as their fortunes improved.

This change in the significance of worldly possessions was accompanied by a change in the goods themselves. The village house that George Collier and I rented in 1963 lacked such modern conveniences as indoor plumbing, a gas stove, a washing machine, and a refrigerator. Our house did have one of the few flush toilets in town, but we had to bring water in buckets from the village fountain in order to flush it. And the tiny, two-burner gas stove we bought was the envy of village women, who cooked with wood stoves and over open hearths.[2] When I returned to Los Olivos in the 1980s, most of the people I met did have indoor plumbing and kitchen appliances. And, with the exception of a few elders, they praised modern conveniences. When reminiscing about their childhood homes, friends my age tended to lament the "misery" and poverty their parents had endured. In the 1980s, most adults younger than sixty seemed to have difficulty imagining how people could have lived without running water, indoor bathrooms, and household appliances.

I also noticed a dramatic change in the dress and demeanor of married women. In the early 1960s, married women tended to wear drab, shapeless clothes and most were in mourning. Although they were always neat and clean, women did not try to maintain youthful figures. Most appeared matronly; a few were very thin. When I returned to Los Olivos in the 1980s, I found that married women my age and younger were wearing shapely, colorful outfits. Many told me they were dieting to lose weight or to avoid putting it on. I also noticed that married women participated in public amusements, unlike wives in the 1960s (and many older women in the 1980s) who commonly stayed home. On long summer evenings, wives dressed in fashionable outfits to join their husbands and friends for drinks at outdoor bars, strolls to the highway, and dancing at fiestas (see J. Collier 1986). No longer did only unmarried people participate in Sunday paseos. In the 1980s, teenagers and novios were joined by young parents pushing baby strollers, middle-aged couples enjoying the evening air, and even some elders taking their prescribed exercise.

In this chapter, I suggest that these changes in marital possessions, women's dress, and couples' amusements contributed to, and reflected, an underlying transformation in the cultural concepts people used to understand and manage conjugal relations. In the early 1960s, when inheritance appeared to be the main determinant of a family's income, people envisioned marriage as a partnership between owners of property, who managed and protected their merged assets to provide as large an inheritance as possible for their children. In the 1980s, when both villagers and emigrants participated in the wider national market for jobs and commodities, people envisioned and enacted marriage as a partnership between workers with different capacities, who pooled their efforts to make a home for themselves and their children.

Although I have labeled this shift as one from a vision of spouses as co-owners to a vision of spouses as coworkers, married couples during both periods of fieldwork were, of course, simultaneously owners and workers. Couples jointly owned their lands, houses, furniture, and so on and both worked to make a living and a home. Nor do I want to suggest that households changed from units of production into units of consumption. As already noted, most families during both visits relied on wage labor to survive. But I do want to explore an apparent shift in people's experience of family property. In the 1960s, property appeared to be the major determinant of a family's status. The houses and furniture that newlyweds received from their parents, along with the fields or stores they inherited at parents' deaths, constituted the property that determined not only their incomes and lifestyles but also their occupations and working conditions. Twenty years later, the relationship between household and work appeared to be reversed, in the sense that a couple's work now determined their household possessions. In the 1980s, the wages or profits earned by a husband and wife shaped how much a couple could spend on their house, furniture, and children, even as their shopping and housekeeping skills affected the value they obtained for their money.[3]

I thus suggest that Giddens's observation about "modern" people being "forced" to follow "lifestyles" (1991, 81) reflects less a change in the number of choices open to people than a shift in the assignment of responsibility for lifestyle choices. In the 1960s, villagers' lifestyles appeared to be "handed down" because a married couple's parents were held responsible for the amount of property they passed on to their children. In the 1980s, in contrast, lifestyles appeared to be "adopted" by the couples themselves because they were held personally responsible for the amount and quality of their furniture, food, and entertainment.

This chapter on changing conjugal relations contrasts with the previous chapter on changing courtship customs in two ways. First, it is not arranged in chronological order. I both begin and end by discussing marriage in the 1960s. Second, the chapter devotes more space to the 1980s than to the 1960s. Although this chapter, like the previous one, documents the changes I observed between my two visits, it is concerned less with exploring why people shifted their understandings of marriage than with exploring a conflict between my sense that women lost power relative to their husbands and the assertions of people I interviewed that husbands and wives had become more equal. After a first section tracing changes in how and when couples acquired marital property, I turn to exploring why I, as a feminist anthropologist from the United States, experienced the changes as detrimental to women's power and autonomy. Then, in the third and fourth sections, I explore why it might have made sense for people from Los Olivos, both male and female, to disagree with me. I begin by considering the behaviors that people cited as evidence for their claim that women's status had improved and finally return to my field notes from the 1960s to explore why—given how people talked and acted at the time—it made sense for people in the 1980s to remember women as having been oppressed.

## CHANGING RELATIONS OF MARRIAGE AND PROPERTY

In class-divided[4] and class societies, marriage is legally defined as a relationship between a husband and wife in respect to property (broadly construed)—in contrast to classless societies where marriage is primarily imagined as a relationship between men (or their social equivalents) in respect to people defined as women (see J. Collier 1988, 226). In Spain, marriage laws for at least the past two centuries have focused on the rights of a husband and wife: rights to hold, manage, and transact in actual property, rights to children (conceived as authority over them), and a married woman's right to hold (and to confer) the privileges of citizenship (see Sponsler 1982). The law portrays all of these rights as something that an individual can "have," rather than as obligations flowing from the marital bond. Not surprisingly, the most important rights (as reflected in the amount of legal ink spilled over them) are those related to what I have called "actual property"—the economic factors of land, labor, and capital that, in class-divided societies, appear to determine a person's lifestyle and social influence.

If marriage in class-divided and class societies is a relationship about property, then differences in people's experiences of how property is acquired should affect their understandings of what marriage is about. I thus begin this chapter with a discussion of changes in how married couples acquired the property that affected their lives. I explore how people's efforts to "hang on" to inherited property in a social world dominated by landed elites encouraged them to envision husbands and wives as co-owners of joined inheritances managed by the husband. And I consider how people's efforts to advance in a capitalist employment market dominated by industrial and financial entrepreneurs encouraged them to envision marriage as the union of a breadwinner and a homemaker who worked together to create a home for themselves and their children.

In the 1960s, before emigration drained the village of young people, courting couples commonly tried to acquire and furnish a complete house before marrying. No weddings occurred during the nine months I spent in Los Olivos in 1963–64. But shortly before I left I was invited to see the house being prepared by a bride and groom from wealthy, landowning families who planned to marry in the summer. Sally Price, who visited the house three times that summer, provided the following account of her final visit on the eve of the wedding—"the formal occasion when the whole *pueblo*, not just those who were helping with preparations, could come and see what was described as the richest wedding house in many years."

> The house was "shown" by 3 or 4 smiling female hostesses—either aunts or the mother of the bride and the *madrina* [godmother]—who encouraged all admiring remarks by pointing at each and every object and asking, "*¿Le gusta esto?*" [Do you like this?] and then agreeing heartily with the inevitable answer. On this final showing, all the lights in the house were turned on (even though it was a bright, sunny day), all the windows were open, and

the cupboards were opened to show off the china, glassware, or linen they held. The walls (each about 2 feet thick) were freshly whitewashed and the arches joining all the rooms were newly painted a cheery turquoise. The living room was furnished completely with wicker chairs and tables. A glistening glass chandelier hung from the ceiling and a few modern Japanese prints (in almost flourescent colors) adorned the walls. The floor, as in all the rooms, was tiled. On the left, one turquoise door led to the basement, another to the attic. To the right of this room was the master bedroom. The furniture, provided by the novio, was heavy, thick, and dark . . . a huge double bed with massive headboard, a tremendous (6–7 ft. long?) armoire with two doors for her, two for him, a matching dresser with its overpowering mirror, and two bedside tables . . . all of the same depressingly dark wood. The bed had been made with a yellow blanket covered by an almost transparent white spread—all ruffled and embroidered with a separate piece to cover the pillow. On one bedside table lay a lifelike Christchild in its manger, on the other stood a serene Virgin. Over the bed hung a bleeding Christ on the cross. The dresser was topped by an embroidered doily, a globe of plastic flowers, and still another mirror—this time a small round one at the center of a decorated plate on a stand. Heavy curtains shut off the room from the street, and on the far wall, transparent white curtains separated it from the *aseo* [the lavatory]. The *aseo* was a spacious room, set up with a washstand and a whole array of enamel pans which were to serve as sinks. New plastic pails and pitchers stood ready for use, and several bottles of perfume were set out before the mirror. A wall coat rack displayed all of [the bride's] new aprons. A small *cuarto de soltero* [bachelor room] was furnished with a single bed—we remarked that in an American house, a young couple might have planned this for children, but they said it was for taking a nap in the afternoon (because it was away from the "noise" of the street) or for when the couple was having a fight and wanted to sleep in separate beds! A softly smiling Virgin looked over the bed, which was covered with a plain white bedspread. Its only other furniture, a 5-drawer dresser, was crammed with [the bride's] linen, all carefully packed in tissue paper.

Behind the living room was a large dining room with a huge, heavy table in the middle. A modern plastic chandelier hung over the table and several modern prints spotted the walls. Two built-in, glass-doored cabinets were left open to display their china and glassware (I counted 12 place settings of one pattern . . . there was a whole variety of several other types of china in addition). Between these two cabinets was a large sideboard topped with a 5–6 ft. long mirror. The doors to this were also opened wide and showed off more of the same china. Two colorful plastic candleholders stood on the side board and held two fake candles of twisting green plastic. (The candles were admired perhaps more than any other single decoration.) A small breakfast room also sported a gaudy plastic chandelier and looked out over the back corral through windows with glass panes. Its table and chairs were all in green and white plastic and another plastic flower in a globe sat on the table. The pantry was a small room whose walls were covered with racks for a huge array of pots, pans, and kitchen cups of tin. There was a tall earthenware urn in the corner for bread, as well as cannisters of sugar and other staples. The fattest *bacalao* [dried codfish] ever seen by the girls in our family was in the corner and 8 hams and numerous *chorizos, morcillas,* and other sausages hung from the ceiling. Finally, the small kitchen had a cozy fireplace with various bric-a-brac on the mantel and a number of decorated wooden spoons, etc., were nailed on the walls. The "sink area" was newly tiled and the *mesa camilla* [round table equipped to hold a brazier] complete with floor-length green cloth, was set up with pitcher and glasses. This "open house" lasted until that night and [the bride and groom] joined the aunts and [the bride's] mother to act as hosts.[5]

When I interviewed villagers about inheritance, they commonly distinguished between items transferred at the time of death and those acquired at marriage—between "inheritance" proper and what might be called "trousseau" or "marriage gifts."[6] Valuable properties, such as houses, agricultural land, and commercial enterprises, were inherited. Even if parents allocated particular houses, fields, or businesses to individual children for their use, these items were considered part of the parental estate, to be divided equally among all children after the death of the surviving parent, or in anticipation of such a death. As mentioned in the previous chapter, people occasionally had to move out of houses they had occupied for years, or to relinquish enterprises they had become skilled at managing, when heirs decided to draw lots after failing to agree on a division.

The household furnishings, clothes, tools, and foodstuffs that a couple acquired at marriage—and which they displayed to fellow villagers before the wedding—were not considered part of their inheritances. These items, even when transferred to the bride and groom by their respective families, were theirs to keep. When I asked villagers to tell me what a bride and groom were expected to contribute to the furnishing of a house, they invariably replied that the groom provided the bedroom furniture and stocked the pantry while the bride contributed "all the rest."[7] They often joked that grooms in Los Olivos—unlike those in Seville who were expected to provide most of the household furnishings—contributed only *la cama y el chorizo* (the bed and the sausage).[8]

Grooms had to provide their own metaphorical "sausages," but it was actually the groom's mother, along with the mother of the bride, who assumed primary responsibility for furnishing a wedding house.[9] A young man's mother began saving money for the bedroom furniture when her son became engaged even though they did not shop for the furniture until the couple had acquired a house. The Prices report that a young man's mother bought "material periodically during [her son's] *noviazgo*" even though she did "not get together with her friends to make it into clothes until a month or two before the wedding" (1966a, 312).[10] Two young men told Richard Price that "a man needs a minimum of 25,000 pesetas to furnish the bedroom—bare bones only—and buy the required amount of clothes" (at a time when male agricultural day laborers earned around 350 pesetas a week).[11]

A young woman's mother also saved money to buy "all the rest" of the household furnishings that a bride was expected to contribute. Even before a girl reached puberty, her mother began buying items for her hope chest (*ajuar*), particularly cloth for the young woman to sew and embroider. The bride who married in the summer of 1964, for example, "started sewing for her wedding at the age of 12." She was twenty-nine when she married, "having been informally [engaged] to [her suitor] since 14, formally since 17."[12] "Only the hand-sewn portion" of this bride's trousseau included "10 tablecloth and napkin sets, 27 extra napkins, 25 monogrammed towels, 18 sets of top sheet, bottom sheet, and pillowcases, 6 monogrammed sanitary napkins, 15 nightgowns, 17 personally designed pastel underwear sets of slip, brassiere, and underpants, 10 cloth lunch sacks for her husband, 10 dishtowels, 5 extra pairs of underpants, 5 aprons, and an ironing board cover" (Price and Price 1966a, 312). By the time this bride married, she had also collected several blankets, bedspreads, dishes, and ornaments. Many of these items were gifts from family members, friends, and her novio.

When Sally Price wrote that "the whole" village was invited to "come and see . . . the richest wedding house in many years" she captured the significance of the event. Whatever messages visitors were expected to receive while admiring a wedding house, they were specifically invited to assess the wealth expended on the furnishings. A couple's wedding house testified to their expected lifestyle. On the surface, a wedding house displayed the achievements of the newlyweds: the bride's embroidery skills and the young couple's diligence in earning money. But because the labor of unmarried young people belonged to their natal families, the furnishings of a wedding house actually testified less to the achievements of the bride and groom than to how well their parents had been able to provide for their children. By noting the quality of the bedroom furniture, for example, villagers could learn whether the groom's parents had been able to save the money he earned, and add some of their own to it, or whether the groom's parents had been forced to spend most of his earnings to meet daily consumption needs. Even a bride's embroidery skills testified less to her abilities than to how well her parents had managed their household labor force. For example, when Sally Price admired the hope chest of a novia whose embroidery was widely recognized as the most beautiful in town, two women told her "that the explanation for such fine work is that all she ever does is sit and sew. Her mother brings her lunch when it's lunch time, dinner when it's dinner time, and she goes to bed when it's bedtime, but other than that, all she does all day everyday is embroider."[13]

A wedding house testified to the achievements of the newlyweds' parents in another sense as well. In the early 1960s, no one could hold a newly married couple accountable for the size and quality of their joined properties. Their inheritances were an accident of birth. But people could—and did—hold parents responsible for the size and quality of the wedding houses they provided for their children. The differences between a couple's own wedding house and the furnishings they contributed to their children's wedding houses provided the most eloquent testimony possible of a parental couple's success—or failure—in having preserved, and enhanced, the inheritances they had received from their own parents.

Given that parents were judged by the wedding houses they provided for their children, villagers in the 1960s understandably talked of marriage as requiring "sacrifices."[14] Parents had to sacrifice themselves to save for their children's weddings. At a festive pig-killing, for example, some older women watching teenage girls giggle together remarked that the girls would stop laughing when they married and had other things to think about. And, as I noted in chapter 2, young men told Richard Price that marriage required a man to take on economic responsibilities that inevitably entailed problems and worries. The sacrifices required of parents, however, differed by sex.

Married women fulfilled their obligation to sacrifice themselves by visibly giving up the pleasures enjoyed by unmarried girls, particularly public amusements. In the first few months after the wedding, a bride might go out with her husband in the evenings. The couple who married in the summer of 1964, for example, continued to participate in Sunday evening paseos. But as time passed, and particularly when a bride became pregnant, villagers expected a woman to stay home. A mother had no culturally valid reason for seeking pleasure in the streets and many culturally valid reasons to avoid any appearance of pleasure seeking. A married woman's (symbolic) confinement to her home was multiply determined.

In the 1960s, when I interviewed villagers about wedding customs, they told me that brides dressed in black.[15] Black, of course, was the color of mourning. Indeed, villagers said that brides wore black because a woman always needed a good black dress for attending funerals, whereas a white dress was useless after the wedding. The custom of wearing black, however, had more than practical significance. The somber color and purpose of a black wedding dress symbolized, in condensed form, a bride's abandonment of girlhood pleasures. If unmarried girls dressed in bright colors to attract the attention of potential suitors, then a married woman who dressed in her best clothes in public for any reason except attending a funeral could be suspected of seeking an adulterous lover. And if an unmarried girl spent her days thinking about acquiring things for herself, such as pretty dresses, perfumes, and items for her hope chest, then the married woman who appeared to want more than one good black dress opened herself to accusations of putting her desires ahead of her obligation to save money for her children's inheritances. For a married woman to dress up in public was, by definition, to call into question the legitimacy of her children. For a married woman to spend money on clothes, perfumes, and amusement for herself was, again by definition, to selfishly waste the money she should be saving to furnish her children's wedding houses.

Married women were also expected to make their wedding furnishings last a lifetime. After her wedding, a woman was supposed to accumulate household items for her children's wedding houses, not to make her own workload easier. As a result, women who married before 1965 expected to live and work in houses whose furnishings—except for the bedroom—represented the accomplishments of their natal families, not those of their husbands.

In the 1960s, married men sacrificed themselves by taking on the obligation to manage the household formed by the joined inheritances of a husband and wife. A husband had to assume responsibility for administering the family's lands, labor, and capital assets in such a way as to maintain a lifestyle appropriate to the family's status while protecting, and hopefully enhancing, the property his children would inherit. In contrast to unmarried men, who could quit jobs they did not like and refuse to obey employers who insulted them, married men with children had to keep working and to accept an employer's insults if the family's livelihood was at stake.

But if men, like women, had to sacrifice themselves, men could not afford to stay home and avoid public amusements. A man had to spend time in bars in order to fulfill his role as manager of the family's property and labor force. As one woman explained, "the man who runs a business finds his [customers and workers] in the bar and the man who works [for wages] finds employment there."[16] In the 1960s, men spent very little time at home. One woman whose father left home early in the morning told me that he did not even spend evenings with his family. He "goes straight to the cantina on returning from work in the fields, at around 7 in the evening. He attends the upper bar. He stays there until around 9:30 or 10:00 when he goes home to supper. After that he goes to bed."[17] The Prices, too, observed that men's lives centered "on work and recreation with male friends" (1966a, 310).

But if men's lives centered on "work and recreation," these two activities carried different moral values. A man's "work" benefited his family; his "recreation," although necessary for managing the family's assets, could be interpreted as benefiting only himself. The quotation from *Doña Perfecta* at the beginning of this chapter suggests how easily a man's "recreation" could slide into squandering the family's wealth. Doña Perfecta's husband, Don Manuel María José, saved his wife and child from poverty only by dying before he could waste his entire fortune on gambling and loose women.

After 1965, as young people left the village for urban jobs and the market for Los Olivos produce declined, villagers reworked their understandings of marriage in light of their changing experiences. Although people continued to talk about men's responsibility for the economic well-being of their families, workers' hopes for upward mobility, combined with the declining value of Los Olivos property, encouraged people to think of husbands less as managers of family properties than as breadwinners whose earnings supported household dependents. This change occurred rapidly and dramatically. Unlike Los Olivos courtship practices, which apparently changed throughout this century, becoming increasingly formal before being transformed after 1965, the understanding of households as the source of a family's wealth appears to have had a long and stable history before increased emigration and the demise of the village farming economy transformed households from economic assets into economic liabilities.

George Collier's (1987) analysis of political conflict in Los Olivos before the Spanish civil war of 1936–39 suggests that village men who joined the socialist syndicate wanted to think of themselves less as individual workers who sold their labor power to employers in order to feed their families than as managers of household assets that included the labor power of family members.[18] This understanding was still prevalent when I arrived in Los Olivos in 1963. As I discussed in chapter 1, even people belonging to the majority of families who worked for wages experienced the amount of property a family owned as the major determinant of its members' lifestyles and occupations.[19]

After 1965, however, the young men who emigrated to seek urban employment found themselves faced not with a single type of job—agricultural day laborer—at a single salary but with an array of jobs requiring different skills and offering different amounts of remuneration. Although most emigrants from Los Olivos began with "unskilled" jobs at minimum wages, they were surrounded by perceived opportunities for advancement. As they or their friends began finding better jobs, it soon became obvious to everyone that the amount of money a family had at its disposal depended less on the property that a husband and wife had inherited from their parents than on the type of job held by the principal wage earner, usually the husband. Because employers claimed to hire and pay workers according to their skills and dedication, a man's job appeared to depend less on his family connections than on his personal traits, such as his intelligence, ambition, credentials, and acquired knowledge.

At the same time, Los Olivos newlyweds were finding it increasingly difficult to set up and display wedding houses. Couples who emigrated before marriage were unable to display their possessions to fellow villagers even if, as happened to one bride, her female relatives secretly visited her rented urban apartment to arrange her furnishings so that she could realize her dream of starting married life in an established house. Many of the courting couples interviewed by the Prices in 1964 fared less well. Because several married sooner than they had expected, they had few possessions to arrange in their rented apartments. It was one of these brides who later joked that George Collier and my propertyless arrival in Los Olivos in 1963 heralded a new age for villagers—one in which they, too, would marry with "nothing."

The ideal of setting up a completely furnished house before the wedding did not die out, but newlyweds no longer expected their furnishings to last a lifetime. One couple whose wedding I attended in the early 1980s proudly showed me through the village house they had renovated and furnished with many of the latest appliances, including a gas stove, washing machine, and large color television set. A few years later, however, this couple had to move to an urban area because—they reported—the husband could not earn enough money in the Sierra de Aracena to support his growing family. This couple left their wedding furniture in the village house for use during vacations and bought new furniture for their city apartment. Other emigrants moved their wedding furniture to urban apartments. But they, too, wished for replacements. In 1983, I visited a woman from a wealthy village family who had taken her wedding furniture with her when she moved to the city. I thought her rustic furniture was lovely, but she spent the visit apologizing for the fact that her husband's inability to find a good job had prevented her from replacing her old tables, chairs, and sideboard with more stylish items.[20]

Not everyone born in Los Olivos, however, wanted to replace old wedding furniture or to acquire the latest household appliances. I found that older people, particularly those born before 1925, seemed happy with what they had. A village friend who was born before 1920, for example, never complained about her lack of a modern bathroom, even though she complained about many other things. And an emigrant I interviewed told me that his parents did not use the refrigerator he had bought for them. His mother, he said, preferred to shop every day.

Although this difference between older and younger people may represent a generational contrast between seniors who already had enough possessions and juniors who still needed to furnish their houses, I think it reflects a more profound shift in parental roles. As I discuss in the next chapter, villagers who were born before 1925 reared their children in a social world where it made sense for parents to avoid buying conveniences for their own households in order to save as much money as possible for their children's inheritances. After emigration and the collapse of village agriculture, however, people born in Los Olivos lived in a social world where children's futures appeared to depend less on the amount of property they inherited than on the kinds of jobs they obtained. As a result, it no longer made sense for parents to avoid spending money on household conveniences. Rather, parents who refused to replace outworn furniture or to buy new appliances appeared to be depriving their children of physical comforts and social advantages the family could afford.

## THE INCREASING DEPENDENCE OF WIVES

When I interviewed people from Los Olivos about changes in the experiences of married couples, they commonly emphasized improvements in women's lives. As I discuss in the next section, they observed that housewives no longer had to avoid public amusements but could go out in the evenings with their husbands. In addition they pointed out that husbands, instead of spending all their free time in bars, tended to spend evenings at home with their wives and children. Finally, they praised labor-saving household appliances for lightening women's workloads. Some people also noted that women no longer had to do the agricultural labor their mothers and grandmothers had performed.

If I questioned people's optimism and pushed them to give me examples of how women's lives might have deteriorated, they tended to comment less on changes over time than on the drawbacks of urban living. This focus on rural-urban differences made sense for them, given that their primary experience of change had been the massive emigration of former villagers to urban areas. But their tendency to interpret temporal changes in terms of spatial variations did make it harder for them to notice changes that had affected everyone born in Los Olivos, regardless of where they lived.

When I asked about the problems of "modern" housewives, for example, people commonly began by describing city apartments as "cages," an appropriate metaphor given their physical appearance (square and stacked in high-rise blocks like chicken coops on a truck), but also because of the limitations that urban apartments imposed on housewives (and the elderly) who lacked outside employment. I, too, was impressed by the constraints that urban living imposed on housewives. They had no reason to leave their apartments except to restock the refrigerator from time to time—in contrast to village housewives, whose daily tasks took them outside their houses to tend gardens, feed penned animals, wash clothes at the fountain, shop for food, or visit sick relatives.

Moreover, urban mothers were trapped by their need to watch children. Unlike mothers who remained in the village, where every teenage girl was a potential child minder, urban mothers had to tend their own children or make special arrangements for child care. And, unlike village mothers who could allow children as young as three or four to play in the streets unattended, secure in the knowledge that neighbors would call if a child wandered too far or fell down, urban mothers had to accompany their children on excursions outside the apartment. No wonder so many of the people I interviewed portrayed urban housewives as "prisoners" in their homes.[21]

But if people could list the problems of urban housewives, most remained convinced that women's lives in general had improved greatly. After all, one had only to notice all the labor-saving devices avilable to "modern" housewives. Friends, for example, constantly reminded me that during my first visit to Los Olivos no one had running water, gas stoves, refrigerators, or washing machines, whereas such conveniences were common in both village and urban homes by the 1980s.

Almost no one questioned the idea that labor-saving devices did, indeed, save the labor of housewives. Only a few older women and I doubted it. Some of my older friends from the 1960s focused on the disadvantages of modern conveniences. They observed that tap water has a funny taste, gas cooking stoves do not heat rooms, refrigerators grow mold, and washing machines mangle clothes. A few also joined me in questioning whose labor was, in fact, saved. Many of the tasks performed by machines, such as cooking food, washing clothes, and cleaning houses, had commonly been performed not by housewives but by their unmarried daughters and nieces, or by servants in wealthier households. Between my two visits to Los Olivos, the falling age of marriage, combined with young women's need for schooling and their access to jobs that paid far more than housework, had deprived married women—in both the village and the city—of the young (or poor) female labor force that had once been theirs to command.[22]

I also noticed four other changes in women's situation that were not mentioned by the people I interviewed—at least as far as I can remember. All of these changes reflect what I perceived as a decline in the status of wives relative to their husbands. All four were brought about by the transformation of husbands from managers of family properties into family breadwinners, and by a shift in what children needed to succeed from inherited property to human capital. These changes affected all married women, not just those who emigrated to urban areas.

First, married women seemed to have lost the separate identity signified by the furnishings in their wedding houses. In the early 1960s, wives lived and worked in houses that reflected the accomplishments of their parents and their own embroidery skills. Because wives were expected to avoid buying new things in order to save money for their children's inheritances, they spent their lives surrounded by objects that represented and reflected their identities as daughters of their parents—even as their husbands lived and worked with land and tools that reflected their identities as sons. By the 1980s, in contrast, the houses that women tended were showcases for displaying a husband's achievements. As suggested by the lament of the urban housewife who wanted to replace her wedding furniture but had been unable to do so, the location, size, and furnishings of an urban wife's apartment testified not to her individuality but to her husband's (or to the couple's joint) earning power. Even the houses of village wives told more about the achievements of their husbands than about those of a woman's parents. Because successful villagers redesigned and redecorated the old houses they had inherited or bought, unchanged houses came to signify a husband's failure.

Second, married women in the 1980s appeared to have lost their ability to enhance, or to detract from, their family's status in the social hierarchy. On my first visit to Los Olivos, when villagers talked about a family's standing as determined by inheritance, a wife contributed approximately half the family's property, her chastity guaranteed both her children's legitimacy and her husband's "honor" among his barroom equals, her sacrifices and work preserved and enhanced her children's inheritances, and—if she were fortunate—she might bring additional property into the family by caring for a childless older person who would leave her a house or fields upon death. In the 1980s, however, the wives of factory workers, semiprofessionals, and village farmers had few ways to increase or decrease a family's status. A wife's infidelities might cause her husband emotional anguish, but they were not likely to affect his ability to keep or do his job. The government agencies and large corporations that employed most migrants[23] and the banks that extended credit to small farmers and entrepreneurs had little interest in the sexual activities of their employees or borrowers. Similarly, a wife's housework and child care might bring joy to her family, but her saving, scrimping, and even her work in the family business had less impact on her family's disposable income than her husband's job promotion or his successful completion of a business deal. Obtaining paid employment did allow a wife to contribute to her family's income. But most mothers found it difficult to combine a factory or office job with their household duties, or to find employment at wages greater than the expenses of child care and a wife's forgone scrimping.

Even the work done by housewives who remained in the village appeared to contribute little to the family budget. The vegetables and animals a village wife raised did improve the family's diet and cut food costs, but such housewives appeared to be saving money rather than earning it. Only the few wives of farmers or store owners who did agricultural or selling tasks that someone else would have been hired to perform actually seemed to be earning money. For village women in the 1980s, as for their emigrant sisters, a woman had to hold a job that paid wages or earned profits if she was to be credited with making a significant economic contribution to her family's welfare.[24]

Third, wives in the 1980s had become economic dependents of their husbands. Unlike wives in the 1960s, who usually kept the family property if their husbands died or decamped, few women in the 1980s could replace a dead or departed husband's earning power. Even women who held paying jobs or ran small stores were economic dependents in the sense that they would have had a hard time maintaining their standard of living if something happened to their husbands. Very few Los Olivos husbands had, in fact, abandoned their wives and children. But divorce was a hotly debated topic in the 1980s and people talked in hushed voices about the few mothers who had been left to rear young children alone.

Finally, children's changing needs put mothers in a position where they had to hang onto their husbands. In the 1960s, when children's futures depended on the amount of property they inherited, children might suffer emotionally at the loss of a father, but mothers were usually capable of managing and preserving the joined properties that constituted the children's inheritance. Even the children of agricultural wage laborers, whose mothers might appear to have been as economically dependent on a husband's earnings as the wives of wage workers in the 1980s, did not suffer a drastic decline in expectations or living standards if their fathers died or departed. As children of wage laborers, they would have had to become wage laborers in any case. And their widowed mothers could provide for them almost as well as if their fathers were present because landowners in the 1960s liked to employ widows, who could be hired to do a man's work at less than a man's wage.

Once a child's future appeared to depend more on personally acquired "human capital" than on inherited property, however, a mother needed her husband's earning power and credit rating if she was to provide her children with a better education and lifestyle than she could afford alone. Once a husband's income appeared to be determined by his personal capacities, rather than by the size of the household property he managed, a mother could no longer benefit her children by sacrificing herself. Instead, she had to persuade her husband to sacrifice himself, in the sense that she had to persuade him to spend the money he earned through his labor to provide benefits for his family—rather than spending his earnings on fast cars and women. In the 1980s, a mother had to worry about the health and happiness of her breadwinner in a way that her own mother had not had to worry about the health and happiness of the husband who managed their joined inheritances.

But if changing economic conditions transformed wives from adults who contributed more or less equally with husbands to the well-being of their families into economic dependents who, like their children, needed the support of an adult breadwinner in order to survive, the increased power this shift granted to husbands did not come without a price. In contrast to the manager of a family household, who was not held responsible for his family's poverty unless he had wasted his and his wife's inherited resources, a breadwinner was held responsible for his family's income. He received credit if the family income rose, but he was also blamed if the family income fell or if he failed to achieve the level of income attained by those who started out with approximately the same resources. Moreover, a breadwinner had far more chances to fail than did the administrator of a family household. Whereas most men could manage to avoid losing status in a social system where men strived to preserve the family properties and reputations they and their wives had inherited, only some men could succeed in a social system where men competed for apparently unlimited wages and profits. Unlike a household manager whose authority came with his role, a breadwinner had to earn the respect of his family and friends.

Although I have attributed the development of the "male breadwinner family" to changing economic conditions, the conditions I stress differ from those commonly stressed by others. Instead of asking why employers and workers excluded women from opportunities for paid employment outside the home (Creighton 1996), I have focused on changes in the meaning of people's work. Men became "breadwinners,"

I suggest, less because mothers were denied opportunities for paid employment than because the shift from inherited property to occupational achievement made a husband's income the most important factor determining the lifestyles and opportunities of his wife and children.

## EXPERIENCING MARRIAGE IN THE 1980s

None of the villagers and emigrants I interviewed in the 1980s shared my pessimistic impression that wives' status had declined relative to their husbands.'[25] Instead, they argued the reverse, claiming that wives who had once been subordinated to their husbands had become their husbands' equals. In this section and the next, I explore the truth behind their claim, focusing in this section on how the people I interviewed in the 1980s talked about the equality between husbands and wives, and in the next section on how people in the 1960s talked about women's subordination to their husbands.

When people in the 1980s argued that husbands and wives had become more equal, they commonly mentioned two changes. First, they observed that wives were now enjoying pleasures that had formerly been restricted to their husbands, such as going out in the evening to sample the public pleasures of street life. They also observed that married women could now spend the family money on things for themselves, such as pretty dresses, perfumes, and labor-saving appliances. Second, they observed that husbands had given up some of their former privileges, particularly the privilege of going out alone in the evenings. They pointed out that most men under the age of sixty no longer spent all their free time in bars or, if they did, they felt guilty about it. And several people observed that husbands in urban areas often helped their wives with the housework.

The changes in married women's appearance and behavior were dramatic. In the twenty years between my first and second visits to Los Olivos, married women apparently went from trying to emulate the Virgin Mary, who sacrificed herself for her Son, to emulating the "modern woman" of magazine and television advertisements, whose beauty stimulated male desire and whose housekeeping skills earned her family's admiration (see J. Collier 1986). The change in men's behavior was less dramatic, but also significant. Not only did formerly "resigned" husbands turn into ambitious job seekers, as I discussed in chapter 1, but men whose fathers had spent all their free time in bars told me that they regretted the hours spent apart from their wives and children.

People discussing the dramatic changes in women's dress and demeanor commonly attributed them to women's release from traditional constraints. Just as people discussing changes in courtship customs commonly portrayed the new practices as reflecting what fiancés had wanted to do in the past but had been prevented from doing by fear of social sanctions, so they portrayed married women as having become free to do what their mothers wanted to do but had refrained from doing because they lacked cash and feared the neighbors' gossip.

Housewives in the 1960s, as I discuss in the next section, complained endlessly about their hard work. In the 1980s, in contrast, housewives bought labor-saving appliances. Mothers in the 1960s constantly lamented their sacrifices. In the 1980s, mothers, like their unmarried daughters, bought pretty dresses, danced all night, and visited bars. Even the changes in husbands' behavior could be interpreted as desired by women. In the 1960s, wives complained about the time and money their husbands wasted in bars. In the 1980s, men spent many evenings at home and often took their wives with them when they went to drink beer on weekends. No wonder the people I interviewed in the 1980s experienced such changes as reflecting not only a wife's growing equality with her husband but also her freedom to enjoy pleasures her mother had only dreamed about.

But if the villagers and emigrants I interviewed attributed the changes to loosening constraints, I follow my project of exploring how people's participation in the national market for jobs and commodities encouraged them to "think for themselves" rather than worry about "following social conventions." In particular, I suggest that the new behaviors of wives and husbands reflect not their freedom to act out desires people once repressed but the development of new requirements. When women born in Los Olivos tried to emulate the "modern woman" of magazine and television advertisements, and when husbands stayed home in the evenings, they did so because their adoption of a discourse of occupational achievement encouraged them to imagine—and to enact—marriage as a symbolic partnership between a breadwinner and a homemaker. Married couples in the 1980s were as constrained by cultural assumptions as their parents. But the assumptions were different.

In both the 1960s and the 1980s, people born in Los Olivos contrasted the *casa* (house) to the *calle* (street). But participation in the market economy altered people's experience of the casa. In the 1960s, the casa was a family's property (houses and lands) whose quality and size determined the income, activities, and lifestyle of family members. In the 1980s, in contrast, the casa designated a home, whose quality and size was determined by the wages and profits earned by a husband and wife. No longer did the work of a married couple appear to be determined by the needs of their casa. Instead, couples could create the kind of home they wanted. They were limited only by their imaginations and earning power.

Participation in the market economy also changed people's experiences of the cultural contrast between "work" and its opposites. Although some of the older people I interviewed in the 1980s continued to use the contrast between *obligación* and *diversión* that I discussed in the previous chapter, most of the younger people used a cultural contrast between *trabajo* (work) and *descanso* (rest, leisure).[26] And "work" appeared to have shifted location. In the early 1960s, obligaciones were associated with the casa, diversiones with the calle. Family members worked to maintain the family property; men and unmarried girls went out into the street to seek amusement. Only those with too little property to support the family had to seek wage work in the calle. In the 1980s, in contrast, trabajo was associated with the calle; descanso with the casa. People left home to earn wages or profits in the marketplace; they returned home to rest, recuperate, and enjoy time with family and friends.

But if "work" appeared to have switched locations, the situation was actually more complex. The cultural contrast between trabajo and descanso had different implications from the contrast between obligación and diversión. In the 1960s, everyone may have experienced the obligaciones associated with maintaining a family's property and reputation, but only some people were obliged to "work." Those rich enough to hire others could fulfill their household obligations by telling servants and workers what to do. In the 1980s, in contrast, "work" was the source of a person's income and social status. Even those who spent their time telling others what to do portrayed the giving of orders, along with the responsibility for seeing that assigned tasks were done, as the "work" that they did.

Most important, the contrast between work and leisure encoded a distinction not between required tasks and having fun but between activities that earned money and those that did not. The central importance of wages and profits for determining a family's income and lifestyle ensured that the most visible and talked about forms of "work" were activities undertaken for the express purpose of earning money. As a result, the descanso associated with the home came to encode two potential oppositions to income-earning work: actual rest (cessation of activity) and activities undertaken for reasons other than earning money (i.e., because one "wanted" to do them). The "home" encoded both meanings of descanso. On one hand, it was the place of rest. On the other, it was the place of desire.

Conchi, the young woman who thought that twelve-year courtships were "not normal" told me on another occasion that she could not

understand why her parents had married one another. They never
sought each other's company, she said. Her father, before his death,
spent all his free time in bars. Her parents rarely spoke to one another.[27]
Conchi's amazement reflects, I think, her experiences as a member of
the generation who participated in the national market for jobs and
commodities. Once the home came to be experienced as the location of
both "rest" and "love," couples who loved one another had to want to
spend their leisure hours together.

Men's desire to spend time with their families came out particularly
strongly in stories told by emigrants who had become truck drivers. My
field notes from one interview report that

> Adolfo said he regretted the ten years he spent making long-distance trips
> across Spain. The work was terrible, both because of the long hours and
> dangerous road conditions, but also because those years were crucial ones
> for the growth of his children. His job not only took him away from his
> family but also left him in a bad mood when he came home. (Adolfo's wife
> chimed in to say that when he returned from one of his long trips, he would
> only get mad at his family.) Adolfo agreed, saying that he came back tired
> and ill-humored. Finally, reported Adolfo, he requested a job transfer that
> meant a serious reduction in pay, but that allowed him to spend more time
> with his family. Now he comes home in the early afternoon, in time for the
> large midday meal. It is hard living with less pay, he said, particularly be-
> cause of his children's school bills, but now he has time to help them with
> their homework.[28]

Another truck driver told a similar story, reporting that he refused to
make further long-distance trips after his second child was born.

For most of the villagers and emigrants I interviewed in the 1980s,
leisure time had become family time. Many couples told me that they
spent their evenings at home together watching television. Sometimes
they would visit friends or relatives or, more rarely, go out. On long
summer evenings, many couples from Los Olivos joined crowds strolling the streets of cities and towns, pushing baby strollers or holding children by the hand, often stopping at bars for beer and snacks.

When I asked couples how they spent their weekends, I usually heard
stories of family outings. This was particularly true of those who lived in
urban areas. For example, one couple whose jobs allowed them full
weekends said that "they often take their children to the *campo* (countryside). Andrés said that he has a friend from work who has a *casita de
campo* (country house) that he is constructing on some land he bought
about 50km. from the city, and the family often goes out there. While
the women fix *paella* for them to eat, the men work on the house and

the children play. Estebana (Andrés's wife) emphasized that they use their weekends to do things with their children. On other weekends they take the children to the park so that they can play on the grass and ride their bicycles. They may also take the children to the movies if there is an appropriate children's film."[29] Parents also planned vacations together with their children. Some couples, particularly those with two jobs, told of making complex arrangements to ensure that their vacation times coincided.

One Sunday in 1983, George Collier and I joined a group of families from Los Olivos who lived in the Barcelona area for a picnic in the "country" (on public land where a freeway crossed a river). Even though the picnickers divided into groups by sex and age (the men played cards, the women prepared lunch and then knitted, and the children ran around), it was clear that no married person would have attended the picnic alone. It was a family outing. The whole point was for family members to spend a day in the country together.

I noticed that even couples who lived in Los Olivos, or who were there on vacation, spent leisure time together. Several people told me that the older pattern of couples spending leisure time apart persisted in the village. They were partly right. Village men did spend large amounts of time in the bars while their wives relaxed in homes with their female kin. Vacationing emigrants tended to adopt this pattern to some extent. Men on vacation usually spent mornings in the bars or out hunting, while their wives did the housework. Nevertheless, both villagers and emigrants tended to join mixed-sex groups on summer evenings. Men whose fathers had sat outdoors only in front of bars and only with other men joined women in carrying chairs outside to sit by the front door chatting with friends and relatives. And women whose mothers never went inside bars if they could help it accompanied their husbands to drink beer around bar tables.[30] In the 1980s, married couples were also the most enthusiastic participants in village festivals and religious pilgrimages, where they drank spiked punch and danced to popular bands.

But if most of the villagers and emigrants born after 1940 shared Conchi's assumption that couples married one another because they wanted to be together, they seemed reluctant to draw the conclusion that couples who did not enjoy each other's company should get a divorce. One young mother, for example, observed disapprovingly that "modern girls don't believe in marriage. They think marriage is just a contract and that couples should live together if they are in love and only as long as they are in love."[31] Like the other villagers and emigrants who told courtship stories about finding the unique other meant for them, this young woman rejected the idea that marriage was only a "contract" between two parties for the fulfillment of personal goals. Even though couples married for love, she implied, they should not be free to end a marriage if they decided they were not in love after all.

I noticed that the couples I interviewed in the 1980s were loath to admit disappointment in marriage. When I asked people to tell me when they had been happiest (phrased as when when they had had *más ilusiones*), I found that people born after 1940 seemed to have a harder time answering this question than their elders. Older villagers invariably told me that they were happiest before assuming the heavy obligations of marriage and child rearing. One young woman whose husband was not present at the interview also observed that "one enjoys life more before marrying." Couples, however, seemed to resist any temptation they might have felt to celebrate premarital bliss. Most avoided saying they had been happier before the wedding by declaring, diplomatically, that every life stage has its joys and sorrows. One man observed that "before marrying we had the joy of anticipating marriage, now we have hopes for our child."[32] And one woman said that "although love goes after the wedding, affection grows." When her husband teased her for sounding like an old woman who had been married "200 years," she asserted—and he assented—that "it takes work to make a better life."[33]

I was intrigued by the idea that marriage "takes work." Not only was the phrase familiar to me from my experiences growing up as a North American, but it seemed to capture the sense in which "modern" persons had to "produce themselves." In the 1980s, married couples talked in a way that implied they had to constantly work on their relationship. They could not simply rest secure in their love. This vision of marriage as a project contrasts markedly with the vision put forward by villagers in the 1960s. At that time, people commonly portrayed marriage as requiring resignation and endurance—not "work." One friend, for example, told me that "if the marriage encounters problems, a woman has to stick them out; she can never return to her parents' house once she is married."[34] Indeed, couples often set up a "bachelor room," like the one furnished by the novios who married in 1964, where an angry spouse could retire alone. In the 1980s, in contrast, most of the younger people I interviewed talked about having to learn to get along together. One young woman observed that early marriage is always hard because you have to "adapt to each other."[35]

Young couples also talked about the "work" required to feed, clothe, and shelter family members. Husbands, in particular, said they "worked" to support their families. Andrés, the young man who talked about spending weekends with his children, declared earlier in the interview that "all his life he had worked hard to put together his home."[36] Indeed, it made sense for people from Los Olivos to assume that men worked to support their families. Once people participated in the wider national market for jobs and commodities, there appeared to be a direct link between the money a man earned and the lifestyle of his wife and children.[37]

Wives also talked about "working for" their families. Andrés's wife, for example, said that she, too, "worked" to make a home. But house-work was clearly a problematic concept. In the 1960s, when people commonly used a conceptual opposition between obligations and diver-sions, a woman's housework was her obligation, just as a man's farming, wage work, or business activities were his obligation. At that time, both husbands and wives performed the duties required of them by the size and quality of their joined inheritances. In the 1980s, however, when people commonly contrasted work that earned money to activities that did not earn money but were undertaken for one's own benefit or plea-sure, housework did not fit easily into either category. On one hand, housework appeared to fall on the leisure side of the work/leisure di-chotomy: it did not earn money and was performed in the home, the site of a worker's rest and desire. On the other hand, housework was clearly work, in the sense that it had to be done whether or not the person doing it found it restful or pleasureful. Housework was a housewife's duty and she could not pursue other relaxing or pleasureful activities until her chores were completed.

Most of the young couples I interviewed in the 1980s seemed to treat household tasks as work when contrasting housework to resting or hav-ing fun. Andrés's wife, Estebana, for example, reported that "although she has never told Andrés's father, Andrés does help her occasionally with the housework. He will help with dishwashing when she has a lot of work and they want to go out, and he will also help her with the shopping. It would not be right, Estebana said, if only Andrés had fun."[38] Several urban husbands admitted helping their wives. I also ob-served husbands setting tables, washing dishes, disposing of garbage, and even cooking meals. When men reported helping their wives, they commonly implied that they did so because it would be unfair for a hus-band to enjoy rest or leisure while his wife worked, particularly if the wife also had an income-earning job. Like Estebana, several of the younger wives I interviewed praised their husbands for helping around the house. (In the 1960s, in contrast, these women's mothers and aunts had told me that a good husband was one who did not meddle in his wife's affairs.)

Despite people's recognition that housework was a form of work, they more often characterized housewives as "not working" if the woman did not hold a paying job outside the home. One young mother, for example, lamented that "I have no work" when talking about how she hoped to find paid employment when her youngest child entered nursery school. Once her children no longer needed constant supervision, she said, she wanted to "work" in order to contribute to the family's income and to relieve her "boredom."[39]

Boredom, in fact, was a frequent complaint of young mothers who did not "work." While knitting with the women at the picnic outside Barcelona, I listened to them arguing over whether or not one of the group, who was pregnant with her first child, should return to her factory job after the birth. The expectant mother was adamant about working. She said she would be bored if she had to stay home, cooped up in her tiny apartment. And, besides, she observed, jobs were scarce in the 1980s. If she left this factory job, she would have difficulty finding another when her child was older. I was intrigued by this notion of boredom, both because I had been bored when confined to the home with small children and because my field notes from the 1960s suggested that housewives at that time never complained of it. My sense that boredom was a new problem was confirmed by an argument I overheard between a widow who lived in the village and her two daughters, both of whom held semiprofessional urban jobs. The widow argued that a married woman belongs in her casa. It is wrong for a woman to work in the calle, she said. Her daughters argued that they would die of boredom if they had to stay inside the casa. What would they do all day? The widow countered that a woman can always find things to do in her casa. The younger women expressed horror at wasting their time knitting.

I found this argument particularly amusing because the widow, in fact, spent almost no time inside her house. She was seldom home when I knocked on her door. But she managed to stay inside her "casa" because it included not just her dwelling but also the fields she shared with her siblings and the stalls where she kept her animals. I suspect she also extended her idea of casa to include the house where her mother and unmarried siblings lived. The "homes" that her daughters imagined, in contrast, were contained within the walls of their tiny, urban apartments. For the widow, the "street" peopled with strangers began outside the properties in which she held inheritance rights. For her daughters, the "street" began in the hallways outside the doors of their apartments.

Although this argument clearly reflects the different experiences of village and urban housewives, I think it also captures an important shift in the social significance of housework. In the 1960s, a woman's housework mattered, as I discovered one spring day in 1964 when I told the housekeeper that she did not need to clean the green mold off the outer, street walls of the house. She gently informed me that she was not cleaning the walls for me. She was doing it because if she did not, other village women would criticize her.[40] At that time, village women had an audience for their housework. The entire female population of Los Olivos took note of how well a woman kept her house and used that knowledge when assessing the status and reputation of her family.

In the 1980s, in contrast, women's housework, whether done in a village house or an urban apartment, had little significance for a family's social standing. People might criticize a sloppy housekeeper and admire a good one, but it was the income family members earned through market participation that determined the family's social status relative to others they cared about. I think, therefore, that housework became "boring" less because it differed in amount or location from the housework done by village women in the 1960s than because housework suffered from the contrast with paid employment. Once the money that people earned through participation in the national market appeared to be the most important determinant of a person's social standing, the workplace became the primary site for negotiating identity. People who were deprived of income-earning work were thus deprived of opportunities for asserting and becoming who they "were."

It thus seemed to me that women who married and bore children in the 1980s sacrificed far more than their mothers had. Instead of assuming shared responsibility for maintaining the family's property and reputation, as housewives had done in the 1960s, a woman who took on the burdens of housework and child care in the 1980s jeopardized her opportunities to participate in the social sphere where wealth and reputations were acquired, contested, and asserted. In spite of her labor-saving appliances, pretty clothes, helpful husband, and occasional outings, a wife who stayed home in the 1980s was condemned to the "boredom" of a "meaningless" existence.

The villagers and emigrants I interviewed in the 1980s seemed to recognize, on some level, that housewives who gave up paid employment were indeed sacrificing themselves. They often observed, for example, that it was hard for a woman to quit her job in order to stay home with her children. But this perception of housewifely sacrifice was difficult to maintain in the face of constant evidence that others sacrificed more. Housewives in the 1980s, for example, appeared fortunate in comparison to their mothers, who had not only lacked labor-saving appliances but also complained endlessly about their "sufferings." At the same time, a housewife's sacrifices must have seemed insignificant compared to those of her husband. Whereas a wife could stay home, a husband had to leave home—the site of leisure and desire—in order to perform physical or mental labor, dictated less by his preferences than by the demands of his employer, profession, or the marketplace. In addition, a husband who gave money to his family visibly sacrificed the opportunity to spend "his" income for other purposes.

When I was in Los Olivos in 1983, I saw a play on television called "*Papa quiere ser libre*" [Father Wants to Be Free] about an urban upper-middle-class man who wanted to leave his wife, two children, and mistress of eighteen years in order to elope with one of his daughter's friends, a girl who was working as the family's maid to pay for her university education. My field notes suggest that the play captured many of the assumptions and fears expressed by people from Los Olivos. The female characters were stereotypes. The seductive "maid" was immoral, ruined by her university education. The unsympathetic daughter urged her mother to be "modern"—to find a job and stop crying about the loss of her husband. The mercenary mistress worried about her children's futures—"Papa," she said, earned only enough money to support two homes, not three. The wife was the heroine of the piece. She claimed to be a "traditional" housewife whose primary concern was her husband's happiness. After the mistress persuaded "Papa" to stay home and fulfill his responsibilities, the wife intervened, telling the mistress that if "Papa" stayed, he would be doing so only because he was resigned, not because he wanted to. The play ended with "Papa" walking out the door to meet his university student.

None of the villagers I spoke with the next day appeared to have trouble understanding the play's title, "Father Wants to Be Free," even though villagers in the 1960s had talked of men as inherently "free" whereas women were "tied down" by fear of losing their honor. Between the 1960s and the 1980s, "freedom" and "constraint" appear to have switched sexes. Actually, of course, the shift was more subtle. In the 1960s, men were inherently more "free" than women because they could not bring bastards into the family. And a husband demonstrated his "freedom" by continuing to enjoy the pleasures of the street after marriage had confined his wife to the home. In the 1980s, in contrast, both men and women were born "free," but men gave up their freedom when they took on the heavy burdens of supporting a wife and family. At marriage, a husband lost his freedom to do what he wanted. His wife, in contrast, became free to quit her job and stay home doing what she pleased.

Although I did not think to question people about their perceptions of the wife in the play, it seemed to me that the "traditional" sentiments she expressed were actually quite "modern." They were more like those I heard from women in the 1980s than the sentiments expressed by women in the 1960s. On my first visit to Los Olivos, most of the married women I met seemed to expect their husbands to be as "resigned" as they to the heavy obligations of marriage. At that time, people had to do what was expected of them, but they could think what they wanted underneath. On my return twenty years later, in contrast, I heard several young wives talking about wanting to please their husbands. Many described cooking special dishes, and some reported trying to finish the housework before their husbands returned home so that they could give them full attention. Like the supposedly "traditional" wife in the play, these young women talked in ways that suggested husbands should support their wives and children not because married men had to "resign" themselves to fulfilling their responsibilities but because they wanted to. In other words, wives in the 1980s, unlike those in the 1960s, had to take on the task of making their husbands happy.

But if young women in the 1980s portrayed themselves as personally "wanting" to please their husbands, they seemed to realize—at least on some level—that they were not free *not* to want to make their husbands happy. In 1983, for example, I overheard a group of young mothers comparing diets and joking that if they did not keep their figures, their husbands might leave them for slimmer, more attractive women. None of these mothers, to my knowledge, was actually worried that her husband might leave her. They were indeed joking. But every villager and emigrant had heard about the woman whose husband had abandoned her and their children to move in with a younger woman he met at his workplace.

Women's jokes about diets, in which they conjured up a worse alternative to dieting, reveal, in a particularly striking way, the pattern I have been describing of how people in the 1980s went about producing accounts of their actions that portrayed them as "thinking for themselves." In contrast to villagers in the 1960s, who commonly said they were simply following social conventions (as revealed by the fact that their neighbors would criticize them if they did otherwise), people in the 1980s commonly tried to explain why they, as individuals, had decided to do what they did. These explanations often took the form of listing, explicitly or implicitly, one or more alternatives that were less desirable than the chosen one, particularly if the chosen activity was something that everyone had good reason to suspect the person might not have wanted to do. Dieting, for example, might be miserable, but it was far worse to be abandoned by a husband. Or, to return to an example given earlier, the novia who suffered through soccer games might have preferred to go dancing, but her novio could have had worse passions than rooting for the local soccer team.

Women's efforts to "want" what their husbands wanted were particularly apparent during discussions of family vacation homes. By the 1980s, several couples from Los Olivos had become wealthy enough to invest in seaside condominiums and country retreats, or in renovating the village houses they had inherited. Men were invariably proud of such investments. They signified the family's wealth and the husband's commitment to his family. Women, however, seemed ambivalent. Vacation homes were houses that required care. Even though most husbands in the 1980s helped their wives with the housework, a husband's help was rarely enough to compensate his wife for the doubling of her workload that occurred when the family purchased a vacation home or renovated an old village house. During informal discussions in the 1980s, I heard many women talk of dreading holidays, known in Spanish as "days of rest" [días de descanso]. They expected little rest because they knew they would have to clean the vacation home of its accumulated dirt. One woman whose "vacation home" was a large old house in Los Olivos was particularly bitter about the amount of dirt that accumulated between visits. Nevertheless, women joined their husbands in "wanting" vacation homes. They, too, proudly displayed pictures of seaside resorts, mountain retreats, and renovated village houses. Women did not need to point out that the alternatives were worse. After all, the family could have been too poor to buy a vacation home, or—worse still—the husband could have used his income to support a mistress rather than investing in a vacation home for his family.

Although thinking for oneself did require people to imagine less desirable alternatives, I believe that most of the wives I met in the 1980s truly wanted to make their husbands happy. They did not go on diets, cook special dishes, or show enthusiasm for a husband's pet project simply because they were afraid their husbands might leave them. Rather, they dieted, cooked, and enthused because they loved their husbands and these were ways that a wife could show her love for the man who demonstrated his love for her by sharing his money and leisure time with his family. Nevertheless, demonstrations of "love," like "thinking for oneself," required people to imagine alternatives not chosen. It would not count as "love" if the person would have performed the action anyway out of compulsion or self-interest. A husband's economic support, for example, counted as love primarily because he could have spent his earnings on things only he wanted, such as a sports car or a mistress. Similarly, a wife's dieting, special dishes, and enthusiasm for a vacation home counted as demonstrations of love because she could have let herself get fat, been a lazy cook, or demanded hotel vacations.

## EXPERIENCING MARRIAGE IN THE 1960s

Just as people trying to convince me that wives had become more equal to their husbands regaled me with examples of how women's lives had improved, so they also reminded me of women's past "subordination." The grim pictures they painted of women's lives in the 1960s did indeed reflect how villagers had described and enacted marital relations. On my first visit to Los Olivos, the housewives I met constantly bemoaned their "sacrifices" and "subordination"—in contrast to wives in the 1980s, who commonly portrayed themselves as "wanting" to do what they did. In the 1960s, for example, villagers often joked that "divorce begins on the wedding night." Before the wedding, a novio had to visit his novia every evening in her mother's kitchen. After the wedding, a man rejoined his cronies in the bar. Women talked about this change in men's behavior as desertion. One novia told Shelly Zimbalist "that newly married men stay in their houses evenings for a while, but then they start going out to *cantinas* again." This novia expressed the vain hope that her novio would "be different," because, she said, "when [I] am away he goes to bed straight after supper."[41]

Women also portrayed marriage as the moment when a wife became subordinated to her husband's authority. An older woman repeated what she described as "a common saying": "On the wedding night the husband says to the wife that while they were engaged, he tried to please her. But after marriage the husband says, 'I wear the pants.' A wife has to do everything her husband says. Until he says 'yes' she cannot do anything. After marriage, even if the wife is right, her husband gets his way."[42]

Wives also emphasized their sacrifices. As I noted earlier, married women commonly told unmarried girls to enjoy themselves while they could. And married women contrasted their constraints to men's continued freedoms. Two women, for example, reported that wives had few friends because "a [married] woman has more things to do and cannot go out with her friends as she used to." A man, in contrast, could keep his friends because "men, when they come home from work in the fields, dress up and go out and meet their same friends as before in the casino."[43]

In the early 1960s, village women said they accepted the sacrifices of marriage with "resignation." After all, sacrifices and suffering were a woman's fate.[44] Not only did women have to be "tied down" because they could lose their honor, but they had to be subordinated because they could ruin the reputations of others. Men seemed incapable of such evil.[45] An older friend who lamented women's propensity to gossip observed that "men are not as malicious as we."[46] Indeed, it was always easy for people to find a woman to blame for any problem, as suggested by the epigraph at the beginning of this chapter. Doña Perfecta's husband may have wasted his family's inheritance, but it was loose women who tempted him to do so.

Rereading my field notes from the 1960s, however, I see that even then I had doubts about whether women's lives were really as hard as they portrayed them. "From what I have seen," I wrote, "the life of a married woman isn't half as bad as Ebelia and Francisca picture it to be. The women seem to have lots of time to sit around, go visiting, and enjoy themselves. Not even their housework seems to take very much time. Ebelia and the other four women sat around for hours yesterday afternoon just talking. Work was not pressing on them. They don't even have the problem of having always to care for a baby. Babies are in great demand and the mother who gets tired of hers can always take him to a willing relative."[47]

I was also impressed by women's apparent autonomy. Men and women seemed to lead separate lives. Men were rarely in their houses, and when women went to the fields, they appeared to control their own labor. Husbands and wives often did separate agricultural tasks or, if they worked together, they seemed to do so as equals. Finally, I began to doubt whether women were, in fact, confined to their homes after marriage. Not only did their regular chores require them to leave the house for agricultural tasks, feeding animals, shopping, clothes washing, and more, but they regularly visited sickly and housebound relatives in the evenings. Women might complain about men wasting time in bars drinking with their friends, but women spent hours gathered in sickrooms, munching goodies and visiting with other women.[48]

In short, I, like many ethnographers who visited small communities in Southern Europe before the 1970s, was struck by the discrepancy between housewives' "appearance" of subordination and the "reality" of their autonomy and power (see Friedl 1967; Riegelhaupt 1967; Rogers 1975, 1985; Dubisch 1986). Although no villager reported a popular saying equivalent to the one Lison-Tolosana (1966, 151) recorded for Aragón ("The husband commands in the house, when his wife is not at home"), it seemed as true in Los Olivos as in the Aragonese village he described that authority in the household belonged "*de jure* to the husband, *de facto* to the wife" (1966, 149).

Even though the same statement about household authority could be made in the 1980s, the implications of having authority in the household changed dramatically. In the 1960s, the casa was the basis of the family's wealth. Husbands may have assumed full legal authority to manage the joined inheritances of a married couple,[49] but a wife's association with the household ensured her direct access to the family's economic resources and the power they conveyed. Moreover, because household property was symbolically held in trust for the children, a mother enjoyed considerable protection against dispossession. Should a husband want to abandon his family, he would have had a hard time doing so without simultaneously abandoning the property that was the source of his wealth.[50] Moreover, wives were protected from a husband's mismanagement. Because everyone in the village knew which fields or enterprises had been inherited by which spouse, neighbors usually kept a wife informed of her husband's decisions. She thus had time to intervene if she disapproved. By law, a husband may have had the right to dispose of his family's assets, but the women I knew disputed this. When I told one woman that her husband could legally sell the fields she had inherited, she was horrified. "Those fields belong to my children," she declared. "He can't touch them."

Husbands also had few ways to assert their legally and socially sanctioned authority over their wives. Men were rarely in the house. And should a man venture into his wife's domain, she rapidly fulfilled his request, leaving him no excuse to hang around. I noticed, for example, that adolescent boys were sometimes allowed to participate in groups of adult women, joining younger children and girls in listening to conversations and sharing the pastries. But adult men were met at the door and rapidly sent off again. When I asked a neighbor if men ever beat their wives, she told me that "it would be a very low thing to do."[51] Everyone in the village looked down on a husband who beat his wife. They regarded wife beating as a failure of masculine authority, not its realization.

Given the economic security and personal autonomy enjoyed by married women, why did they talk endlessly about their sacrifices and subordination? I believe they did so because in a social world where a family's social standing appeared to be determined by the amount of property it held, those who visibly sacrificed themselves for the family could assert a stronger moral claim to control the family's limited resources than people who appeared to be using those resources to pursue personal pleasures (see also Dubisch 1995, 214–223). Because married women were in a position to sacrifice more than either their husbands or their children, they had more opportunities to claim moral authority than other family members.[52] But if wives could claim moral authority, they also needed to stress their subordination to their husbands. The welfare of the family depended on preserving its inherited property. All family members suffered if the authority and social standing of a husband and father were called into question.

Although no villager told me that married women gained moral authority through sacrificing themselves, the women I knew in the 1960s talked and acted in ways that suggested they understood, at some level, the empowering consequences of "suffering." They avoided, for example, disempowering talk about the benefits of marriage. Unlike novias, who could give good reasons for wanting to marry, I never heard wives mention the benefits of marriage except in contexts where they dismissed them. For example, a woman born before 1920 told me that

"Since the mothers suffered so much in marriage, you would not think they would want their daughters to have to go through the same thing. But no, mothers are happy when their daughters marry."[53]

Married women also boasted of sacrificing themselves more than custom required. I remember one incident in the 1960s that puzzled me at the time. An older woman told me, with evident pride, that she had never left Los Olivos, even to visit the nearby market town of Aracena. I was astounded. I actually thought she was crazy. Only later did I realize that this woman had good reasons to take pride in her achievement. Not only was she informing me that her family was wealthy enough to shop in village stores, where prices were higher; she was also telling me that she was more virtuous than women who visited "sinful" urban centers. Similar messages about family wealth and personal virtue were implicit in the boasts of women and girls who, in the summer of 1965, told Shelly Zimbalist that they were "muy luteras" [intense mourners], implying that they stayed indoors and refrained from participating in social activities for a longer period than most women who had recently lost a relative.

Finally, in looking over my field notes, I realize that many instances where I recorded women talking about their sacrifices were actually occasions when a woman invoked her "obligations" to justify doing what she wanted. Women commonly excused themselves for not staying longer or for refusing to comply with someone's request by referring to their obligations. An older friend, for example, who constantly complained about how boring the local priests were, cheerily responded to my question about why I never saw her in church with the cliché "obligation comes before devotion." I also noticed that some of the stories I heard about women "submitting" to their husbands were actually stories about how the woman got her way. A woman who married shortly after I left Los Olivos gleefully told me on my return that she and her husband had taken an expensive honeymoon against her mother's express wishes. When her mother had complained, this woman said, her husband announced, "after the wedding, I give the orders." So the couple went.[54]

As I came to realize the empowering effects of wives' "subordination," I began to wonder whether husbands' absolute "authority" might entail fewer advantages than people implied. When married couples in the 1980s portrayed themselves as enjoying more equality than couples once did, they talked not only about women's former "sacrifices" but also about men's propensity to spend all their free time in bars. They treated men's barroom attendance as evidence of a husband's power and willingness to defy his wife's wishes that he stay home and avoid wasting the family's money. But men had to spend time in bars, not only because employment contracts were negotiated there, as I mentioned earlier, but also because men had to interact with other men in bars in order to protect their reputations as people who could defend their families and properties.

Unfortunately, I have little information on male bar culture in Los Olivos. Like other women in the village, I avoided entering bars in the 1960s. And neither Richard Price nor my husband wrote much about them in their field notes. Nevertheless, it is my impression that men's actions and concerns did not differ significantly from those reported by ethnographers who patronized male-dominated bars and coffee houses in other southern European small communities (Brandes 1980; Dreissen 1983; Gilmore 1987; Herzfeld 1985; Papataxiarchis 1991).[55] Stanley Brandes, who studied an Andalusian town in the 1970s, observed that men there were "concerned above all with two problems of identity: their place in the social hierarchy and their relationship to women" (1980, 6). He suggested psychological reasons for their concerns. My experiences in Los Olivos lead me to suggest some cultural reasons why men might have worried about these two problems of identity.

In the early 1960s, men had good reason to worry about maintaining their place in the social hierarchy. The standard of living represented by a couple's wedding furniture, which was displayed to the whole village, was difficult for a husband to sustain, harder to enhance. Wedding furniture represented the lifetime savings of the newlyweds' parents. Married couples, both before they acquired their inheritances and after they had more than two children, faced the problem of trying to maintain, with diminished resources, the standard of living exemplified by their wedding house. As a result, the most common experience of husbands who assumed responsibility for managing a household's property was one of trying to hang on to the family's inherited resources.

Although some ethnographers of small Spanish communities have portrayed class and honor as incompatible or conflicting principles of stratification (e.g., Lison-Tolosana 1966, 108–109; Corbin and Corbin 1987, 132; but see Davis 1977, 90), I argued in chapter 1 that economic and moral worth are always interrelated. Class may be based on the unequal distribution of property while honor is based on the equal distribution of social worth, but those who are "doing well" inevitably enjoy more input into defining what counts as "doing good." I thus suggest that men's concern with equal honor has to be understood in relation to the unequal distribution of productive property in a social world where inheritance appeared to be the main determinant of a family's wealth.[56] In a stratified village such as Los Olivos, where married couples had difficulty maintaining the standard of living established at their weddings, all married men were equal in the sense that all had something to lose. All men could fear dropping down the social hierarchy even if they began in different places.

This fear of losing status, I suggest, gave men a good reason to spend time in bars. Not only did men negotiate work contracts there, but a man had to go out in public to display his ability and willingness to defend what he claimed as his. No manager of a family's property could afford to stay home. Because a husband had to protect his and his wife's joined inheritances, he had to appear ever ready to fight anyone who might try to plow an extra furrow into his field, pasture animals on his lands, divert water from his irrigation ditches, cheat him of his wages, and so forth. He had to engage in frequent public displays of virility, assertiveness, and hospitality (see Corbin and Corbin 1987, 57). Many ethnographers of rural communities in southern Europe have analyzed men's barroom interactions as performances (see particularly Herzfeld 1985). They have observed that, instead of talking to each other or exchanging information, men in such communities usually talked at each other as each man tried to enact the powerful, invulnerable, individual he wanted others to think he was (Brandes 1980, 115–136; Corbin and Corbin 1987, 54).

At the same time that men displayed invulnerability, they also benefited from emphasizing their equality with other men. In a social world where every man could fear losing status, each man had reason to avoid interacting with others who might treat him as an inferior.[57] As a result, men could maintain cooperative relations with one another only by ensuring that each man was given an opportunity to prove his invulnerability.[58]

But if men's fears of losing status forced them to spend time in bars, the time they spent there also gave them good reason to worry about their relationships with women. I do not doubt that many, if not most, of the men I met in the 1960s wanted to spend time in bars. I certainly enjoyed the time I spent in bars drinking with friends on my return visits to Spain. But husbands in the 1960s must have known, on some level, that frequenting bars put them at a moral disadvantage relative to their wives. When Brandes observed that Andalusian men worried about their relationship to women, I think he captured not only men's fears that their wives might cuckold them but also men's recognition that, by spending money on drinks for themselves and their friends, they became open to accusations of "wasting" the family's limited resources on pleasures only they enjoyed.

In Los Olivos, as in the town Brandes studied, people often observed that widows were better off than wives (Brandes 1980, 87).[59] Some older women I overheard discussing a man's terminal illness, for example, "commented on the good fortune of his widow who would be left free to enjoy herself."[60] When I asked a friend born before 1920 why widows in Los Olivos did not remarry, she replied, "why should a widow want to remarry? Why should she want to put up with a man once she has her independence? Look at Remedios. Her husband was very bad, but now that he is dead, Remedios gets her widow's pay to do with as she likes. She gets to live in peace."[61] Some villagers went so far as to suggest that wives might want their husbands to die. One woman told me that if a man got drunk and failed to return home at night, "his family will not come to look for him. He will die sooner and cease to be a burden if they leave him to lie out in the streets."[62]

But if women often complained about the time and money men spent in bars, and portrayed widows as better off without their wastrel husbands, wives did not openly challenge a husband's moral and legal right to rule his family. No one benefited by calling a husband's authority into question. As long as he was alive, a husband and father represented the household in public. If he lost credibility, his wife and children suffered. Their property might be vandalized, they might lose their credit in stores, and the children might have difficulty finding appropriate marriage partners. As a result, the wives I knew not only deferred to their husbands, particularly in public, but also stressed their subordination.

Although women might celebrate the benefits of widowhood in the abstract, they were visibly distressed by the idea of benefiting from the death of a loved one. None of the widows I spoke with expressed joy at her supposed release. Remedios, the widow whose neighbors all said she was well rid of a bad husband, told me what a good man he had been and how much she missed him. I heard only one wife, whose marriage was widely regarded as one of the most unfortunate in the village, say that she looked forward to the day when her husband finally drank himself to death.

In summary, I believe that husbands in the 1960s were analogous to the novias I described in the previous chapter. Both experienced vulnerability while being constantly reminded of their dominance. On one hand, everyone asserted that husbands, like novias, enjoyed power and moral authority over their loved ones. On the other hand, both knew that the wives and novios they supposedly dominated actually enjoyed autonomy and moral superiority. In the 1960s, novias expressed their insecurity by crying at the slightest pretext. Although I did not frequent bars, I imagine that husbands in Los Olivos expressed their insecurity through the kinds of barroom jokes, pranks, and riddles that Brandes recorded in the Andalusian town he studied (1980, 73, 137).

Husbands also took practical steps to escape their moral predicament. Many surrendered control of the family finances to their wives. A man who turned over all his and his children's[63] income to his wife, and spent only what she doled out to him for amusement, could partially escape being accused of "wasting" the family's resources on prostitutes, gambling, and drink. When I asked villagers and emigrants about family budgets in the 1980s I found that most people said their mothers had handled the family finances, distributing allowances to the husband and children on weekends and holidays (see also Lison-Tolosana 1966, 148; Salamone and Stanton 1986). The major exceptions were people who had grown up in wealthier families, or in families with political connections that experienced upward mobility after the civil war. Such people tended to report that their fathers had allowed their mothers to control only the funds needed to sustain the family's standard of living.

In this chapter, I have focused on parents, ignoring the experiences of adults who did not have children, either because they never married or because they remained childless. In the 1960s, however, there were many childless adults in Los Olivos owing to high rates of nonmarriage and late marriage. But the experiences of childless adults, like those of parents, were shaped by the prevailing understanding that property should be managed for the benefit of those who would inherit it. Parents who had legitimate children could always appear to be sacrificing themselves for the benefit of their heirs. People without children, in contrast, were never able to claim the obligations that conferred full adult status. Their lack of children who could not be disinherited deprived them of any purpose in life beyond their own pleasure.

Childless adults could—and of course did—act selflessly. But even when they adopted heirs, or sacrificed themselves for others, their ability to choose their heirs and beneficiaries always made it possible for unsympathetic others to construe their acts as motivated by personal desire rather than by obligation. The plight of childless adults is nicely illustrated in the nineteenth-century novel *Doña Perfecta* by the character of Doña Perfecta's unmarried brother-in-law, Don Cayetano Polentinos. The novelist introduces him as a "distinguished savant and bibliophile" (Pérez Galdós 1960, 35), but portrays him as a man who wrote silly histories and misunderstood the tragedy unfolding around him. His childlike dependence on Doña Perfecta captures the sense in which adults without children, whatever their achievements, remained forever barred from becoming full participants in the social world of responsible adults.

## CONCLUSION

At the beginning of this chapter, I suggested that the transition from spouses as co-owners to coworkers reflected a change in people's experiences of property. In the early 1960s, when villagers lived in a social world where inherited property appeared to be the major determinant of family members' activities, incomes, and lifestyles, people tended to imagine husbands and wives as co-owners of their joined inheritances, managed by the husband. When people participated in the national market for jobs and commodities, where a family's income and lifestyle appeared to depend on the money workers earned for their labor, people tended to imagine husbands and wives as coworkers who pooled their assets to realize shared goals.

These two ways of imagining marriage were reflected in the laws promulgated by the Franco regime and revised after his death by democratically elected legislators. During Franco's dictatorship, laws enforced the vision of husband and wife as a single legal body represented by the husband. At marriage a woman lost her separate identity as a citizen as well as the right to manage any valuable properties she owned or inherited. The democratically elected legislators, in contrast, imagined marriage as an equal partnership. When they reformed the civil code in 1981, they eliminated the articles distinguishing between the powers of a husband and wife. "Both parties now have the same rights in terms of control and management of the property each brings into the marriage" as well as the same rights over the community property they purchase or earn after the wedding (Sponsler 1982, 1599). Married women also keep their citizenship and the right to vote.

These two visions of marriage were also reflected in laws concerning adultery. During Franco's dictatorship, adultery was a crime. It carried a penal sanction. The standards for determining whether the crime of adultery had been committed varied by sex. A married woman could be charged with adultery if she had sexual intercourse with any man not her husband, whereas a married man could be charged with adultery only if he had sexual intercourse with a married woman, knowing that she was married, or if he had continual relations with an unmarried woman in the home he shared with his wife or in a notorious manner outside the home (Sponsler 1982, 1617). In other words, it was not a crime for a married man to have affairs with women he thought were unmarried as long as he did not destroy his family's reputation in the process. These laws, of course, reflect the vision of society as dependent on the orderly transmission of inherited property. Adultery was a crime because it harmed everyone, not just the immediate victims. The separate standards for men and women reflect their different potentials for disrupting inheritance lines. Adultery was always a crime for a woman because she could bring bastards into the family. But adultery was not a crime for a man unless he knowingly risked begetting bastards on another man's family or if he committed adultery in such a flagrant manner that it jeopardized the inheritances and reputations of his legitimate heirs.

In 1978, when democratically elected legislators reformed the penal code, they dropped all the articles pertaining to adultery. In Spain, adultery is no longer a crime for either women or men (Sponsler 1982, 1617). This removal of adultery from the penal code reflects, of course, the vision of marriage associated with a social world where people appear to achieve the statuses they enjoy. Once individual achievement seems more important than inherited property for determining a person's social status, adultery poses no threat to the social order. It may be a personal tragedy. It may be morally wrong. But it is hardly a crime. Moreover, once status depends on personal achievements, there is no reason to distinguish between a husband's and wife's adulteries. For either spouse to engage in outside affairs is to betray the trust of the other. People may find it easier to excuse a husband's adulteries, on the basis that men are "naturally" more promiscuous than women. But if couples marry because they love one another, then neither spouse can engage in extramarital affairs without calling into question the adulterer's commitment to the marriage.

Although no villager or emigrant from Los Olivos discussed these changes in the civil and penal codes with me, most of the younger people I interviewed in the 1980s shared the premises behind the changes. One man who lived in Barcelona did mention law to me. According to my notes, "José said that there is a law in Catalonia giving a married woman control over her own property, so that her husband could not dispose of it. When I asked if there was not such a law in Andalusia, José laughed and said that I had to understand there was this thing called *machismo*, and that *andaluces* had *más machismo*.[64] There, [he said], the man controls all.[65] Nevertheless, José felt that the Catalonians, in allowing a woman to control her own property, were much more advanced and '*civilizados*' than the *machista andaluces*." Clearly José shared the vision of Spain's democratically elected legislators that—at least among "civilized" people—marriage should be an equal partnership between spouses who pool their assets.

But if "modern" spouses pooled their assets, their assets were no longer of equal value. When I first visited Los Olivos, couples tended to bring equal assets into marriage because vigilant parents discouraged marriages between young people who expected unequal inheritances. By the 1980s, however, the "assets" of husbands were usually far more valuable than those of wives. In the capitalist market, men could earn money for their "productive" labor. But the market did not pay women for the "reproductive" labor they expended in caring for their children and homes. In this chapter, I have drawn on this insight to suggest that, between my two visits to Los Olivos, wives lost power and autonomy relative to their husbands. In the 1960s, the Franco regime may have given husbands full legal authority over their wives and children, but wives, at least in Los Olivos, were not subordinated. In the 1980s, the democratic legislators may have granted wives the same rights as husbands, but the problems that a mother faced in combining paid employment with child care turned most mothers into de facto economic dependents of their husbands (see Cowan 1990; S. Sutton 1986). For women, the shift from inherited property to occupational achievement did not signal an end to male domination. Rather, it marked a shift from overt—and often ineffectual—political domination to covert—but quite effective—subordination through the workings of a supposedly "free" market (see also Seccombe 1992).

Although the mothers I interviewed in the 1980s were—like mothers of young children in the United States—only one man away from destitution, none seemed to adopt an overtly subservient role. They seemed far more independent and assertive than I or most of my North American female friends. When interviewing married couples in the 1980s, I heard many wives interrupt, contradict, and argue with their husbands in ways that, had they been North Americans, would have signified an imminent divorce. One wife, for example, broke in on her husband's narrative, told him he was wrong, and proceeded to state her views, ignoring his protests. Another wife burst out laughing in the middle of one of her husband's pronouncements, told him he was stupid, and pointed out that he had stated the opposite opinion on a previous occasion. Although these interactions do reflect differences between Spanish and English linguistic rules for taking turns, they also suggest that Spanish wives enjoyed more opportunities to assert their opinions than I ever felt were allowed to me (see also Tannen and Kakava 1992).

When trying to understand why women from Los Olivos were virtually unanimous in portraying their lives as improving, I think it is important to remember not only the evidence they presented about women's current equality and past subordination but also Foucault's and Giddens's insights about the "attitude" of "modernity." In the 1980s, women (and men) really did seem to take themselves as objects of "a complex and difficult elaboration" (Foucault 1984, 41). Given that most of them had, in fact, experienced a dramatic improvement in their standard of living, it made sense for them to portray their lives in terms of a "trajectory of development from the past to the anticipated future" (Giddens 1991, 75).

This sense of life as a "trajectory of development" was brought home to me one afternoon in Barcelona when I visited Clara, a woman whose sister Pilar had asked me to look her up. Pilar, who lived in Los Olivos, told me that she was worried about Clara. Knowing that I was about to leave for Barcelona, Pilar begged me to look in on Clara and to comfort her because—said Pilar—"she works in the street, poor thing."[66] I immediately envisioned Clara dressed in black rags, miserably sweeping the dirty streets of Barcelona. I was, of course, utterly wrong. When I finally went to "comfort" Clara, I found an enthusiastic middle-aged woman dressed in nice clothes with a stylish hairdo. She proudly showed me around her modern apartment, pointing out the nice furniture and calling my attention to her children's diplomas on the walls. Clara did indeed work for a janitorial firm cleaning office buildings. But far from lamenting her job, she talked enthusiastically about how her salary, combined with her husband's earnings, had enabled them to purchase the possessions we were admiring. She also regaled me with future plans for improving their living standard and for enhancing her children's educational opportunities. Clearly Clara felt empowered, rather than disempowered, by the shift from inherited property to occupational achievement.

## CHAPTER FOUR

# Children: From Heirs to Parental Projects

Doña Perfecta to her daughter Rosario, who has just
defied her:

"I'll teach you the duties of a daughter, which
you have forgotten."
*(Pérez Galdós 1960 [1876], 225)*[1]

WHEN I RETURNED to Los Olivos in the 1980s, many of my friends
complained that "today's youth no longer respect their elders." They
observed that young people no longer used the formal *usted* (you) when
talking to their parents, but addressed them informally as *tú*. Adults'
major complaint, however, was that young people, "now talk back to
their parents" and to other adults. My friend Felisa, for example, illustrated her contention that today's children no longer respect their elders
by telling me that she had recently observed an older boy hitting a
younger child. When she told the boy to stop, he rudely replied, "what's
it matter to you?" Another older woman, who overheard a teenager telling her mother that she did not intend to remain in Los Olivos when she
grew up, burst out, "Now youth talk about whether they do or do not
want to do the work their parents tell them to do. When I was young,
[we] did what our parents told us."[2]

Villagers and emigrants commonly blamed "modern" culture for corrupting children. They reported that television, the lure of urban entertainments, and the bad examples set by "hippies" and "drug addicts"
had undermined young people's respect for their elders. Several villagers, particularly older women, described "today's youth" as "ruined."
"They only want to go off to the city and have fun," complained an
older friend.[3] I heard only one villager blame parents for children's alleged "loss of respect." After listening to an older woman declare that
"modern" culture had corrupted young people, a single woman in her
early thirties countered with the argument that children now "talk back
to their parents" because parents are not demanding respect from their
children. But even this young woman ultimately accused "modern" culture. "Things are changing so rapidly," she said, "that parents are not
taking the time to educate their children in respect."[4]

I, of course, plan to suggest that children's alleged loss of respect reflected less the corrupting influence of "modern" culture, or parents' failure to discipline their children, than a shift in parents' perceptions of what their children needed to succeed in adult life. When children's futures appeared to depend on how much inheritance their parents could provide, parents had to prevent their children from behaving in ways that might prejudice their chances of marrying someone of equal or greater inheritance. As people said, parents had to "subjugate" their children to ensure that girls, in particular, kept their honor. In the 1980s, in contrast, when children's futures appeared to depend on their own achievements, parents had to identify, and then to foster, each child's unique abilities. Instead of "subjugating" their children, parents had to "prepare" them for adult life. Parents had to listen to their children to discover their likes and dislikes.

The contrasting verbs "to subjugate" (*sujetar*) and "to prepare" (*preparar*) capture, in another form, the distinction I have been drawing between "following social conventions" and "thinking for oneself." In the 1960s, a good parent prevented a child from acting on passing "whims." In the 1980s, a good parent "prepared" the child to "become independent" (*independizarse*). But as I highlight the contrast between "subjugating" and "preparing," I do not want to suggest that parents in the 1960s did not try to prepare children for adult life. They did. It is just that when inherited property appeared to determine a child's future, "preparing" a child meant forcing the child to follow accepted social conventions (regardless of what the child might be thinking or wanting underneath). Similarly, parents in the 1980s did subjugate their children, in the sense that they actively punished behaviors they regarded as undesirable. Once a child's future appeared to depend on how well a child was prepared to compete in the capitalist market for jobs and commodities, parents had to prevent their children from indulging in such self-destructive behaviors as refusing to study or taking drugs.

The contrast between subjugating and preparing is well depicted in the nineteenth-century novel *Doña Perfecta*. As suggested by the quotation at the beginning of this chapter, Doña Perfecta believed it was her obligation to teach Rosario "the duties of a daughter." Instead of listening to Rosario's pleas for understanding, Doña Perfecta prevented Rosario from acting on her love for Pepe Rey by locking Rosario in her room and setting the servants to guard the house. Pepe Rey's father, in contrast, encouraged his son's whims: "the boy used to amuse himself by building earthen viaducts, mounds, reservoirs, dams and ditches in the patio of the house, then turning on the water and running it among those fragile works. The father let him do it. 'You'll be an engineer,' he used to say" (Pérez Galdós 1960, 18).[5] In Pepe Rey's social world, good parents noticed and encouraged their children's productive capacities. But parents also had to subjugate children who exhibited "unnatural" or inappropriate desires. Had Pepe Rey amused himself by destroying his toys rather than building viaducts, for example, one suspects that his father would have been less accommodating.

In this chapter, I suggest that these different parental strategies correlated with contrasting images of children's "natures." During both my visits to Los Olivos, people imagined children as separate beings with wills and desires of their own. But over time children seem to have changed from "animals" who needed control into "miniature humans" who needed encouragement. In the 1960s, parents had to squash their children's animal appetites until the children became old enough to understand, and to follow, human social conventions. In the 1980s, in contrast, human infants, unlike animals, had the capacity to become rational beings, capable of thinking for themselves and making their own decisions. As a result, parents had to foster and channel their children's desires.

Finally, I suggest that these different parental strategies encouraged the development of different subjectivities in children. Young people whose parents "subjugated" them to prevent them from acting on personal whims must have come to experience themselves as having inner desires that had to be suppressed in favor of following social conventions. Moreover, they must have experienced knowing and following social conventions as the behaviors that conferred adult privileges—including the right to tell others what to do. Children whose parents encouraged them to express and develop their inborn talents, in contrast, must have come to experience themselves as having inner desires and abilities that could be channeled into productive activities. Instead of attending to what others were saying in order to master social conventions, such children had to learn to attend to their own inner desires, sorting out the ones to be cultivated from the ones to be suppressed. For such children, it was not mastering social conventions, but rather learning how to think for themselves that earned them adult privileges.

This chapter is divided into three sections and a conclusion. In the first, I compare my impressions of parent-child relations in the 1960s and the 1980s. I then discuss the transformation in people's experience of schooling from the 1960s, when villagers commonly regarded schooling as a privilege of the wealthy, to the 1980s, when education had become a prerequisite for adult success. In the third and longest section, I explore the dilemmas experienced by parents in the 1980s who wanted to "prepare" their children for adult independence. Finally, in the concluding section, I consider a parental dilemma that I experienced but which people in Los Olivos seem to have avoided.

## PARENTING IN LOS OLIVOS

When George Collier and I arrived in Los Olivos in 1963, with our two-month-old baby and a copy of the latest edition of Dr. Spock's *Baby and Child Care* (1957), we and the villagers we met were struck by differences between their and our treatment of infants. We always spoke softly to our baby, and to any infants we held, waiting for the baby to respond and then adapting our actions to the infant's reactions. Villagers, in contrast, spoke loudly to infants, and often initiated actions without observing the infant's response. If a baby started to cry while being jounced or tickled, the adult was likely to jounce or tickle harder, often reducing the infant to screaming hysteria in the process (see also Friedl 1962, 78–81). My husband and I, with righteous indignation derived from frequent reading of Dr. Spock, were appalled by villagers' apparent insensitivity to infants' moods and desires.[6] We thought that villagers treated babies as playthings rather than as individuals with their own personalities and needs.[7]

Our reading of Dr. Spock also led us to disapprove of what we perceived as adults' tendency to lie to children (see Hirschon 1992). When children begged for candies or toys, they were often told there weren't any, even when the desired object was in full view. Adults also bribed children with promised rewards that we (and probably the child) knew the adult had no intention of providing. And adults often tried to frighten children into obeying with stories of evil people or fearful animals. One evening, for example, Sally Price observed some adults trying to quiet a crying child by "pointing to the one street light and banging on the door, saying that witches would hear him and come get him."[8]

In the 1960s, schooling seemed to be a low priority for many village parents. Richard Price wrote in his field notes that "many boys here do not go to school till the required age of 14. And those who do—who are only perhaps half—rarely go twice a day, as they should. Fathers take kids out of school to help them work, to guard flocks, etc., often at the age of 8 or 9. The teacher doesn't care too much, and besides, what can he do."[9] I noticed that parents also kept older girls out of school to help in family enterprises, to earn money as part-time maids, or to care for infants and toddlers. Even younger children were often prevented from attending school functions until they had finished their chores.

Some parents did sacrifice themselves to keep their children in school. One friend was furious when her thirteen-year-old daughter was expelled from school along with the other girls her age in order to make room for entering six-year-olds. She railed—uselessly—against the fact that she would now have to pay the teacher for private lessons so that her daughter could obtain the primary school certificate she needed to pursue further education. I also noticed that the wealthiest families in Los Olivos not only kept their children in primary school but also sent their teenagers away to obtain secondary, and even more advanced, degrees in cities.

In the early 1960s, when villagers talked about "educating" a child, they rarely meant formal schooling. Instead, they considered children "well educated" when they knew how to behave properly. María José, an unmarried young woman, told Shelly Zimbalist in the summer of 1965 that the parents of a daughter had to "subjugate" her from childhood in order to give her an "education."[10] Parents failed, María José observed, when their "daughters did many things they shouldn't and their parents did not scold them." In her view, children who talked back to adults were "uneducated." If their parents had given them "more education," observed María José, "they would have had more fear of their parents, more respect."

María José's concept of "education" presumed a particular understanding of children's maturation. She told Shelly that girls passed through three stages before reaching adulthood: "[First there] is infancy, when they are small, younger than seven. After that they are girls, who have more understanding . . . more knowledge. Afterwards they are young women of fifteen or older, who no longer go to school and who dress up and do the things of *muchachas* [i.e., prepare their hope chests and begin courting]; then they reach womanhood and marry."

In María José's view, the years between seven and fourteen were crucial for "educating" a child. Unlike infants, school-age children had "understanding." They could act on their desires and they could learn. If not properly "subjugated" (i.e., prevented from doing what they wanted), they could develop bad reputations that would harm their chances for marriage. María José asserted that "If, from childhood, a girl is not deprived [of liberty], she will be the same [i.e., act freely] when adult." As an example of bad parenting, María José described two sisters—Juana and María—whom she characterized as *locas* (crazy, uncontrolled) because their parents allowed them "too much liberty." "Juana," she said, "is becoming a young woman, passing from girlhood to womanhood. She has very little shame around boys. She runs about freely with them. And María is younger, but even so is the same. They become worse every day . . . they are girls the whole world will talk about. Perhaps they are good,[11] but they allow themselves that freedom and they will suffer as they become older. Now they act without using their heads. They don't think if what they are doing is right."

Although María José spoke only of girls (in response to Shelly's questions), I felt that her observations applied equally to boys. The villagers

I knew spoke of boys, too, as passing through four stages, beginning as preschool "infants" who turned into more knowledgeable schoolboys. After leaving school, boys became youths who worked for their fathers and courted girls until they married and established separate households. Although villagers commonly permitted boys more freedom than girls, a boy who was allowed to shirk tasks and talk back to adults could also harm his chances for making a good marriage by becoming known as someone who was not "formal" or "serious."

In the early 1960s, the parents I observed did appear to educate their children by subjugating them. They constantly scolded them. Parents spent more time—at least in public—yelling at children than talking with them or trying to understand a child's viewpoint. I often noticed caretakers playfully scolding infants and toddlers, knocking objects out of their hands and mouths, saying *es caca* [it's shit]. And adults—passersby as well as parents—frequently yelled at older children who were not doing what adults wanted. I also noticed that answering back tended to elicit more scolding. Children who tried to defend themselves were usually yelled down, slapped, or physically dragged away.

Children also appeared to learn adult tasks primarily by observing working adults and then surreptitiously imitating them.[12] Children rarely asked questions or received verbal instructions. When the village barber, a man born before 1920, told George Collier how he learned his trade, he said that "first he watched [the existing barber] for about a year. Then he swept and cleaned [the barbershop]. Then he was given the oldest razors to sharpen every day, using the sharpening stone. Then he watched the clipping, and then, finally, began trying the clipping, with little children, with kin, and finally with other people."[13] The barber concluded by observing that in his youth one had to "learn in infancy rather than in adulthood" [aprender con baba y no con barba], unlike "modern" youth who spend many years in school learning an occupation.

But if my husband and I, as loyal followers of Dr. Spock, disapproved of villagers' parenting techniques, we were charmed and delighted by village children. I was particularly impressed by Los Olivos toddlers. Rarely did I see them cling to their mothers or whine for attention. Instead, they spent hours playing quietly in corners. I interpreted children's behavior as a rational response to parental practices. The best way for a small child to escape scolding or interruption was to remain unnoticed.

Village children, particularly boys, appeared to enjoy an age-graded children's world separate from the world of adults. Children of approximately the same size played together in sex-segregated groups and learned the games and activities appropriate to the next stage from slightly older children. Because I often took my baby to sit in the plaza, I had many opportunities to observe boys' play groups: "There are the older boys, ages ten to thirteen or so, who play marbles together. Then there are younger boys, from seven to nine, who play ball. Younger than they are the ones who are about five or six years old and who mostly rough-house. The youngest boys are the little ones around four or five. They play with toy horses or imitate the older boys. There are fewer girls who play in the plaza."[14] Nevertheless, I did observe one group of girls, aged around eight or nine who played hopscotch, and some pre-schoolers who tried to imitate them. And I noted that when spring arrived, girls between the ages of three and fourteen often gathered on warm evenings to play round games with dancing and singing.

Village children also performed small acts of resistance. They rarely talked back to scolding adults but they often ignored them. One little girl allowed her mother to call her several times before finally pretending to hear her. And a little boy, who was scolded for chasing some calves drinking at the fountain, threw stones after the herder when he turned his back to leave the area. Children also sought opportunities to escape parental supervision. Some children sent to move the family pigs from one field to another stayed away for the entire afternoon. And children "lied" to adults, particularly when parents demanded to know who had performed an act of which the parents disapproved. Children also kept silent about accidents that might elicit scolding.[15] Finally, older children routinely disobeyed government and church regulations. A friend, for example, told me that every year teenage "boys held a Carnaval party [with stolen chickens], and that the girls went dancing in November [the month of mourning] when they were not supposed to." Her tone of voice suggested that adults expected teenagers to disobey at least some social rules.[16]

Although my American upbringing and reading of Dr. Spock led me to be particularly disapproving of what I perceived as villagers' tendency to "lie" to children, I also wondered if "lying" might not be partially responsible for fostering some of the personality traits I most admired in village children and adults—their self-reliance and focused presence. Village children, for example, appeared to take upon themselves the responsibility to figure out what was going on. I often observed older children sitting quietly, listening to adult conversations, taking care not to be noticed and so sent away. And villagers of all ages seemed acutely aware of their social and physical surroundings. I seldom saw people distracted or preoccupied.

When I returned to Los Olivos in the 1980s, I was again charmed by the children and appalled by some of the adults' parenting techniques, particularly by what I experienced as mothers' force-feeding of infants and toddlers. Although I remembered mothers in the 1960s complaining about their babies being "bad eaters,"[17] my field notes contain no hint of the dramatic mother-child battles over food that I observed in the 1980s. On one particularly painful occasion in 1983, a toddler who refused to eat her yogurt was reduced to screaming hysteria. As she gasped for breath between howls, her mother took advantage of her open mouth to shovel in another spoonful. The child's grandmother seemed to find this scene as painful as I did. But she sided with the mother in observing that because the child would not eat her yogurt voluntarily, it had to be shoved down her throat if she was to obtain proper nutrition.[18]

Members of the grandparental generation in 1983 seemed to pity young parents, rather than to blame them, for their children's eating problems. In fact, they often cited children's resistance to eating as evidence of how bad children had become. In the past, elders observed, children ate what they were given. All family members ate from the same large bowls placed in the center of the table. "Modern" children, in contrast, had their own special likes and dislikes. In the 1980s, elders said, mothers "had to cook" separate dishes for each child.

As will become obvious, I was less impressed by the changes in children than by the changes in adults' willingness to cater to children's individual whims. Whereas parents in the 1960s seemed to ignore their children unless a child was misbehaving, the parents I met in the 1980s seemed focused on helping their children get ahead. My notes from that period describe many families as "child-centered." Not only did mothers of infants seem obsessed with ensuring that their children obtained proper nutrition, but all the parents I met seemed focused on helping their children to "prepare" themselves for adult jobs. For example, my field notes from one interview report that "Ana Belén said that she wanted her daughters to 'prepare themselves for some job.' She thinks that modern children need to 'become independent' from their parents. Ana Belén said that 'before, children depended entirely on their parents,' but that now things have changed and children should be able to get work for themselves."[19] "Preparation" usually meant schooling. Guillermo, for example, proudly observed that because all of his children had graduated from secondary school, they were "more prepared" than he and his wife, who had only finished primary school.[20]

In interview after interview during the 1980s, when I asked parents how they spent their leisure time, they invariably talked about spending it—or sacrificing it—for the sake of their children. One emigrant couple, for example, forcefully replied that for them the children came first: "everything is for them."[21] Guillermo told me, "We have been poor, but we have taken full advantage of our time. We have had no luxuries, no privileges except for our children: school, school! I don't want them to be like me [i.e, an unskilled laborer]. That is my point of view. For me, luxuries don't exist. I even despise luxury."[22]

As Guillermo's statements suggest, parents in the 1980s were concerned about their children's education. When parents talked about their lives as a "battle," the battle was not to put food on the table, or even to get ahead, but to provide their children with as much education as they could obtain. One father, for example, said that "I fight hardest to support my children's education" and went on to describe confrontations with his children's teachers. When parents in the 1980s talked about their sacrifices, they usually referred to what they had given up in order to purchase educational opportunities for their children. One man, for example, said that although he wants a larger car, he will not buy one because "the children come first."[23]

The high value that Los Olivos parents placed on schooling was demonstrated by one couple my husband and I interviewed in Seville. These parents, although quite poor, were spending a considerable amount to provide their teenage daughter, Isabel, with educational opportunities. My notes from this interview report that "Isabel is now in the second year of [secondary school], but her parents have also spent a lot of money on subsidiary studies. They paid so that she could take a course in typing—and she seems to type very well, given the noises we heard from the back room. [Isabel's parents] also spent 50,000 pesetas (which they could probably ill afford) to buy Isabel a casette course in English [which she apparently abandoned]. Finally, [the parents] are paying for private lessons for Isabel in the subjects she failed last year. Apparently she has three subjects to redo, one of which is mathematics."[24]

## THE TRANSFORMATION OF SCHOOLING

This shift in parental strategies—from taking children out of school to doing everything possible to keep a child in school—reflects a transformation in the meaning of schooling. As villagers and emigrants began participating in the national market for jobs and commodities, people whose parents had perceived schooling as an adornment of wealth, available primarily to those with the money and leisure to obtain it, became parents who perceived schooling as a requirement for their children's occupational advancement.

In his historical study of Los Olivos, George Collier observed that during the first quarter of the twentieth century, "schooling in Los Olivos had been a privilege of the wealthy, controlled by the pueblo's elites and affiliated with the Catholic Church. . . . Boys had attended class in the school owned by [the father of the village priest], and were taught first by his son and later by a private teacher. Girls had attended a school run by [the] wife of a wealthy property owner . . . this was another devout family whose son was a clergyman . . . the schoolteachers had charged students 15 centimos per day, an amount poor families could not afford. Only the rich had attended" (G. Collier 1987, 91–92).

The declaration of the Second Republic in 1931 brought few changes to Los Olivos schools. "The disassociation of public schools from the church . . . simply meant that the Town Council now paid rent for what had previously been private school quarters and paid the salaries of teachers who had previously charged fees. . . . For the most part, poor children had continued not to attend school since their families counted on the income [boys] could earn tending pigs and goats in the countryside" or girls could earn as servants (G. Collier 1987, 92). One woman, who reached school age during this period, told me that the girls' school was "very bad." Because girls were primarily taught to sew, knit, and crochet, "she learned what reading and writing she knows after leaving school."[25]

Schooling was not simply a privilege of the wealthy. As I noted in chapter 1, landed elites also used schooling as a justification for their domination. By the beginning of the twentieth century, formerly competing "traditional" and "progressive" elites in the Sierra de Aracena had joined forces to forge a consolidated justification for rule, fusing religious discourses with scientific ones "to communicate the notion that the possession of 'knowledge and wisdom' created an unquestionable right to social power" (Maddox 1993, 128). According to elites, schooling imparted "Culture" (with a capital C). Those who lacked schooling remained "brutes."[26]

Political advocates for the working class apparently accepted this elite ideology. Before the Spanish civil war of 1936–39, "Lack of schooling and of access to schooling on the part of the working class was one of the ills that the Socialist press repeatedly lamented" (G. Collier 1987, 92). When Los Olivos finally acquired a socialist mayor in January 1933, he "set out to improve and broaden education substantially, in accordance with current Republican policy and ideology. He began to spend municipal moneys on refurbishing school buildings and facilities . . . and he began to teach evening classes as part of a national adult literacy campaign. It was in these evening classes that many poorer adolescents and young adults who could not attend school by day [or whose parents had not been able to afford school fees during the 1920s] acquired basic literacy" (G. Collier 1987, 92). By teaching workers to read, the socialists hoped to replace the ruling oligarchy with a republic of "cultured" citizens. The socialists wanted to transform society; they did not want just to help individuals climb the existing social ladder by acquiring economically valuable skills or credentials.

After the civil war, the Franco regime "reformed" the schools again, purging the curriculum of leftist ideas, instituting religion classes, and advocating a policy of required attendance until age fourteen. Villagers remember the years between 1940 and 1960 as a time when all children learned basic literacy, but only the rich obtained further schooling. Several villagers from poor families reported that they attended school for only two or three years because, beginning at age eight or nine, they had to earn their food and help support their families by working in the fields (if boys) or as servants (if girls). Schools remained segregated by sex, and girls were forced to spend many hours learning religion and domestic arts. When Antonio looked back on his childhood experiences in Los Olivos, he observed that the greatest crime committed by the Franco regime was to permit a whole generation of poor children to grow up without education.

When I arrived in Los Olivos in 1963, I found that parents' strategies for securing their children's futures tended to vary by wealth, with both the wealthiest and the poorest seeking schooling while people belonging to the middle ranks focused on improving the family properties their children would inherit. At the top of the village hierarchy, the wealthiest families, particularly those with Falangist political connections, were using their resources and their privileged access to state scholarships to pursue the old elite strategy of ensuring that their children acquired the education that both justified and enabled privileged status. Many were trying to prepare their sons (and sometimes daughters) for nonmanual professions—unless the children proved to be hopeless students. Given the low level of village elites, however, most parents seemed to be looking no higher than careers in elementary school teaching, a nonmanual profession that did not require university attendance.

Parents at the bottom of the social hierarchy, who owned little or no land, also valued schooling. Most were trying to help their children stay in school as long as their funds, and the child's grades, made continued schooling possible. Without diplomas, the children of poor families appeared doomed to become unskilled wage laborers. In the 1960s, I met several poor parents who were scrimping and working extra hours in order to obtain private tutoring for promising youngsters. Although some children of poor parents aspired to become primary school teachers, most seemed to want training for semiprofessional or manual occupations. They hoped to become nurses, secretaries, plumbers, car mechanics, truck drivers, and so forth.

Parents of the middle wealth rank, in contrast, seemed to put a low priority on schooling. Those who owned enough land to provide all or most of the family's needs commonly took their children out of school around the age of eight or nine to guard flocks, perform farming chores, or help watch younger children. At that time, these parents had little reason to value schooling. Not only could parents whose children became farmers look forward to having their children near them in old age, unlike parents whose children became professionals, but it also seemed practical for children to learn the farming techniques they would need to manage the lands they expected to inherit. Most important, of course, children from landowning families appeared to benefit by contributing to the value of the family properties that would someday be theirs. As I noted in chapter 2, villagers who calculated a teenager's wealth for the purpose of assessing marriageability focused not on years of schooling but on the amount and quality of land a young person expected to inherit.

After 1970, however, emigration and the collapse of village agriculture transformed the apparent return on an investment in schooling. As emigration raised the wages of agricultural workers and as prices for Los Olivos fruit declined, farming turned from a preferred occupation into one that promised a life of hard labor and poverty. Schooling, which had once seemed a luxury, became a necessity. As the 1970s advanced, lack of schooling became the primary factor responsible for preventing unhappy farmers from escaping to city jobs. At the same time, the academic degrees obtained by those who had gone beyond primary school appeared responsible for the steady, and relatively lucrative, incomes they enjoyed as schoolteachers, nurses, mechanics, and so on.

By the time I returned to Los Olivos in the summer of 1980, all village parents valued schooling. Years of schooling had replaced inherited land as the villagers' preferred criterion for predicting a young person's future status. I noticed, for example, that the landowning parents of one village girl not only did not break off but actually encouraged her engagement to a young man from one of the village's poorest families who was attending a university. This young man also did a lively business during the summer months, tutoring local youngsters whose parents feared they might fail the exams for obtaining a primary school certificate. By 1980, most Los Olivos teenagers seemed to be attending secondary school in Aracena, although the failure rate was high because (I was told) the village primary school did not "prepare" children as well as primary schools in larger towns and cities.

As the 1980s advanced, the high rate of unemployment in Spain, especially among young people, led many villagers and emigrants to observe that schooling no longer guaranteed a lucrative job. Parents, in particular, were often bitter that youngsters who had worked very hard to obtain advanced degrees and certificates were not able to find jobs in their specialties. But if everyone recognized that schooling did not guarantee a good job, they also recognized that failure to obtain schooling almost certainly guaranteed a bad one. In the 1980s, responsible parents of all wealth rankings tried to help their children achieve as much schooling as the child's grades and the parents' resources permitted.

## THE DILEMMAS OF "MODERN" PARENTING

As the parent of teenagers myself in the 1980s, I was struck by similarities between the doubts voiced by Los Olivos parents and the parental dilemmas I experienced. We all wanted to help our children succeed in life, but were uncertain how best to do so. It seemed to me, however, that such doubts were new for Los Olivos parents. Those I met on my first visit had seemed certain how to help their children succeed. They knew that their children's futures depended on the amount of property that parents could accumulate. In the 1980s, parents also seemed to know what their children needed: education. But education differed from inherited property in at least two crucial respects. First, a family's property was owned and managed by the parents, whereas education was acquired and controlled by the children. Second, a family's property remained under the control of parents until their deaths, whereas parents lost control over the money they spent on schooling. On my first visit to Los Olivos, the economic interests of parents and children appeared to coincide. Parents benefited both themselves and their children by protecting and enhancing the family's property. In the 1980s, in contrast, the economic interests of parents and children appeared to diverge. Not only did parents fail to derive any direct economic benefits from the money they spent on education for their children, but the children could want to spend their parents' money for purposes other than those desired by parents. For example, Isabel, whose parents were spending a large portion of their meager earnings to provide her with educational opportunities, did not want to study the subjects her parents preferred. My field notes from the interview report that

> When [George Collier and I] asked about Isabel's plans for the future, [Isabel's mother] called Isabel herself to come talk with us. But before Isabel arrived, [her mother] said that she thinks Isabel wants to study "Public Relations" and she [the mother] does not approve. And indeed, Isabel, when summoned, did answer that she wanted to study "Public Relations." When we asked what kind of work this would lead to, she said that it meant work "on ships." From further conversation, we gather that girls who study "Public Relations" are looking forward to careers as hostesses—on ships, in

luxury hotels, or as airline stewardesses. Part of the schooling involves learning languages. Isabel obviously likes both the glamour of such jobs and the fact that they involve traveling. [Her mother], however, does not think much of such jobs. She clearly wished Isabel had wanted to study something else, such as nursing (but Isabel gets sick at the sight of blood), or teaching (but Isabel does not want to do that), or office work (except that Isabel does not want to spend her days typing in an office).[27]

In the 1980s, as in the 1960s, parents from Los Olivos seemed to judge their own success in life by how well they provided for their children. One middle-aged couple, who spent most of the interview talking about "how they had worked to educate their children, to give them professions," pointed to their children's diplomas (framed on the wall) as proof that their lives had been worthwhile.[28] And one father of young children said that "if the children come to nothing, if the schooling doesn't work well for them, then all [my and my wife's] sacrifices will have been for naught and I would see my life as a failure."[29]

Nevertheless, parents recognized that they had little control over the use their children made of educational opportunities. After one man said that his goal in life was to give his daughters the schooling he had been denied, his wife added, "if they want—we cannot force them."[30] When I was attending a wedding in Los Olivos, I overheard a discussion in which one man proudly declared that "his daughter, who was studying to become a teacher, was a very dedicated student." Another man immediately commented that "children must be left to do what they want to do, since it is their lives that are at stake."[31]

Given parents' doubts about their ability to control the use their chldren made of educational opportunities, several parents understandably qualified the hopes they expressed. The parents of one toddler, for example, said they "would have to wait and see how she did in school and what she liked" before deciding how much, and what kind of schooling, they would try to obtain for her.[32] Another father, who said he hoped his young children would eventually attend a university, went on to observe that "nowadays there is more selectivity at all levels of schooling and only those who are worthy get through. Who knows if [my children] will make it?"[33]

Many parents, in fact, linked their willingness to provide schooling to the child's abilities and diligence. One mother observed that as long as her son "brought her good grades," she would be "willing to sacrifice herself to help him keep studying."[34] Other parents told of making explicit contracts with teenage children. One village father, for example, said that when he sent his son to secondary school in Aracena, he told him that "studying costs money and that if [the youth] failed two courses, then he would have to stop studying to come work in the fields."[35] A mother observed that her daughter could continue "studying only so long as her grades were good. Once her grades failed," she would have to quit school to work in the family business.[36]

Explicit contracts, however, did not seem to relieve parents of a sense of failure if their children dropped out of school. Parents understandably regretted watching their children condemned to unskilled labor.[37] Nor did explicit contracts seem to relieve parents of their sense of responsibility for educating their children. One mother who said that her parents had not objected when she quit school to take a job not only blamed them for her failure to acquire more than a primary education but also implied that she would object strenuously if her children tried to follow her example. Despite people's observation that parents could not force a child to study, several parents reported trying to do exactly that. They told of inflicting punishments or of withholding treats until a child achieved some educational goal. The emigrant mother of a teenage girl whose teachers had reported that the girl "did not show promise . . . because she did not pay attention" nevertheless refused to allow her daughter to drop out of school. She forced her daughter to stay home to study for exams, even though the girl was eager to attend the village wedding of a cousin.[38]

But if parents forced their children to study, they also worried about losing their children's affection if they pushed them too far. Most of the villagers and emigrants I interviewed were obsessed with the topic of "hippies" and "drug addicts"—the living reminders of parental impotence. One village mother, after pitying the parents of a "hippie" couple from Madrid who had settled in Los Olivos, observed that "nowadays, children do what they want, and parents have to endure it lest their children stop being willing to visit."[39] She obviously hoped her children would not become "hippies." But if they did, she implied, she—like the unhappy parents of the couple who had settled in Los Olivos—would have to "endure" their behavior if she wanted to remain in contact with them.

Several of the parents I interviewed seemed caught between a desire to help their children become independent and a fear of losing their children. One emigrant father sadly observed that "the unity of the family is a primary value in life that is disappearing today."[40] Parents wanted their adult children to become economically self-sufficient. But people also attributed children's disregard of parental wishes to their ability to support themselves. When villagers talked about the urban "hippies" who had settled in Los Olivos and nearby villages, they commonly mentioned young people's separate bank accounts as the major factor allowing them to pursue a lifestyle contrary to their parents' wishes and values.

Indeed, most families from Los Olivos who had adult children living at home reported keeping separate financial accounts. One woman, whose mother had managed all the family money when she was a child, told me that she handled only the money for household expenses. Her working daughter contributed a small amount for room and board but kept most of her earnings. The daughter bought her own clothes, had recently bought a car, and was making payments on an apartment.[41] Adult children also treated their parents' earnings as belonging to the parents. One village teenager, for example, speculated that her urban cousin rarely went out because the girl had not been able to find a job and did not want to ask her parents for the spending money she felt she should be earning.[42]

Given children's need to become economically independent, some parents tried to keep their children's loyalty by building bonds of affection. A good friend told me that "children in Spain do not share trust [confianza] with their parents—they do not tell them things." "But," my friend told me, "I am trying to develop trust with my son so that he will tell me" his concerns. She reported that she was speaking openly to her son in the hope that he would speak openly with her.[43]

Most of the Los Olivos families I met in the 1980s seemed to have succeeded in maintaining family unity. Both my husband and I were impressed by the strong bonds we observed between parents and their adult and nearly adult children.[44] One afternoon in Los Olivos, for example, I found myself alone with a teenage girl who began interviewing me about my college-age children. She said she wished that she, like they, "could go off to another city and learn to take care of herself, rather than remaining beneath her parents' roof." But clearly such independence was out of the question. She told me that her family was devastated when her eldest brother left home for military service. One evening, she forgot that he was away and set his place at the table. Her parents and siblings were so upset at seeing the unused place setting that they could not eat. This teenager implied that, however much she might wish for independence, she could not inflict such pain on her family.[45]

Although most Los Olivos families seemed to enjoy family unity, people's sense that families were dissolving reflects, I think, the shift from a situation in which there was a coincidence between the economic interests of parents and children to a situation in which their economic interests appeared to diverge. No villager or emigrant actually told me that the economic interests of parents and children conflicted. But such an understanding was suggested by their discussions of family planning. In the 1980s, I noticed that both critics and defenders of birth control justified their positions in terms of parental "selfishness." Several couples, for example, reported that although they would have liked to have large families, they felt it would be selfish to have more children than they could adequately "prepare." A vocal critic of birth control accused parents of small families of selfishly hoarding their money for adult pleasures rather than spending it on having more children. By invoking notions of parental "selfishness," both proponents and critics of birth control implied an inherent conflict between parents and children over scarce family resources.

In the 1960s, in contrast, people arguing over birth control had focused not on parental selfishness but on parents' ability to repress their sexual desires in order to follow social conventions. At that time, most villagers pitied children who had to divide a parental property with many siblings. The birth rate, which fell drastically during the difficult years of the Spanish civil war and World War II, rose again during the 1950s, but never reached prewar heights. Few Los Olivos parents heeded the pronatalist rhetoric of the Franco regime, and those who did found themselves criticized by their neighbors. Several people, for example, told me that one prolific couple were "animals" who had been unable to control their sexual desires. Parents who had more than four children commonly defended themselves by saying that they had never interfered with God's will by practicing birth control. In the 1960s both supporters and critics of family planning claimed to be suppressing their personal desires in order to do what was required of them by God's social order.[46]

In the 1980s, most of the families I interviewed were aware that parents sacrificed their economic interests in order to provide for their children. In the 1960s, of course, parents—particularly mothers—had also talked about sacrificing themselves. But the sacrifices were different. On my first visit to Los Olivos, the sacrifices that parents made to maintain and enhance the family property benefited all family members, especially the parents. In the 1980s, in contrast, the money that parents spent for their children's support and education did not enhance the value of the parents' economic assets.[47]

Although both parents sacrificed for their children in the 1980s, mothers sacrificed far more than fathers. A father merely sacrificed money he could have spent in other ways. He kept his job and with it his ability to continue earning money. A mother, in contrast, faced an impossible choice. If she stayed home with her children, she gave up her opportunity to become a self-supporting adult. But if she kept her job, she could not provide her children with the motherly care that children "needed" to realize their potential. None of the people I spoke with in the 1980s told me that the "needs" of mothers and children were in conflict. But they did recognize that something was "wrong" with mothers.

María, for example, commented to me that "it seems women today are always tired." "Today's mothers," she observed, "who rarely have more than two children, seem to tire more easily and to complain more frequently than their grandmothers, who not only had more children but also worked in the fields as long as men and then did the housework after coming home." "Perhaps," María speculated, "today's mothers are tired because now there are more 'points'," as suggested by a television program she had seen recently. When I asked María to explain, she told me that "children now have to be 'more fixed-up,'" and thus require more care and more changes of clothes than children did when she was young.[48] Indeed, children in the 1980s did seem to require more care. I observed that mothers not only fixed special dishes for each child but also put up with other inconveniences. One mother who lived in a tiny urban apartment kept a dog she loathed because her son wanted a pet.

It was children's need for schooling, however, that really increased the workload of mothers in the 1980s. One woman summed up the observations of many people when she told me that as a child she had been a "slave" to her mother, whereas as an adult she was a "slave" to her daughter. Indeed, as I noted in chapter 2, unmarried girls in the 1960s usually spent their days doing housework for their mothers. They washed the family clothes, mopped the floors, and often did the cooking and cleaning up. In the 1980s, in contrast, many mothers told me that they did all the housework in order to leave their daughters free to pursue an education or a paying job. One woman said that although she suspected her teenage daughters claimed to have schoolwork in order to avoid being asked to do housework, she nevertheless "never asks them to do anything; their studies come first. 'At least you study,' I tell them."[49] Another mother told me that she never had time to knit and crochet, the common afternoon activities of village women in the 1960s, because she had to spend her afternoons as well as her mornings doing housework. "One cannot count on the children's help," she said. "They have their studies and their jobs."[50] Daughters echoed these observations. One young woman told me that she had not learned how to cook or care for a house until she married. She observed that "now the girls who go to school, and then go on to work, do not get into the habit of helping their mothers with the housework. They continue to act as children, letting their mothers take full care of them."[51]

These women's comments point to the conflict between mothers' and children's interests that I see as the deeper cause of mothers' problems in the 1980s. It was not simply that mothers had to do all the housework in order to leave their daughters free to pursue education and careers. Rather, it was through encouraging daughters, as well as sons, to become economically independent that mothers endorsed the vision of responsible maturity encouraged by people's participation in the wider national market for jobs and commodities—a vision that could not be realized by mothers who gave up paying jobs in order to stay home with their children (see also Doumanis 1983). The conflict between working for pay and being a good mother was, I believe, new to women from Los Olivos. In the 1960s, the villagers I met seemed to evaluate mothers less on the quality of motherly care they provided than for the inheritances they accumulated. For example, an older friend's favorite standard of motherly virtue was a woman who—as far as I could tell—had spent almost no time with her children. She had several, all born before the civil war. But because her husband died when the children were young, she had supported them by working from dawn to dusk as an agricultural wage laborer, leaving the older children to take care of the younger ones. "But all her work paid off," my friend observed admiringly, "her children are now married and established in life."[52]

In the 1980s, however, a mother could not leave her children alone all day without incurring condemnation. Once children needed "preparation" more than inheritances, "good mothers" had to provide their children with the individual attention that each child needed to develop his or her unique abilities (see Doumanis 1983, 107). When interviewing women who emigrated from Los Olivos, I noticed a difference between mothers whose children reached adulthood by the 1980s and those whose children were still young. Mothers of older children seemed not to have experienced the conflict between caring for children and working for pay. One woman, for example, proudly told me that throughout the years her children had been growing up she worked long hours as a domestic servant, either taking her children with her or leaving them in the care of a cousin who was slightly older than they. Clearly this woman took pride in helping to earn the money that had enabled her children to pursue higher education. Mothers of young children, however, seemed unsure what to do, particularly if their own mothers had sacrificed to enable them to study for a profession. All of them said they wanted what was best for their children, but they seemed torn between staying home, in which case they had to give up their jobs, or working for pay, in which case they could not personally provide the care they thought their children needed.[53]

Moreover, as people who were expected to think for themselves, mothers of young children in the 1980s had to justify whichever less-than-ideal option they chose. In contrast to the mothers I met on my first visit to Los Olivos, who could claim to be merely fulfilling their "obligations" whatever they did, a mother in the 1980s had to explain why she, as an individual, had decided that the option she chose was best for her children. As a result, mothers who decided to keep their jobs were constantly reminded of the care they were not providing for their children, whereas mothers who decided to stay home were constantly reminded of their failure to earn money for advancing their children's careers.

Finally, it seemed to me that mothers in the 1980s suffered because of the changing meaning of women's housework (see also Doumanis 1983). When I first visited Los Olivos, the work that women did in their homes seemed as necessary for wresting a living from the family's property as the work their husbands did in the fields. But when the jobs that family members held became a better predictor of the family's income and lifestyle than the amount of land a husband and wife had inherited from their parents, most of the work that women did in their homes appeared unproductive (or reproductive) because it did not earn an income. In the 1960s, self-sacrificing mothers, like their hard-working husbands, could claim the prestige accorded to responsible, productive adults. But after people from Los Olivos began to participate in the national market for jobs and commodities, mothers who stayed home became as economically dependent on a husband's wages as the children they cared for. In the 1960s, women—like men—could become both good adults and good mothers. In the 1980s, in contrast, women—but not men—had to choose between being responsible adults and being responsible parents. Mothers could not be both.

In summary, although both mothers and fathers in the 1980s experienced a conflict between the economic interests of parents and children, this conflict was more acute for women than for men. A father might have to spend his money on supporting his family, but he did not have to give up his opportunities to realize himself through working for pay. In fact, it was by earning an income that a man fulfilled his fatherly obligations. But a mother could not simultaneously realize herself and prepare her children for self-realization. In a social world where people were supposed to realize their inner capacities to the fullest, the personal interests of mothers and children inevitably conflicted. If a mother gave up her career to stay home with her children, she sacrificed her opportunity to realize herself as a unique individual. She also condemned herself to becoming an economic dependent of her husband rather than a self-supporting adult. But if a mother realized her own productive potential through paid work, she deprived her children of the motherly care they needed to prepare them for adult achievement.

This situation was, of course, exactly the opposite of that experienced by parents in the 1960s. Not only did the economic interests of parents and children tend to coincide at that time, for everyone benefited when the family's property was protected or enhanced, but fathers were more likely than mothers to experience a conflict between their needs and the needs of their children. The money that fathers spent in bars, for example, appeared to be taken from the family's limited supply. And when an elderly man refused to relinquish control over the family's properties to his adult heirs, he appeared to be depriving them of the opportunity to become economically independent.

## CONCLUSION

Although I was impressed by similarities between the dilemmas I experienced as a parent and the worries expressed by Los Olivos parents in the 1980s, I did notice one striking difference. One day, when a friend was telling me about a young drug addict who had been jailed, she expressed pity for the young man's mother rather than the blame I expected. Instead of wondering what the mother had done, or failed to do, that led her son to turn to drugs, my friend burst out, "What a tragedy for the mother! What she must be suffering!" I also noticed that people never blamed the parents of the "hippie" couple who had settled in Los Olivos, even though they expressed horror at the hippies' lifestyle. One woman, for example, told me how nice the parents of one hippie had seemed when they came to visit. She, too, expressed pity for the parents and commented on how much they, as members of the professional class, must be suffering to see their child living in squalor.

Given that the villagers and emigrants I interviewed talked about sacrificing themselves to "prepare" their children, and even talked of evaluating their own success in life by their children's achievements, I had expected them to hold parents responsible for how their children turned out. I thought they would praise the parents of successful children for having reared them well and criticize the parents of school dropouts, drug addicts, and hippies for having ruined them. But they did not—at least in my hearing. Instead, they seemed to praise and blame the children.

I noticed, for example, that parents whose children had turned out well did not claim credit for their children's successes. Rather, they talked about the children's characters. One mother "emphasized how studious all her children were, and told me that I would not find other children like them in the city. She said that her children 'never go out' (*no salen a ninguna parte*). All they do is study. And in reference to her eldest, she said that her daughter is not a 'modern' girl (*no es una niña de hoy*). Today, 'there is so much liberty' (*está la vida muy libertina*), but her daughter is not that way. When her daughter is not studying, she stays home and does housework or knitting."[54] Another mother told me that her adult son "is neither profligate nor dissolute." He is not like so many city boys, who "spend and toss" their money away the day they earn it.[55]

When parents of successful children did claim credit, it was usually for having provided their children with educational opportunities and good examples. My notes from an interview with a couple whose adult children had all obtained higher education report that:

> Alberto talked about his children's goodness and concern for their parents as all coming "from inside" (*sale de adentro*). He and his wife, he said, had never forced the children to study nor scolded them when they stayed out late in the evening with friends. "My children have always behaved well with me and I with them." Josefina went on to stress how the goodness of her children derives from the example they get from their parents at home. She kept emphasizing that she and Alberto get along well together and never fight. Because both she and her husband "interact with well-mannered people at work" (*tratan con gente de educación*), they have learned never to use bad language or to yell at people. Josefina said that there is no scolding in her house. "My children have never had a bad example at home, ever" (*mis hijos no han tenido mal ejemplo en la casa nunca*).[56]

When children turned out badly, people commonly blamed the children. It was their own fault if they had succumbed to the corrupting influences of "modern" culture. My friend who told me about the jailed drug addict, for example, said that he had been too weak to resist the pressures of his companions. Even the parents of problem children seemed to blame the children, albeit covertly. One father explained his son's bad grades at school by observing that the boy was only interested in playing soccer, which the father described as "the opiate of the young."[57] Another mother, whose daughter had dropped out of secondary school, told me that the girl did not like her classes and preferred to work instead. A few parents even praised their children for dropping out of school. One father proudly reported that his son had decided he should work rather than waste more of his parents' money on schooling, given that in the 1980s even university graduates were having difficulty finding good jobs.

When the villagers and emigrants I interviewed did blame someone other than the child for a child's school failure, they tended to accuse inept or uncaring teachers. One father told of confronting the secondary school teachers who had failed his son, telling them that they could fail the boy for not knowing the material but not for a lack of studying. He had seen his child spend long hours poring over his schoolbooks.[58] And a mother explained that she had taken her teenage son out of secondary school after deciding that the teachers there only helped students who had personal connections.[59]

Finally, I noticed that no one seemed to expect the children of "bad" parents to turn out badly. For example, my friends who talked with me about a young man whose father regularly drank too much and fought with his wife commonly pitied the youth for having had to endure such a miserable home environment. No one, at least in my presence, expressed surprise that such a fine young man could have emerged from such an unhappy home. And although I heard several villagers criticize the "hippie" mother for sending her little girl to school in dirty clothes, no one—at least in my hearing—speculated that the child might turn out badly because of such neglect. When trying to understand why people from Los Olivos failed to hold parents responsible for how their children turned out, I wondered if it might be because they seemed to lack a concept of child care. It is difficult to discuss—much less to prove—an absence. But I was struck by the fact that not one of the village or emigrant women I interviewed mentioned caring for children (*cuidando a los niños*) when asked to list her activities. Women did list household tasks such as housecleaning, clothes washing, preparing meals, and so on. They also talked about doing specific things for children, such as feeding and dressing them, walking them to school, or taking them to parks so they could ride their bicycles. But no one spoke of "child care" as a female activity comparable to clothes washing, housecleaning, or even knitting. A good mother, it seemed, kept her children clean, well fed, safe from harm, and provided with encouragement to discover and develop their abilities. But she did not have to "rear" them. Children grew by themselves.

Looking back at my field notes from the 1960s, I can see continuities in people's concept of parental responsibility. During neither of my visits did people seem to expect parents to "rear" their children. Rather, they expected parents to provide a safe and healthy environment for the children to grow in. In the 1960s, parents had to "subjugate" their children to prevent them from harming themselves physically or socially. In the 1980s, parents had to provide their children with the nutritional and educational opportunities they needed to "prepare" themselves for earning a living. But in neither period did parents have to worry about harming their children by failing to provide proper "care."

The difference between my concepts of child care and those implicit in how people from Los Olivos talked about rearing children was brought home to me one day in a beauty parlor, when I picked up a copy of the Spanish magazine *Ser Padres* [Being Parents]. I was fascinated to observe that although several articles in the magazine were based on articles in foreign journals, none seemed to threaten parents with dire consequences if they failed to provide proper care for their children. For example, I remember one article on children's nightmares that advised mothers how to comfort a frightened child. But the article's authors never hinted that if a mother failed to follow their advice, her child might suffer lifelong sleeping problems. Similarly, another article offering advice on how to tell a child about God never hinted that if parents failed to instill proper religious feeling, their children might grow up to join some dreadful cult. Even the articles on food failed to threaten mothers with the illnesses their children could contract if they did not feed them properly.

This Spanish magazine struck me as having a very different tone from the parental advice books I read when my children were young. I learned that children faced a series of crises. If parents failed to provide proper guidance, a child could suffer permanent emotional damage—be condemned to a life without basic trust, a sense of self-worth, or an ability to establish mature sexual relationships. I remember being so terrified by one book on child care that I never finished reading it. Recalling the guilt and fear instilled in me by the books I read, I envied and admired parents from Los Olivos for what seemed to me a far healthier attitude toward their children's needs.[60]

## CHAPTER FIVE

# Mourning: From Respect to Grief

Doña Remedios

> always dressed in mourning . . . even though her
> widowhood was now an old, old story.
> *(Pérez Galdós 1960 [1876], 195)*[1]

IN THE 1980s, when I interviewed villagers and emigrants about changes that had occurred since the 1960s, they inevitably mentioned the decline in women's use of black mourning dress along with changes in courtship customs. Long formal courtships and extended mourning periods were the two customs that, in everyone's minds, exemplified past practices that had been abandoned. In the old days, people told me, women wore black clothes for several years after the death of a close relative. "Today," one woman observed, "no one dresses in black."[2] This was an exaggeration. Young women still wore black clothes after the death of a close relative, particularly when in Los Olivos. But women born after the civil war mourned for shorter periods and did not wear the heavy black shawls, veils, and stockings that women in mourning had worn in the 1960s.

The change in costume was, in fact, less dramatic than the shift in how people talked about mourning customs. Villagers in the 1960s, and older people in the 1980s, said that women wore mourning clothes to "show respect for the dead." In the 1980s, in contrast, women born after the civil war talked about grief for the departed. My field notes from one conversation with an older woman report that her daughter Lola broke in on her mother's description of past mourning customs to announce that "wearing black is a stupidity (*tontería*). It is a backward custom of rural villages (*un atraso de los pueblos*)." Lola declared that she, herself, would never wear black. "After all," she said, "one doesn't feel a death any less deeply whether one wears black or not."[3] For Lola, as for other women of her generation, mourning was not about showing proper respect for the dead. It was about the personal grief experienced by people who had lost a loved one. Understandably, Lola and her contemporaries thought that women who continued to dress in black long after a death—like the fictional character Doña Remedios—must be hypocrites. How could someone continue to feel deep grief for a death that had occurred many years before?

In this chapter, I focus on the misunderstandings that were occurring in the 1980s between older villagers, who had lived most of their lives in a social world where status appeared to be inherited, and their adult children who had moved into a social world where status appeared to be achieved through market competition. Whereas most of the villagers who had been born before 1920 were reconciled to the disappearance of long formal courtships, and accepted the fact that children in the 1980s needed to be "prepared" rather than "subjugated," elders were understandably worried about whether or not their adult children would show them the respect they thought they were due. Seniors wanted their children to care for them in old age and to mourn them properly when they died. Meanwhile, their adult children, who were born after the civil war, agonized over how to make their aging parents understand that they loved them and were doing all they could. This struggle between the generations was particularly painful for me to watch because, as someone not involved in the conflict, I could see how each side talked past the other. The "respect" that parents wanted and the "love" their children offered were impossible to reconcile because they reflected different understandings of how to be a good person.

This chapter is divided into four sections. I begin by discussing the conflict between people born before 1920 and their adult children over the care that elders expected their children to provide. Then I describe changes in mourning customs before explaining the close relationship between mourning and inheritance in the 1960s. Finally, I return to misunderstandings between older and younger people over relatives' obligations to mourn and care for one another.

## CARING FOR THE ELDERLY

In 1983, when I was interviewing Bartolomé and Isabel, a married couple who had emigrated to Barcelona, they began talking about Isabel's elderly parents. My husband and I were particularly fond of Isabel's parents because they had been very kind to us in the 1960s, and we regularly visited them every time we found ourselves in Los Olivos. We had therefore heard Isabel's parents complain about the fact that their only daughter and her husband were refusing to return to the village to take care of them. Obviously the younger couple felt guilty. Bartolomé, in particular, kept returning to the theme that his wife's elderly parents were welcome to come live with them in Barcelona. He and Isabel kept a special room in their apartment ready for them. But the older couple

would not come. Instead they wanted Bartolomé—and especially Isabel—to return to Los Olivos to live. "But we cannot do that," said Bartolomé. "Every family has its own life, and we have to live ours." Bartolomé emphasized that he came to Barcelona, not for his own benefit
but for the sake of his family. "In the village," he said, "you cannot make
enough money to support a family." Isabel then broke in to say that her
children needed her in Barcelona. She could not abandon them to return to Los Olivos to care for her aging parents.[4]

The guilt experienced by Bartolomé and Isabel and the righteous anger expressed by Isabel's parents were hardly unique to them. Their
quarrel reflects the fact that massive emigration had drained Los Olivos
of the young people aging parents had expected to care for them. The
generational conflict, however, was not over whether young people
would provide care or not. Bartolomé and Isabel were eager to care for
Isabel's parents. Most of the adult children I met in the 1980s said they
would never think of allowing their parents to end up in an old-age
home, cared for by strangers. Instead, the conflict was over where the
care was to be provided. Isabel's parents, along with most members of
their generation, wanted to be cared for in their own homes in the village. Adult children, in contrast, wanted their aging parents to come live
with them in the cities to which they had emigrated.

Most of the working adults I interviewed in the 1980s stressed rural-
urban differences when trying to explain why elders wanted to remain in
Los Olivos. In the village, people said, elders lived surrounded by the
kin and friends they had known since childhood. Elders also had their
gardens to putter in and their animals to care for. City apartments, in
contrast, were like "cages," particularly for older men. Whereas older
women could help their daughters, or daughters-in-law, with the housework and child care, older men had nothing to do except, perhaps, walk
their grandchildren back and forth to school. Although older men in
cities did pass time in local bars, people stressed that drinking and playing dominoes with recent friends was not the same thing as passing time
in the village bar with friends known since childhood. Indeed, I heard
stories of at least two widowers who had returned to the village after
having tried to move in with urban daughters. And when I visited people in cities, they would often point out lonely old men sitting on park
benches.[5]

The joys of country living, however, could not explain the righteous
anger expressed by older people whose children refused to return to the
village to care for them. The elders I met in the 1980s did not just want
to stay in the village. They thought they had the right to be cared for in
their own homes. In particular, elders thought that they were entitled to
the same kind of care they had provided for their own parents. What had

changed, of course, was the role of inherited property in determining a family's social status. In the past, when people's incomes and lifestyles appeared to be determined by the amount of property they inherited, elders who retained control over the family property usually enjoyed the respect and obedience of prospective heirs. By the 1980s, however, the jobs that people held, rather than the properties they expected to inherit, appeared to determine their incomes. Adult children still wanted to care for their aging parents. They loved them, after all. But adults wanted their parents to recognize the sacrifices that children made when taking elders into their urban apartments.

No one baldly stated that adult children in the past had done what their elderly parents wanted because parents retained control of the family property until they died. Indeed, the villagers I met in the 1960s, like those I met in the 1980s, expected children to want to take care of the parents who had cared for them. In 1963, for example, one woman told me that Los Olivos was such a traditional community that "even the [grown] children don't want to leave their parents."[6] She was right. Married women, I noticed, usually spent several hours a day in their mothers' houses. And when Richard Price asked one young man whether he intended to emigrate, he replied, "How could I think of leaving Los Olivos to live? My father, who started with less than nothing, has always brought us up well, given us good food, decent clothes, a good home. Not like a millionaire, but *vamos.* Could I abandon him now after all he has done for me, just at the time when the doctor says he can no longer work?"[7] Nevertheless, this young man did, in fact, emigrate two years later.[8]

People did link inheritance to obedience, however, when explaining why some elders failed to obtain the care they wanted. In the 1960s, I heard many King Lear-like stories of elders who relinquished control over their property and then found themselves mistreated by their heirs. One friend, for example, had no sympathy for a widow whose son-in-law remodeled her house against her express wishes. If the widow had not divided her property while still alive, my friend told me, her daughter's husband would not have been able to make alterations without her consent. This friend, like other villagers who told similar stories, concluded with the moral that if parents wanted to ensure proper care in old age, they should retain control over their property until they died.

In the 1960s, people also linked inheritance to care when discussing childless seniors. They expected elders without living children to seek care from younger relatives to whom they would then will the bulk of their property. I heard many stories about childless people who established close relationships with women of the succeeding generation, usually nieces but occasionally cousins. When one elderly widow without close relatives began spending her days in the house of her mother's sister's daughter, for example, everyone expected the younger woman to care for the older one when she became ill and to inherit the bulk of her property after her death.[9]

Finally, villagers were most explicit about linking care to inheritance when discussing the arrangements made by childless seniors with unrelated caretakers. One woman, for example, told Shelly Zimbalist about an elderly couple who were "sick and needed someone to take care of them. They offered to leave all their *capital* to their nephews in exchange for care, but none of [the nephews' wives] was willing. Therefore, [the couple's] offer was accepted by another [woman]—who is not family or friend or anything—and they made a will leaving her their *capital*."[10]

Because women rather than men actually provided the physical care that elders needed, women in the 1960s were in a better position than men to acquire inherited property from distantly related or unrelated elders.[11] When interviewing people from Los Olivos, I learned of at least three women who had obtained significant properties by caring for an elderly person who willed them property in return. Some elders without female relatives did approach male relatives for care, as suggested by the story Shelly heard, but men could accept such offers only if they could convince their wives or daughters to provide the care that elders needed. I did, however, hear of some enterprising nephews who were able to accept an elderly aunt's offer of inheritance by hiring a female servant to nurse her.

Not surprisingly, I found that most of the elderly villagers I met in the 1960s were still living in their own homes cared for by children or by younger relatives who lived either with them or in nearby houses. On my return in the 1980s, in contrast, I found that many elders had moved, or anticipated moving, to urban areas in order to obtain care from a child (usually a daughter). Although young people's emigration to urban jobs was obviously responsible for this shift in where elders found caretakers, I also discovered that elders' experiences varied by birth cohort. Most of those who were born before 1900 were able to obtain care in Los Olivos, even if they lived into the 1980s, whereas most of those born after 1900 had either followed their children to urban areas or expected to do so.

In 1984, when I used the genealogical census to trace the fates of elders, I realized that most of the people born before 1900 had been able to stay in the village because their children were already mature adults, with children of their own, by 1965. As a result, few of their children had emigrated, and several of those who had tried to emigrate after 1970 were forced to return to the village when they could not find urban jobs. Of the thirty-two villagers born before 1900 whose histories

I could trace,[12] only five had had to leave the village, and of these five, four had been born in the last years of the century, between 1897 and 1899.[13] In contrast, only nine of the twenty-five elders born between 1900 and 1909 whose fates I could trace had been able to remain in Los Olivos or expected to be able to remain there, although another four, who had left the village, hoped to return there to die.[14] In 1984, it was still too soon to tell what would happen to villagers born between 1910 and 1919. Although most were retired by then, they were still active and able to care for themselves. Significantly, more than half of them were living in Los Olivos. Of the twenty-eight whose whereabouts (or final days) I could trace, only twelve lived outside the village, near or with children who had emigrated.[15]

Because most of the seniors who needed care in the 1980s, or who expected to need care in the near future, were people whose parents had been able to remain in their own homes, cared for by daughters, daughters-in-law, or nieces until death, seniors in the 1980s understandably felt that their children should return to the village to care for them. Isabel's elderly parents, for example, rightfully pointed out that because Isabel's children were grown, Isabel should be able to leave them. Isabel's daughter, although still unmarried, was in her early twenties. She was fully capable of taking care of herself as well as doing the housekeeping for her father and younger brothers. But Isabel was also right when she said that her children needed her. Her daughter, after all, held a full-time job. How could she do the housework as well? And the boys were still in school. They needed a mother at home to do the housework and the cooking.

Sadly, Isabel and her parents talked past one another. Isabel's parents stressed how hard they had worked to provide Isabel with a respectable inheritance. Indeed, Isabel's and Bartolomé's combined inheritances put them in the small group of *propietarios* when they married in the 1950s. By the 1980s, however, children did not need village inheritances. Instead, they needed time to study and pursue their careers. Whereas Isabel's mother had consolidated, and even added to, her children's expected inheritances by caring for her elderly relatives, Isabel would have harmed her children by leaving them to do all the housework while she returned to the village. As Isabel said, she was more than willing to take on the extra work of caring for her elderly parents in the city. She loved them, and they had done so much for her. But caring for them would be a burden. Isabel's mother may have obtained a material benefit for herself and her children by caring for seniors, but Isabel could expect no such benefit for herself and her children. If Isabel welcomed her aging parents into her home and tenderly cared for them, it could only be because she loved them.

## MOURNING CUSTOMS

When I returned to Los Olivos in the 1980s, everyone commented that mourning customs had changed. Miguela, an older woman who had been born before the civil war, told me that when her husband died in the 1960s she had to wear *velo y mantón*, referring to the square black veil and heavy wool shawl that women in deepest mourning were expected to wear in addition to black dresses with long sleeves and heavy black stockings. Indeed, Miguela was still wearing this outfit when I interviewed her in 1983, because another close relative had recently died. "But now," Miguela told me, "no velo or mantón. Women in mourning now just wear a black dress, black stockings, and a black sweater."

At this point, Miguela's daughter, Fernanda, entered the room. Fernanda exclaimed that "before, it was too much." She went on to tell me that as a teenager in the 1960s she had been forced to wear mourning for seven years after the death of her father. "My youth was wasted," she lamented. "Those years will never come back. And mourning serves no purpose." When Fernanda left the room, I tried asking Miguela why women in the past had observed such oppressive mourning practices. Miguela answered laconically, "it was the custom." When I tried to press Miguela for a fuller explanation, asking her why people should have had such a custom, she only shrugged. "When I was a child," she told me, "my mother used to dress me in black whenever one of my uncles died." "But now," she said, people "have become modern. They don't wear black" when a distant relative dies.[16]

Although I was disappointed by Miguela's laconic observation that "it was the custom," I later realized that she had, in fact, given me the standard explanation advanced by members of her generation. It was also the most common explanation I heard in the 1960s. At that time, I met several women who complained about mourning requirements, such as one friend who bitterly remarked that "here they bury the living with the dead."[17] But even women who complained about mourning requirements nevertheless took care to put on the black clothes they thought their neighbors expected them to wear. I also realized later that Miguela's daughter had given me the standard explanation offered in the 1980s by members of her generation for why young women were refusing to wear black mourning clothes. Fernanda's assertion that "mourning serves no purpose" was echoed, in various forms, by several of her contemporaries.

Mourning requirements did seem excessive in the 1960s. At that time, villagers summarized full mourning dress, or "heaviest" mourning (*luto más pesado*), with the phrase "veil and shawl" (*velo y mantón*). As

Miguela reported, a woman in heaviest mourning, such as one who had recently lost a husband or parent, was expected to wear a black dress with long sleeves, heavy black stockings, a large square black veil, and over all, the heavy wool mantón. After a few months, a woman could shed her mantón when in her own home, but was expected to keep on her veil and to wear a black apron. During the period when a woman was in heaviest mourning, she was expected to wear this costume every day, during the hot summers as well as the cold winters. Later, after the required period of deepest mourning had passed, a woman could begin to don "lighter" black clothes. She could substitute a black sweater or crocheted shawl (*manto* or *toca*) for the heavy, blanketlike mantón and a smaller round veil for the large square one. As the mourning period neared its end, she could finally abandon her veil and begin to wear a short-sleeved black dress and clear stockings.

Mourning costume also varied by age. When girls were still children, between the ages of four and fourteen, their female relatives dressed them in black after the death of a parent, sibling, or grandparent. But little girls were not required to wear veils or heavy shawls. Once she reached the age of courtship, however, a girl was expected to don full mourning costume, although girls younger than twenty might wear the lighter crocheted shawl in place of the heavy wool mantón.[18] Fully adult women, whether married or not, were expected to observe heaviest mourning, including the mantón. In the early 1960s, most women who had passed the age of forty never wore anything except black dresses. As one friend commented, women of that age were always in mourning for someone, since their parents and parents' siblings were reaching old age. In the 1960s, people also expected widows to continue wearing black stockings and black veils for the rest of their lives. Indeed, one elderly widow, when I met her again in the 1980s, proudly told me that she had not worn anything but black for the past thirty-eight years.

Villagers in the 1960s also expected a woman's behavior to correlate with her costume. A woman in heaviest mourning, with velo y mantón, was supposed to stay in her house, with the doors and windows closed. When chores required her to leave her home, she was supposed to avoid the public gaze as much as possible—to draw water from the fountain at hours when few people were around, to wash clothes in the privacy of her walled garden or after dark at the public wash fountain, and to send a child on errands rather than to venture out to the stores herself. A woman in heaviest mourning was also expected to shun entertainment.[19] In the first year after a husband or parent died, a woman was expected to silence her radio and to avoid Sunday Mass, although she might attend early morning weekday Masses (which were usually attended only by women in mourning). Women in heaviest mourning also avoided happy occasions. They did not attend baptisms or weddings.

But they could visit the sick and offer condolences to the recently bereaved.[20]

After a woman discarded her veil, she might begin to watch public entertainments, but not participate in them. Villagers distinguished between *distraerse* (to distract oneself) and *divertirse* (to amuse or enjoy oneself). A woman in light mourning could distract herself, but she could not actively enjoy herself as long as she wore black clothes. An unmarried young woman, for example, might watch other couples dance, but she could not participate in the dancing herself.

Men, in contrast to women, did not have to wear black clothes or to remain indoors after the death of a close relative. When in mourning, a man was expected to wear only a small black band on his sleeve or pinned to his lapel. He was also expected to avoid going to the bar for a few weeks or months, depending on his genealogical closeness to the person who died. A widower, for example, was expected to wear a black armband and to shun the bar for a year. When Shelly asked a woman, "Why do men have less stringent mourning requirements [than women])?" she replied, "Because men can't wear black. And since there are no amusements here except the bar or casino, they refrain from going for a little while, and that is the mourning they observe."[21] Men, like women, were allowed to "distract" themselves after the period of deepest mourning had passed. They could watch others enjoying themselves but, like women, were expected to refrain from participating in the pleasures they observed.

In the 1960s, as in the 1980s, people said that mourning customs had been stricter in the past. Just as Miguela reported that when she was a child her mother had dressed her in black whenever one of her uncles died, so a woman told Shelly in 1965 that "mourning used to be a lot stricter than today." In her youth, she reported, "young children mourned for aunts and cousins."[22] Another older woman reported that when she was young (before the civil war), women in mourning had to wear the *pañuelo*, a black head cloth tied under the chin, rather than the loose black veil common in the 1960s.[23]

People in the 1960s, like those in the 1980s, reported that mourning requirements were becoming even "lighter," both in the number of relatives mourned and in items of clothing.[24] In 1965, for example, one woman told Shelly that "grandparents and uncles don't really count any more," to which a younger woman laughingly appended, "that's now lazy mourning."[25] Another woman told her that "Change takes place because of styles . . . one person wears less black and the others follow; people today are more modern."

Although people attributed the lightening of mourning requirements in both the 1960s and the 1980s to the fact that people were becoming "more modern," I noticed a subtle shift in the explanations people offered for why younger women were reluctant to follow the heavy mourning practices of their elders. Looking back at field notes, I can see that people in the 1960s tended to suggest two explanations for change, both of which evoked the conceptual contrast between following social conventions and giving in to personal whims. One friend, for example, offered a "personal whim" explanation when she suggested that "young women" were adopting the "little round veils" used in Aracena because they enhanced a woman's attractiveness, in contrast to the ugly, square veils commonly worn by mourning women in Los Olivos.[26] And many people advanced a "following social conventions" explanation when they observed that urbanites tended to look down on women in mourning dress as country hicks. Shelly, for example, reported overhearing a conversation in which some young women talked "about how a friend [who moved to the city] had taken off her black clothes because people laughed at her, and everyone [in Los Olivos] thought of the shame she would feel if her father could see her from his grave."[27] Celia, another young woman interviewed by Shelly, who was in deepest mourning at the time but who expected to emigrate shortly, told Shelly that she did not expect to "wear black more than two or so years [in the city] because no one does."[28] She went on to observe that "here [in Los Olivos] I dress for the *pueblo* [village], [but] when I leave [for the city] I will see reality [and] take off my *mantón* right away and my veil soon after."[29]

In the 1980s, in contrast, none of the younger women I interviewed mentioned wanting to look pretty or to avoid their neighbors' criticisms. Rather, they advanced explanations that implied they thought for themselves. "Mourning," they told me "serves no purpose."[30] As I noted earlier, Lola argued that "one doesn't feel a death any less deeply whether one wears black or not." Catalina, a young woman who lived in Barcelona and whose mother had recently died, told me that since her mother was dead, she was not around to care about what Catalina was wearing. Catalina, in fact, was wearing a stylish, short-sleeved black dress with silver threads and black stockings. But instead of talking about what custom required, Catalina explained her outfit by carefully describing her reasoning process. Her elderly aunts, she told me, would be upset if they were to hear that Catalina was wearing colorful clothing so soon after her mother's death. "I love my aunts," Catalina told me, "and I would hate to cause them pain." (Indeed, when I later visited Los Olivos, one of Catalina's aunts did question me on what Catalina was wearing, and I dutifully affirmed that Catalina was wearing a black dress.)

Given younger women's assertion that dressing in black "served no purpose," either for the mourner or for the person who had died, they understandably tended to assume that if their mothers had worn the velo y mantón, it must have been because older women had blindly followed "stupid village customs" rather than thinking for themselves. Older women, of course, tended to confirm this assumption when, like Miguela and my friend María, they asserted that they wore mourning clothes because "it was the custom" and the neighbors would criticize them if they did not conform. Nevertheless, I think that women in the 1960s had a good reason to wear mourning clothes. As I discuss in the next section, women who lived in a social world where inherited property appeared to be the main determinant of a family's income and lifestyle, could protect—and even enhance—the family's properties by observing accepted mourning customs.

## MOURNING AND INHERITANCE

In 1983, when I was talking with Emiliana, an elderly widow who had been born at the beginning of this century, she started complaining about the fact that "nobody wears black any more." I protested, saying that women still wore black. Emiliana replied that maybe they wore black dresses, but they were not wearing full mourning dress. To prove her point, "she told me that she saw Felisa in the cemetery two days after her mother's funeral. Felisa, who lives in Aracena, was dressed in black, but she was not wearing a veil or *mantón*. Emiliana told me that she, in contrast, had worn three years of *pañuelo* when her husband had died, and two years for her brother." Emiliana concluded by lamenting that "the only way you know if someone has lost a relative is by knowing who is related to whom." "Now," she said, that is the only way to know "who a dead person's kin are."[31] Emiliana's lament reflects the fact that, for people of her generation, women's mourning dress signified the kinship bonds through which inheritances passed.[32]

In 1965, when Shelly asked the people she interviewed why women in Los Olivos observed mourning customs that many women—even then—characterized as "excessive," they commonly gave two answers. The first was that other villagers would criticize a woman who did not wear mourning. When Shelly asked Miguela, who was in mourning at the time, "What happens if a woman wears less mourning than is required?" Miguela replied, "she is criticized by everyone."[33] When Shelly spoke with a recent widow, the widow said that although she, personally, agreed with one of her city friends that "it was silly" to wear a velo y mantón, she nevertheless "didn't want to be the first" woman in Los Olivos to abandon the custom.[34] The second, and less frequent, answer to the question why women observed oppressive mourning customs concerned showing respect for the dead. One young woman in mourning responded to Shelly's question "What use is it to wear black?" with the answer "To honor the dead person." When Shelly pressed her to explain what she meant by "to honor," the woman responded that in order to honor a dead person, a woman had "to observe the mourning the dead person was due."[35]

The mourning "due" to a dead person was determined by the genealogical relationship between the mourner and the person who died. In 1965, the villagers Shelly interviewed about the effects of a death on the living commonly used two verbs: *tocar* (to be touched by a death, in the sense of being selected or singled out by it) and *sentir* (to feel a death). "Touching" followed genealogical lines. "(A death) touches through blood," people said.[36] The relatives of a dead person were all touched, whether they "felt" the death or not. And people could feel a death even if it did not touch them.

Touching and feeling were also demonstrated differently. When a woman was touched by a death, she had to wear mourning clothes. As one woman observed, "one wears mourning when one is touched." Feeling, in contrast, was demonstrated by behavior. Josefa, for example, responded to Shelly's question "How do you know if someone has been greatly touched by a death?" with the answer "By the mourning she wears." When Shelly asked, "How do you know if [a woman] really feels [a death]?" Josefa responded, "In that she is very upset; you can see she feels great sorrow."[37]

In the early 1960s, villagers argued endlessly over exactly which items of mourning dress a woman who was touched had to wear and for how long. But they all agreed on the basic principle that a woman's mourning dress should reflect her genealogical relationship to the person who died. The following chart represents my summary of the many lists of mourning requirements that Shelly collected in 1965.

As the chart reveals, those most touched by a death were members of the dead person's family of procreation: wife and children. Next were members of the dead person's natal family: siblings and parents. Although women were required to mourn longer for a husband or parent than for a child, I noticed that women, in fact, wore the heaviest mourning after the death of an unmarried, adult son. One grief-stricken mother never shed heaviest mourning. And even though mothers were not supposed to mourn the deaths of very young children (whose innocence supposedly allowed them direct entry into Heaven), mothers mourned anyway. One woman who lost a toddler wore heavy mourning for four years.[38]

When women were touched through an intervening blood relative, the amount of mourning they were expected to wear reflected the

Degrees of Mourning Corresponding to Genealogical Closeness

| Relationship | Time of "Heavy" Mourning Dress | + | Time of "Lighter" Mourning Dress |
|---|---|---|---|
| 1. Deceased's spouse | 4–5 years | | 3–6 years |
| 2. Deceased's children | 3–4 years | | 3–4 years |
| 3. Deceased's siblings and parents | 2 years | | 2–4 years |
| 4. Deceased's grandchildren | 2–6 months | | 12–18 months |
| ******** | | | |
| 5. Mourner's *tíos carnales* and *sobrinos carnales* (parents' siblings; siblings' children) | 1–3 months | | 6–12 months |
| 6. Mourner's parents- and siblings-in-law | 1–6 weeks | | 6–12 months |
| 7. Mourner's first cousins | few days | | 3 months |
| 8. Mourner's parents' cousins, mourner's *tíos políticos* and *sobrinos políticos* (parents' siblings' spouses and spouse's siblings' children) | none | | 0–3 months |

*Note:* This chart is divided in two parts to reflect the fact that most villagers listed the mourning required of close relatives with reference to the person who died and of distant relatives with reference to the mourner. This chart also reflects people's use of the generic masculine to describe kinship relations even though women were the ones who actually wore mourning clothes.

amount required of that relative. For example, a granddaughter, whose parents were children of the deceased, was expected to mourn more than a niece, whose parents were only siblings of the person who died. Similarly, a woman related to the dead person through her husband was expected to adjust her mourning to his, mourning longer for his parents than for one of his siblings. The least mourning was required of women who were touched through two intervening relatives. A few months of wearing black were enough to indicate the relationship. Finally, no mourning was required after the death of distant relatives.

The villagers Shelly interviewed recognized only one valid excuse for refusing to wear mourning dress when touched by a death: a woman had not received an expected inheritance from the person who died. When some women did not wear mourning after the death of three elderly cousins who had no other living relatives, people explained that "they did not wear mourning or receive condolences because they had been disinherited." Their elderly cousins had left all their property to the un-related woman who took care of them in their old age.[39]

A villager also told Shelly that when people observe less mourning than they should, it is usually because of "a quarrel in the family."[40] Such quarrels usually involved property. One woman who fought with her brother over a walled garden inherited from their parents did not attend the wake after his death or offer condolences to his widow and children. Although she wore mourning dress, villagers expected her to resume normal clothing within a few months.

When villagers talked about inheritances, they also tended to use the verb *tocar*. A dead person's relatives were touched by inheritances in much the same way and order as they were touched for mourning. The spouse of a dead person retained control of the family property until death. And children were the primary heirs, even if they did not receive their inheritances until their surviving parent died. When Shelly asked one woman if a child could refuse to wear mourning if disinherited, the woman replied, "No, [because] no one disinherits a child."[41] This woman went on to observe that "to the parents, all children are equal." Even if a parent has quarreled with a child, she said, parents forgive their children when they are dying.[42]

People who lacked children could will their property as they pleased, but villagers expected the bulk of a dead person's estate to revert to his or her natal family after the death of a surviving spouse.[43] One woman told me that the property of a childless couple would be divided after the death of the second one, with the property that each brought into the marriage reverting to blood relatives.[44] Another villager told Shelly that if a person died without children, the property passed to their nieces and nephews related through blood (i.e., children of the dead person's own siblings rather than of the dead person's spouse's siblings).[45] Nieces and nephews, however, were supposed to inherit indirectly. If a dead person's parents were alive, they were supposed to receive the property. If they were already dead, the property was supposed to be divided among the brothers and sisters of the person who had died.[46] Although siblings could never be primary heirs if the person who died had living children, villagers nevertheless expected people to will small items to their natal kin. One woman Shelly interviewed could recall "no case in which something was not left to a living sibling."[47]

Given the close connection that people posited between a woman's mourning costume and the inheritance she expected to receive, villagers in the 1960s had good reason to observe and comment on what women in mourning were wearing. By observing which women put on which items of clothing in the days following a death, villagers could assess, with fair accuracy, not only the genealogical relationships through which inheritances were supposed to pass but also the quality of relationships among living family members. People could also assess a woman's possibilities for inheriting from distant kin. This information was vital in a social world where inherited property appeared to determine a family's income and lifestyle. Parents assessing the suitability of children's marriage partners, for example, needed to know if a teenager's mother was likely to receive inheritances from one or more childless elder relatives.

It also seemed to me that women had a practical reason for wearing mourning clothes, regardless of what they might be thinking or feeling underneath. People in the 1960s may have talked about mourning obligations as following inheritance (i.e., heirs and probable heirs-of-heirs were obliged to mourn). But it seemed equally likely to me that the reverse was true (i.e., that mourning attracted inheritances). Given the large number of childless seniors in Los Olivos, owing to the late age of marriage and the high rate of nonmarriage, there were many village elders who needed to find women to take care of them. Such elders, I imagined, would understandably examine their female relatives' mourning behavior in order to assess each one's suitability as a candidate for the job of caretaker/heir. No one, of course, told me that women could attract inheritances through their behavior following a death. But it seemed to me that by wearing mourning clothes to show "respect" for the dead, a woman could demonstrate (however unintentionally) both her kinship relation to childless elders and her commitment to fulfilling family obligations at the price of her own comfort.

Shelly's and Sally's field notes from the summer of 1965 contain numerous accounts of people drawing inferences about a woman's character—particularly about her capacity for self-sacrifice—from her mourning behavior. At that time, villagers criticized women for observing either more or less mourning than was required by the mourner's genealogical relationship to the person who died. But the criticisms were different. If a woman observed more mourning, critics tended to accuse her of putting on airs, of acting as if she were better than others. Indeed, women who mourned more than required did tend to boast about their behavior. If a woman observed less mourning than was required by her relationship to the person who died, villagers questioned her commitment to observing social conventions. When Shelly asked Angeles what people said if a woman did not observe proper mourning requirements, Angeles replied "that she has no shame." As an example, Angeles told of a teenager who watched television and attended dances while wearing a black veil for the recent death of her grandmother. Angeles scornfully observed, "That is not mourning; that [girl] is 'crazy' people say; if she is not completely crazy, she is half crazy, because she doesn't think about mourning; she thinks more about boyfriends, about distracting herself."[48]

In a village where, as one woman bitterly remarked, "everyone knows what everyone is doing,"[49] women in mourning had to worry about what their neighbors would say. They could not afford to attend just to their own feelings, however intense or shallow their personal grief might be. Several of the women Shelly interviewed in 1965 were obviously grieving. But they nevertheless seemed to remain acutely aware of how their dress and demeanor appeared to others. For example, two unmarried sisters who were grief-stricken at the recent death of their mother nevertheless monitored their outward behavior. When alone behind the closed doors of their house, the sisters often removed their mantones and veils, and rolled down their heavy black stockings. But they quickly donned them again whenever someone knocked on the door. They always donned full mourning when leaving the house, even if only to slip across the street to the family's shed. One sister even scolded the other for not putting on her veil when she passed in front of an open window.

## MISUNDERSTANDINGS ACROSS THE GENERATIONS

When I returned to Los Olivos in the 1980s, I found that the transformation of mourning customs was far less dramatic than implied by people's statements that "today, no one dresses in black." Not only did younger women like Catalina continue to wear black dresses in order not to upset their elderly relatives, but older women wore lighter black clothing than they thought proper in order to please their children. One day, for example, I noticed that my neighbor, an elderly widow who always dressed in black with a veil over her head, had a new hairdo, had shed her veil, and was wearing a black dress with little white dots on it. When I commented on her appearance, she told me that she was going to visit her children in the city and they wanted her to dress this way. "My children," she told me, "do not like me to wear black all the time. They are ashamed to be seen with me if I wear my veil." So, she told me, she had bought a new dress and had her hair done. But, she assured me, she intended to resume her regular mourning clothes when she returned to Los Olivos.[50]

Even as older women dressed to please their younger relatives, they seemed to misunderstand why younger people wanted them to discard mourning dress. The adult children of my neighbor, for example, never mentioned being ashamed of their mother's black clothing. Instead, they talked about wanting their mother to recover from grieving. My neighbor's children told me that they wanted their mother to have fun when she visited them in the city. They wanted to take her out to restaurants and shows. They did not want her to continue mourning for their father, who had died many years before. Rather, they wanted her to put on pretty clothes and to enjoy the remaining years of her life. They loved her, and they wanted her to be happy.

Younger women also talked of hoping to make their mothers and aunts understand that "mourning serves no purpose." For example, Celia—who as a young woman in 1965 had told Shelly that she did not expect to "wear black more than two or so years" after emigrating to the city "because no one does"—never mentioned wanting to avoid the scorn of her urban neighbors when I interviewed her in the 1980s. Instead, she described the mourning requirements she had observed in her youth as "a village stupidity" and lamented the fact that she could not make her elderly mother understand that she and her sisters did not intend to wear black after their mother died. Celia, like other members of her generation, wanted her mother to realize that it did not matter what her daughters wore after her death. Celia and her sisters would not feel their mother's death any less deeply if they did not wear black. In any case, their mother would not be around to see what her daughters were wearing. So, Celia argued, why should she and her sisters follow a stupid custom when there was no good reason to do so?[51]

Nevertheless, as I observed earlier, young women did tend to wear black dresses after the death of a close relative, even if they wore black only for a short while or only when visiting elderly relatives in Los Olivos. They did so, as Catalina carefully explained to me, because they knew that their elderly relatives would be upset if they did not. None of the elders I spoke with in the 1980s, however, talked about being upset. They never mentioned their own feelings when complaining about the fact that young women no longer wore black dresses. Instead, older people commonly lamented young people's failure to "respect the dead." If they did talk about feelings, the feelings they mentioned were not their own but those of the dead person, for example, "What would Catalina's mother say if she could see what her daughter was wearing!"

In the 1980s, young women were right that their elderly relatives would be upset if they refused to wear black. But just as my widowed neighbor misunderstood her children's reasons for wanting her to wear bright clothing when she visited them in the city, so I think that young women misunderstood their elder relatives' reasons for wanting them to wear black. When trying to understand why older people would be upset, young people usually resorted to the explanation advanced by Antonio: older people had a different "mentality." Instead of "thinking for themselves" (in which case they would obviously realize that wearing black clothes serves no purpose), elders let others think for them. They had minds enslaved by prejudice and superstition.

As a foreigner listening to older and younger women talk past each other in the 1980s, I was disturbed by what I heard. But I could not, at the time, put my finger on what I found so disturbing. Only after completing the analysis in this book did I realize that each generation seemed to be exacerbating the other's fears in their efforts to put the best interpretation possible on the words and actions of relatives they loved. When older women, for example, talked about city customs as a way of understanding why their daughters and nieces did not want to "respect the dead," they were implicitly denying the accusation that young women simply wanted to look pretty and have fun. But elders' efforts to suggest that loved daughters and nieces were following urban customs rather than succumbing to personal whims had the unintended consequence of portraying young people as allowing others to think for them rather than thinking for themselves. Similarly, when young people credited beloved elders with having a "different mentality," their efforts to suggest that elders were, in fact, doing what they wanted had the unintended consequence of suggesting that elders who followed "traditional" customs were giving in to personal whims rather than suppressing their desires in favor of observing social conventions.

Finally, the misunderstanding between older and younger people seemed particularly sad because young people's efforts to convince their elders that they intended to care for them in old age appeared to have the opposite effect of exacerbating elders' fears that their children might abandon them. Because people born after 1935 had spent most of their adult lives in a social world organized by market competition, where knowledge of a person's intentions and abilities was the best guide to predicting future status, young people understandably took every occasion to assure their elderly parents that they loved them and intended to care for them in old age. As Bartolomé and Isabel kept telling me, they loved Isabel's parents and wanted the elderly couple to come live with them in their urban apartment. Talk about personal desires, however, was exactly what people born before 1920 did not want to hear. Having lived most of their adult lives in a social world where inheritance appeared to determine social status, and where a person's respect for social conventions was the best guide for predicting a family's future, elders wanted assurances that their children were capable of suppressing personal whims in order to fulfill onerous family obligations. As a result, children's protestations of love, which were the strongest assurances that children could provide, had the unintended consequence of confirming elders' fears that their children were putting personal desires above duty to the family.

# Identity: From Villagers to Andalusians

> In the casino patronized by the landowning men of
> Doña Perfecta's rural city,
>
> > The debates all boiled down to the superiority of
> > Orbajosa and its inhabitants over all other towns
> > and peoples in the world.
> > *(Pérez Galdós 1960 [1876], 76)*[1]

WHEN I ARRIVED in Los Olivos in the 1960s, the people I met frequently compared their village to surrounding communities and to people from farther away, such as visiting North Americans. They had, they assured me, the strictest and most onerous courtship and mourning customs for miles around. When I returned to Spain in the 1980s, the people I met commonly stressed their identities as Andalusians. They invited me to participate in their festivals, feasts, and pilgrimages in order to appreciate, and to celebrate, their Andalusian heritage. During both my visits, people identified themselves as being from Los Olivos. They emphasized their membership in what they called the *patria chica* (little country) (see Pitt-Rivers 1954, 30). But in the twenty years between 1963 and 1983, they apparently remade their vision of what it meant to belong to the village. In the 1960s, belonging to Los Olivos meant not belonging to other nearby communities. In the 1980s, belonging to Los Olivos meant belonging to a wider region: the Sierra de Aracena and Andalusia as a whole.

In this conclusion, I draw on my experiences in Los Olivos to explore how and why individuals from one small Spanish community remade themselves from villagers who "were traditional" into Andalusians who "had traditions." Many authors have written about an apparent paradox of modernity. Far from producing the cultural homogeneity predicted by modernization theorists, the globalization of Western modernity has spawned the proliferation of ethnic differences and ethnic conflicts (Tambiah 1989; Appadurai 1990; S. Hall 1992; Comaroff and Comaroff 1993). As formerly isolated rural peoples have joined global cultures of capitalism and communication, their participation has not led to a single world culture of modernity but rather to multiple, different, and often antagonistic modernities. Homogenization and differentiation have occurred simultaneously, as self-consciously "modern" peoples have sought to reclaim the cultural heritages that distinguish their ethnic group from other ethnic groups. All "modern" peoples may be alike in "having traditions" but they distinguish themselves from one another by having different ones.

"Modern" peoples' efforts to reclaim their cultural heritages have also created a second paradox noted by many authors: "modern" people often seem to "invent" traditions, or to borrow them from other groups, rather than asking living elders to share their knowledge of the past (see Hobsbawm and Ranger 1983; Handler and Linnekin 1984). This is the paradox I noted in the introduction to this book, when I wrote about Esteban and his wife in Barcelona, who bought the *Gran enciclopedia de Andalucía* for their children rather than asking Esteban's mother to teach them about their Andalusian heritage.

I have already suggested one answer to the question of why members of Esteban's generation might have sought their traditions in books written by intellectuals rather than in the memories of their parents and grandparents. Borrowing Antonio's observation that "modern" people must "think for themselves," I suggested that Esteban and his wife, as self-consciously "modern" people, could not afford to enact or to pass on the "traditions" of their youth because everyone agreed that those traditions required people to suppress their inner desires in favor of doing what others expected of them. The courtship and mourning customs that villagers from Los Olivos celebrated—or condemned—in the 1960s as proof of their adherence to "tradition" had, by the 1980s, become customs that marked their practitioners as "traditional" rather than "modern." No wonder Esteban and his wife were not eager to have Esteban's mother teach her grandchildren about the traditions she remembered.

In this conclusion, I explore other answers to this question by focusing on the traditions that "modern" people celebrated in the 1980s. I begin by describing a religious pilgrimage (*romería*) I attended in the summer of 1984, at which I first came to wonder why the "traditions" celebrated by my "modern" friends were not customs I had seen people practicing in the 1960s. Like many anthropologists of my generation, who have returned to the same community for two or three decades, I found myself faced with the problem of how to analyze, and to write about, celebrations of tradition that—from my point of view—did not seem "traditional" at all. This sense that the traditions celebrated by my "modern" friends had been invented, or at least recently borrowed from the landed upper classes of Andalusia, suggested a different answer to why Esteban and his wife had not asked Esteban's lively mother to teach her grandchildren about their cultural heritage. She was not able to do so. She and her age-mates had never practiced most of the traditions that Esteban and other members of his generation celebrated as examples of their Andalusian heritage.

This conclusion is divided into four sections. After describing the pilgrimage, I consider the problem that apparently invented traditions pose for anthropologists, such as me, who sympathize with modern people's efforts to reclaim their heritages, but who doubt that people's proclaimed traditions are really "traditional." In the third section, I focus on discourses of nationalism to suggest some reasons why "modern" nationalists seem so often to invent or borrow their traditions. And in the final section, I focus on discourses of individual achievement to explore why tradition offers "modern subjects" an effective tool for resisting the secularization and rationalization of contemporary life.


## THE PILGRIMAGE

In August 1984, my husband, an American friend, and I joined two couples from Los Olivos to participate in the annual pilgrimage to a small chapel dedicated to San Bartolomé. The chapel stands in an open field at the intersection of three municipalities in the Sierra de Aracena, a walk of several hours from each center of population. In many ways, this celebration conformed to the picture of an Andalusian pilgrimage depicted on posters put out by the Spanish government to attract foreign tourists.[2] Several of the younger women wore colorful flamenco costumes—tight, long dresses with full, ruffled skirts; fringed shawls pinned in front; and high combs in their piled-up hair.[3] Many of the pilgrims came on foot or horseback, following farm carts decorated with crepe paper flowers and streamers, which carried sacred banners and supplies for the ritual. (Other pilgrims, like those in our group, made the trip more rapidly and comfortably in cars.) Notable events of the day included a religious Mass, followed by an outdoor procession, flamenco dancing, a bullfight, and open-air picnics. Clearly, this pilgrimage was an enactment of "traditional" Andalusian customs. Or was it?

Our group arrived at the site shortly before noon. We parked our cars on the edge of the highway and walked across an open field to the chapel. Our first act was to pay our respects to the saint, whose image, surrounded by flowers and candles, stood on a carrying platform. We did not linger in the chapel, however. After a few minutes of showing respect, José, one of our friends, leaned over to my husband to suggest that they "visit the other saint," meaning the bar that had been set up outside the chapel under a large tent. We all left and—from the sanctuary of the bar tent—watched people assemble for the noon Mass.

After the Mass, which was attended by far more women than men, the saint was brought out of the church to the tune of the Spanish national anthem played by the band. Everyone fell in behind the saint's float. I linked arms with two women friends from Los Olivos, as we walked, counterclockwise, around the chapel. Halfway around, at a point where we could see the distant church of the Virgen de los Angeles, patroness of the Sierra de Aracena, the procession stopped to greet her and to sing a special song in her honor. Then the procession continued around the chapel, finally returning San Bartolomé to his sanctuary, once again to the tune of the national anthem.

Their religious (and patriotic) duties done, the band and most of the worshipers retired to the bar tent for refreshment. After a short rest, the band began to play dance music, primarily *sevillanas* and *paso-dobles*. People of all ages joined in the dancing, but the most enthusiastic dancers were married people in their thirties and forties. Ana, a member of our group and the mother of three children, danced every *sevillana*, actively recruiting partners by persuading other women, her husband, and other women's husbands to join her.

The dancing lasted about an hour. Then the crowd moved down to a field below the chapel to cluster around the "bullring"—actually a circular stone wall, reinforced with branches where the stones had collapsed. Before releasing the "bull"—actually a three-year-old calf—from his box on a flatbed truck, members of the religious fraternity (*hermandad*) that had organized the pilgrimage passed through the crowd, collecting money and offering swigs of spiked punch to contributors. When the bull finally bounded into the ring, all the men who had been strutting around inside quickly jumped the fence. Only the two designated "bullfighters" remained. With an ancient red cape and a tattered blanket, the bullfighters tried to attract the attention of the bull. But the bull had other plans. After circling the ring looking for weak spots in the crumbling wall, the bull got a running start, cleared the fence, and took off across the open fields. The crowd scattered, screaming. Then we all began to laugh. Several young men took off after the bull. The rest of us, still laughing, retired to our picnics.

Our picnic table consisted of a board laid across some beer cases that one of the men in our group had borrowed from the bar. His wife covered the board with a cloth and laid out a superb lunch of local cheeses, ham, and sausages, fresh bread from the village bakery, home-cooked potato omelettes, and crisp, sliced tomatoes from her garden. As we munched, our friends, some of whom lived in Barcelona but were vacationing in Los Olivos, started to talk about how wonderful it was to be in Andalusia. They said that one could not get such cheeses, hams, and sausages anywhere else. They also contrasted the Andalusian character to that of the Catalonians. Andalusians, our friends asserted, know how to enjoy themselves, in contrast to Catalonians who care only about making money. Whereas Catalonians save their best foods to eat in privacy, with only close relatives, Andalusians generously share with everyone (as our friends were indeed doing). With an expansive gesture that took in the entire scene and the day's events, one friend assured us that we were witnessing authentic Andalusian culture. The dances, the music, the food, the colorful costumes, the flower-decorated carts, the bullfight, the hospitality, and the religious devotion—these were the traditions that Andalusians cherished.

I thoroughly enjoyed participating in the pilgrimage to honor San Bartolomé. But if asked whether this pilgrimage was an enactment of traditional Andalusian customs, I would have to reply both yes and no. Yes, in the sense that most of the people present talked about it in those terms. Fully aware and in support of Andalusian claims to political autonomy within Spain, festival-goers treated the pilgrimage as an opportunity to assert, and to enact, their Andalusian heritage. At the same time, I would have to reply that the pilgrimage was not an enactment of "traditional" customs in the sense that several of the customs were not ones that I or my fellow anthropologists had observed twenty years earlier. None of the field notes from the summers of 1963 and 1964 mention a pilgrimage to San Bartolomé (although some older friends in the 1980s did tell me that they had gone in their youth). Nor did any of us see village women dressed in flamenco costumes. At the celebration held to honor the patron saint of Los Olivos in the summer of 1964, Richard and Sally Price observed that every unmarried girl had a new dress. But the dress styles were copied from current high-fashion magazines. Although young people danced all night to music from a local band, no one danced *sevillanas*. The Prices report that whatever the band played, "fox trots, cha-chas, twists, paso dobles, etc., people always did the same kind of dancing: conventional, fairly close, two steps and box steps."[4] In the early 1960s, almost no married women joined the dancing, and the few who did danced only with other women. No woman from the village who had been married more than a few months danced with a man, her husband or otherwise.[5] Finally, there were no bullfights, although such spectacles were held in major towns and older people did report that the village had sponsored bullfights in the past.

As I have returned to Los Olivos in the years following the pilgrimage to San Bartolomé, I have noticed that Andalusian costumes and dancing have become even more elaborate. At San Bartolomé, only unmarried women wore flamenco dresses. Older women and all the men wore regular clothes. But at a pilgrimage to the shrine of the Virgen de los Angeles that I attended in the summer of 1994, I noticed that even matrons of my age were dressed in flamenco costumes, while many of the younger men were dressed in the male counterpart of tight, high-waisted pants, leather chaps, short jackets, and flat-crowned hats.[6] People of all ages also danced *sevillanas*—the only type of dance performed. Most of the young people had taken lessons in order to learn the steps and arm movements, and they avidly competed for prizes in contests held to judge the most skilled dancers.

As an anthropologist who had read about "the invention of tradition" (Hobsbawm and Ranger 1983), my initial reaction to the Andalusian costumes and dances that I saw in the 1980s and 1990s was to interpret them as invented traditions—or at least as traditions that people from Los Olivos had recently borrowed from others, such as gypsies and the landed, upper classes of larger towns. Some of my older friends from Los Olivos also interpreted them this way. One woman born before 1920 laughingly recounted an experience she had in northern Spain when briefly hospitalized for minor surgery. The other women in her ward were talking about regional traditions, and when they learned that my friend was from the province of Huelva, they immediately asked her to sing a fandango for them.[7] The mock horror in my friend's voice as she told this story, and the expression on her face, clearly indicated that she not only did not know any fandangos, but was appalled at the very idea that her ward mates thought she might sing one for them.

## THE PROBLEM OF "AUTHENTICITY"

My reaction to Andalusian dances and music as "invented traditions" forced me to face a dilemma common to many anthropologists and historians whose experiences have convinced them that the heritages people celebrate are not inherited, but who do not want to imply that people's traditions are therefore not "authentic." I, for example, experienced the dilemma as one of trying to reconcile two contradictory goals. On one hand, I wanted to write about what I and many people from Los Olivos experienced as the loss of a "traditional" way of life and its replacement by a "modern" one. On the other hand, I wanted to do so without having to suggest that the Andalusian traditions celebrated by my "modern" friends were really not "traditional." Not only had I enjoyed participating in their pilgrimages and festivals but, like Richard Maddox, I appreciated the vital role these "traditions" were playing in Andalusians' "struggle to build a humane present" (1993, 22).

My dilemma, of course, reflects the politicization of ethnicity in the contemporary world. "Modern" people's efforts to reclaim their cultural heritages are not occurring in a political vacuum. In a world of nation-states, statehood (as well as more restricted forms of political autonomy) rests on a people's having—or constructing—a "nation." For a group to justify demanding self-government, its members must share a territory and culture. "But which culture or what territory? Only a homeland that was 'theirs' by historic right, the land of their forebears; only a culture that was 'theirs' as a heritage, passed down the generations, and therefore an expression of their authentic identity" (Hutchinson and Smith 1994, 4). By the 1980s, Andalusia, like Catalonia and the Basque country in Spain, had "the constitutional status and governmental institutions of an autonomous region." "Questions concerning the political significance of cultural traditions [were] on the minds of many people." "How such questions [were] answered," Richard Maddox observed, would have "both a direct and an indirect bearing on some of the issues and options involved in Andalusian cultural and political identity" (Maddox 1993, 21).

Because my friends from Los Olivos knew as well as I did that the Andalusian traditions they celebrated in the 1980s differed from the customs practiced by villagers in the 1960s, they would probably not object to my portrayal of their "modern traditions" as different from their "traditional" ones. But the question of how to write about apparently "invented traditions" is not so easily solved for some scholars and the peoples they study. Jean Jackson, for example, has written eloquently about the dilemma faced by anthropologists and historians who conclude that the "traditions" celebrated by contemporary activists campaigning for ethnic and indigenous rights are not, in fact, "traditional," but rather reflect modern understandings of what a people's traditions should be. Because Jackson wanted to explore how the Tukanoan Indians of Colombia's northwest Amazon were "learning to change their notions of their own history and culture to achieve a better fit with received wisdom about Indianness," she found herself forced to address "the issue of ethnographic authority—the confrontation between anthropological and native visions of indigenous culture and history" (1995, 3).

Jackson suggests that some of the difficulties she experienced were due to the anthropological definition of "culture" as something that people inherit from the past. Anthropologists, she concludes, should revise their conventional understanding of culture as "a primordial legacy." "Cultures are not static, homogenous systems on which change is imposed" (1995, 20). Instead, anthropologists should treat "culture as something dynamic, something that people use to adapt to changing social conditions" (1995, 18). Cultures come into existence and develop distinctive customs, Jackson observes, through peoples' interactions with others. If anthropologists recognize that culture is always an "improvisation," in which people build on past themes to address present problems, then anthropologists may be able to develop what could "prove to be a more genuinely respectful—as well as correct—view of present-day indigenous groups in their struggles to preserve their self-respect, autonomy, and a life with meaning" (1995, 18).

Recognizing that all cultures reflect creative improvisations may allow anthropologists to avoid the problem of having to imply that some traditions are more "authentic" than others. But redefining cultures as dynamic does not solve the problem experienced by peoples demanding self-government and the anthropologists who sympathize with their causes. In particular, such a redefinition provides no basis for nationalists to pursue their political project of collective self-determination. A vision of cultures as adaptive and ever changing may allow nationalists to discredit "traditions." But such a vision does not allow nationalists to claim the traditions they need to validate their existence as a culturally distinct people.

In the introduction to this book, I noted that Andalusian nationalists commonly reject the memories of living elders, not because they are "traditional" rather than "modern," but because the customs that elders remember reflect the effects of Castilian domination. Acosta Sánchez (1979), for example, argues that Andalusia lost its "traditions" during centuries of Castilian rule. Village customs, such as those I observed in Los Olivos, were not authentic expressions of the Andalusian spirit. Rather, they were reflections of Andalusia's subordinate position in Spain's class structure, as a provider of cheap labor for industrializing northern regions.[8]

This reason for rejecting elders' memories does make sense. Given the length and strength of Castilian domination over Andalusia, there is good reason to suspect that any customs remembered by living elders were indeed creative adaptations to a history of regional subordination. Not only did Castilians rule Andalusia, but they also appropriated many Andalusian customs in the processes of constructing the centralized Spanish state. Maddox, for example, observes that "in Andalusia, unlike Catalonia and the Basque country, the sense of possessing a distinct regional identity has been relatively weak. Indeed, Andalusian identity has historically been intertwined and usually subordinated to representations of Spanish national identity" (1993, 21). No wonder Andalusian intellectuals, such as Acosta Sánchez (1979) and the editors of the *Gran enciclopedia de Andalucía*, portray Andalusia as a territory where people "felt themselves to be Andalusians—but without firm connections to their origins and without elements to focus their regional identities."

The vision of cultures as ever changing, however, provides no basis for nationalists to pursue their project of asserting political autonomy. If people are always creatively adapting their customs and rituals to changing circumstances, then there is nothing to distinguish one "people" from another except their different histories. A history of oppression might suggest a need for more democratic participation in the current government. But it hardly suggests a reason why a group of people needs to govern themselves. After all, if they adapted to domination, then they should have no trouble adapting to shared governance. In short, nationalists who demand self-government have to have "culture" in the "static and homogeneous" sense now being rejected by most anthropologists. They have to have "a culture that was 'theirs' as a heritage, passed down the generations" (Hutchinson and Smith 1994, 4) and that distinguishes them from inheritors of other cultures.

Recognizing the political realities that require nationalists to claim "authentic" traditions, Jean Jackson suggests that anthropologists should endorse the validity of a peoples' own claims. She writes that she "would prefer to argue that if, in 20 years, all Tukanoans have adopted [the] new forms and believe they are and always have been Tukanoan, then these new cultural elements would be 'genuinely' Tukanoan" (1995, 20). By putting quotation marks around the word "genuinely," however, she reveals her doubts about this solution. No matter how much she might like to redefine "genuine" to cover what the people themselves say, her proposed definition is not generally accepted. Nationalists, in particular, have to contest it. They have to argue that their traditions are "genuine," not just because they say they are but because such customs are "authentic" expressions of a cultural heritage handed down from generation to generation.

Given the difficulty of redefining "genuine," Jackson finally concludes that there is no solution to the anthropologist's dilemma "except to accept multivocality." In the end, she argues, the Tukanoans' portrayal of themselves as enacting traditions handed down from the past "is just as authoritative" as her understanding that Tukanoans are reconstructing their history and culture to fit Western notions of what Indians should be (1995, 20). Jackson ends with the statement "I have no final claim to authority in this matter." She claims only a "viewpoint" that carries no more weight than the viewpoints of others.

Unfortunately, the "multivocality" solution does not work either. In an earlier article addressing confrontations between anthropologists and nationalists over the writing of "native" histories, Jonathan Friedman suggests that "the problem is not one of attitudes, but of structure. . . . If one is engaged in 'negotiating culture,' that is, involved in the construal and interpretation of ethnographic or historical realities, then one is bound on a collision course with others for whom such realities are definitive. Culture is supremely negotiable for culture experts [such as anthropologists], but for those whose identity depends upon a particular configuration this is not the case. Identity is not negotiable. Otherwise, it has no existence" (1992, 852). Nationalists cannot accept the idea that their version of history is just as authoritative as the very different versions written by anthropologists or historians. Nationalists have to be right.

Friedman goes on to observe that anthropologists and historians are also engaged in a political project. He suggests that scholars delude themselves if they imagine they are simply writing "objective" histories, in contrast to the politically motivated accounts written by nationalists. Just as nationalists seeking to recover their heritage are concerned to assert a people's right to produce their own identities, so "the academic modernist is . . . concerned to preserve the authority of the scholar, the monopoly of the truth about the world for the sake of knowledge itself" (1992, 853). Friedman argues that "one cannot combine a strategy of empirical truth-value with a sensitive politics, simply because the former is also a political strategy" (1992, 852). Scholars, too, have to be right.

The final irony, however, comes from the fact that nationalists also have a stake in preserving the authority of the scholar. Just as nationalists cannot accept the idea that their own account of history is merely another version, so they cannot allow anthropologists and historians to deny scholarly authority. Jean Jackson's claim that a people's "vision of themselves, whatever that may be, is just as authoritative as the one" proposed by an anthropologist may salve the consciences of scholars who want to write "truths" that conflict with the stories told by those they study. But undermining anthropological authority in this way is of little use to nationalists because they need anthropology—and related social sciences—to validate the vision they form of themselves. Not only do current nationalists live in a world where powerful interlocutors associate "truth" with the kind of "objectivity" that social scientists claim, but the tools that scholars use to find the "truth" were developed by earlier nationalists for the precise purpose of discovering and validating a people's unique cultural heritage.

Nineteenth-century nationalists, particularly those in continental Europe, developed anthropology and related social sciences, such as linguistics and folklore, to discover and authenticate the traditions that nationalists needed to prove their existence as a culturally distinct people. Moreover, nationalists continue to rely on anthropology. When Acosta Sánchez (1979), for example, suggests methods for recovering authentic Andalusian customs, he echoes turn-of-the-century anthropologist Franz Boas in proposing a combination of techniques drawn from linguistics, archaeology, ethnology, physical anthropology, and folklore. This convergence is hardly surprising. Boas was an heir of German romanticism. He brought the techniques that German nationalists had developed for discovering their *Volksgeist* (the authentic spirit of the people) with him to the United States, where he proposed them as methods for discovering the true histories of native peoples, in contrast to the conjectural histories being proposed by the diffusionists and evolutionists of his day (Stocking 1979).

The intertwined histories of nationalism and anthropology thus make it impossible for anthropologists to escape their dilemma by questioning their own authority. If we, as heirs of Boas—and through him, heirs of nineteenth-century German nationalists—argue that our conclusions are no more authoritative than the very different conclusions of those we study, we deprive nationalists of the methodological tools they themselves developed for "objectively" proving that their vision was "true." We leave today's nationalists with only the dubious claim that "insiders" always, inherently, know better than "outsiders."

In summary, I believe that the dilemma experienced by anthropologists who sympathize with peoples' efforts to determine their own destinies but who also want to write the "truth" derives less from the nature of anthropology than from the nature of "modernity." Although we, as anthropologists, must continue to critically examine our concepts, methods, and motives (Jackson 1995; Briggs 1996), as well as explore the global processes that structure our confrontations with nationalists (Friedman 1992), we also need to interrogate "modern" culture. We need to ask why our "modern" tradition requires us to have "identities" that distinguish us as distinct individuals and as members of culturally distinct groups.

## THE MODERNITY OF TRADITION

In an article I wrote with Bill Maurer and Liliana Suárez-Navaz (1995), we argued that "bourgeois law"—defined as the legal concepts and practices developed in Western Europe since the eighteenth century and spread around the globe through colonialism and capitalism—requires people to have "identities" grounded in supposedly natural characteristics, such as sex, race, sexuality, parentage, and place of birth. By declaring all "men" equal before the law, bourgeois law presumes (and thereby constitutes) a space outside, and prior to, law where people differ in abilities, intelligence, preferences, heritage, religion, and customs. Earlier, medieval legal systems had, of course, also constructed people as different. But they had treated such differences as God-ordained, and as the basis for assigning people to the legally defined, hierarchically ordered, status groups that were also ordained by God. It was only when

Hobbes (and later Rousseau) invented social contract theory, and declared that "Nature hath made all men . . . equall" (Hobbes 1991 [1651], 86), that legal rights and natural characteristics acquired different authors. By wresting from God the right to author their own laws, "men" endowed "nature" with independent creative abilities whose laws could be discovered through scientific experiments (Latour 1993).

But if nature erased the legally defined status distinctions of divinely ordained monarchies, nature also endowed "equal men" with different natural characteristics. Social contract theory was exclusionary from its inception. Once "men" claimed the right to make their own laws, they had to distinguish those who were entitled to participate in making laws from those who were not (Kristeva 1991). Over time, the role that supposedly natural characteristics played in separating voters from subjects has varied. In Hobbes's day, supposedly natural characteristics seemed unimportant because ownership of property was the principal criterion. But when working-class men, who owned nothing but their labor, acquired the vote in the middle of the nineteenth century, sex, race, and degree of "civilization" became the most important criteria separating those who could vote from those who could not (C. Hall 1994; Roediger 1991). In the twentieth century, as people in former colonies and indigenous peoples within established states demand self-government, ethnicity has become the primary criterion for distinguishing between citizens who belong to the "nation" and aliens who do not.

Most of the scholars who have analyzed the worldwide rise of nationalist movements have attributed current forms of nationalism to the ideas and institutions developed and propagated by philosophers of the European Enlightenment (Anderson 1983; Gellner 1983; Hobsbawm 1990; Llobera 1994). Hutchinson and Smith, for example, observe that in the view of the "founding fathers" of nationalism "(Rousseau, Herder, Fichte, Korais, and Mazzini) . . . and that of most subsequent nationalists, the movement brought together the vital aspirations of the modern world: for autonomy and self-government, for unity and autarchy, and for authentic identity." They continue, "Nationalism was, first of all, a doctrine of popular freedom and sovereignty. The people must be liberated, that is, free from any external constraint; they must determine their own destiny and be masters in their own house; they must control their own resources; they must obey only their own 'inner' voice" (1994, 4).

The requirement that people "obey only their own 'inner' voice" means, of course, that nationalists must have or find an inner voice to obey. Not surprisingly, they cannot look to socially acquired experience. They must instead turn to characteristics granted by "nature." Just as the ideal of a "free" market for jobs and commodities—which accompanied, and was made possible by, the spread of bourgeois legal concepts and institutions—required competitors for employment and sales to have inner capacities and desires that distinguished them from rivals, so "peoples" who aspired to control their own territories and resources had to have "inner voices" that distinguished them from current sovereigns and other would-be rulers. If a people were to make their own laws, they had to have some basis for deciding which laws to make. They had to have "a culture that was 'theirs' as a heritage, passed down the generations, and therefore an expression of their authentic identity" (Hutchinson and Smith 1994, 4).

But if "modern nationalists" must have a heritage that has been "passed down the generations," why do so many of the "traditions" they cherish seem to be ones that appear invented or recently borrowed? This question is doubly puzzling because invented or borrowed traditions would seem to be precisely the kinds of traditions that would undermine a people's claim to having a culture that is uniquely "'theirs' as a heritage." The answer, I think, lies in the fact that modern nationalists have to embrace both sides of the conceptual opposition between tradition and modernity that came into being with the invention of modernity. Modern nationalists have to find traditions that distinguish them from other nations without marking them as traditional or backward. This task is ultimately impossible. In practice, "having traditions" is indistinguishable from "being traditional" (Nadel-Klein 1991; Herzfeld 1982, 1991; D. Sutton 1994).[9] But the impossibility of the task does not relieve modern nationalists from the obligation to attempt it.

Throughout this book, I have been using Antonio's implied contrast between thinking for oneself and letting others think for one to explore how he and most members of his generation experienced the distinction between "modern" young people and their "traditional" elders.[10] Not surprisingly, the customs that Antonio and other self-consciously modern people from Los Olivos tended to reject as "backward village stupidities" were precisely those that villagers in the 1960s had said they observed because, in Los Olivos, you "had to go through the forms in everything, but underneath you could think what you wanted"—such customs as postponing marriage and wearing mourning clothes for years after a death. The customs that modern people embraced, in contrast, seemed to be those activities that adults in the 1960s had claimed to want to do but said they usually suppressed—such pleasureful activities as dancing, singing, drinking, attending bullfights, wearing pretty clothes, and so forth.[11]

But if Antonio's characterization of modern people as thinking for themselves suggests a reason why members of his generation had to reject many of the customs they had themselves observed in the 1960s, his characterization offers little insight into why modern nationalists so often seem to invent or borrow traditions, rather than simply selecting the less objectionable traditions from the past. Antonio's distinction, for example, cannot explain why Esteban and his wife bought the *Enciclopedia* rather than asking Esteban's mother to tell her grandchildren about the festivals, dances, and picnics of her youth. Given that people in the past had pursued some enjoyable activities, why did members of Esteban's generation seem to agree with the *Enciclopedia*'s editors that Andalusia was a region without usable memories?

At first glance, the "modern" requirement that people think for themselves seems to coincide with the nationalist requirement that a people "must obey only their own 'inner' voice" (Hutchinson and Smith 1994, 4). But the two requirements are slightly different. Antonio's contrast between thinking for oneself and letting others think for one reflects the opposition invented by Enlightenment philosophers between reason and superstition.[12] Or, put into the terms suggested by Conchi, it reflects the difference between what any "normal" person would do and the "backward" customs of people who have not yet "opened their eyes." The nationalist requirement that a people "obey only their own 'inner' voice," on the other hand, reflects the opposition developed by later advocates of European romanticism between reason and emotion. The "inner voice" that nationalists are required to obey cannot speak acultural human reason. Nor can it tell people to do what any "normal" person would do anyway. Neither reason nor human nature provides a basis for nationalists to distinguish people who belong to their nation from people who rightfully belong to other nations.

Looking back at field notes from the 1960s, it is easy to see that most of the pleasures enjoyed by people in Los Olivos did not distinguish them from people elsewhere in Spain. The pretty dresses worn by girls at the patron saint's festival in the summer of 1964 were copied from high-fashion magazines, the band played tunes that were being played over radios around the world, and the dances were ones that were being danced throughout Europe and the Americas. A few items—such as some local foods and the custom of decorating pilgrimage carts with crepe paper flowers—have continued to be treasured traditions. But most of the pleasureful activities remembered by living elders were not ones that could serve to distinguish people born in Andalusia from people born in other regions of Spain or the world. No wonder modern nationalists, like Esteban, felt they could not ask their parents and grandparents for information about their Andalusian heritage. The customs that people in the 1960s had described as distinguishing virtuous villagers from immoral urbanites had to be rejected as "backward village stupidities," even as the activities that people in the 1960s had claimed to enjoy had to be rejected because they did not distinguish Andalusians from other Spaniards.

The requirement that modern nationalists embrace both sides of the conceptual opposition between tradition and modernity also suggests a reason why so many of the traditions celebrated by nationalists tend to fall on the private side of the modern conceptual opposition between private and public spheres. Just as modern nationalists must find traditions that differentiate their ethnic group from others without marking them as blindly following social conventions, so they must find traditions whose enactment does not interfere with their ability to exhibit the acultural human reason that makes them eligible to govern themselves and to participate in international capitalist markets. On a practical level, modern nationalists must enact traditions that do not hinder them from obeying laws and making money. It seems no accident, for example, that many, if not most, of the festivals and pilgrimages celebrated by people from Los Olivos occurred during summer vacations, or were rescheduled for weekends if they were not already national holidays, such as Easter week and Christmas. But it is also true that modernity constructs acultural human reason in such a way that tradition is reason's opposite rather than its embodiment.

Throughout this book, I have been using examples from *Doña Perfecta* to suggest that people who experience social status as inherited tend to have a different conception of human reason from those who experience status as based on individual achievement. For Doña Perfecta and her allies, people exhibited reason by understanding, and following, God's plan for the world. Traditions embodied reason, as suggested by the definition of traditionalism in the *American Heritage Dictionary* as "a philosophical system holding that all knowledge is derived from original divine revelation and is transmitted by tradition." For Pepe Rey and his allies, in contrast, people exhibited reason by thinking for themselves—by rationally calculating the (market) costs and benefits of their actions. Tradition was reason's opposite, as suggested by the dictionary's definition of Enlightenment as "a philosophical movement . . . concerned with the critical examination of previously accepted doctrines . . . from the point of view of rationalism." The European Enlightenment, which created the modernity/tradition conceptual opposition, not only posited a distinction between reason and tradition but also constructed "rationalism" as the conceptual tool for analyzing "accepted doctrines" and exposing them to view. In Andalusia, for example, the scientific study of folklore began late in the nineteenth century, initiated by intellectuals influenced by liberal ideology (Aguilar Criado 1990).

Throughout this book I have also been tracing shifts in people's experience of the public/private conceptual opposition. When social status appeared to be determined by inheritance, villagers in Los Olivos experienced the casa/calle opposition as one between private homes where people fulfilled their obligations and public streets where men and unmarried women went to amuse themselves. Monarchical political theory also portrayed private homes as spaces of duty and constraint. For Doña Perfecta and her allies, homes, like kingdoms, were ruled by patriarchs who enforced God's laws on Earth. But when villagers and emigrants began to participate in the capitalist market for jobs and commodities, homes became the site of workers' rest and leisure. Freedom and constraint switched locations. Not only did workers experience the public sphere as one where they were constrained to obey political and economic laws, but social contract theory also cast the public sphere as one where people were obliged to fulfill the political and economic contracts they negotiated. Homes, in contrast, were spaces of freedom and desire, where workers could relax and where political actors could enjoy the liberties they had not contracted away. It is not surprising, therefore, that so many of the traditions celebrated by my friends from Los Olivos during the pilgrimage to San Bartolomé—the religious devotion to a local saint, the colorful costumes, the *sevillanas*, the informal bullfight, the hospitality, and the consumption of local foods—were ones that people could imagine having been preserved in the privacy of Andalusian hearts and homes (even if not in the particular homes they happened to grow up in).

Finally, the requirement that modern nationalists embrace both sides of the conceptual opposition between tradition and modernity suggests a reason why women are more often cast as the bearers and enactors of tradition than men. Women's association with tradition is overdetermined. Not only do the gender conceptions associated with modernity identify women with the emotion that is reason's opposite, but they also identify women's homes with leisure and desire. Moreover, women's apparent confinement to the home, which supposedly insulates them from "outside" influences, condemns them to conservatism.[13] Women are thus cast both as passive perpetuators of tradition—in whose hearts and homes rational men can seek the "inner voice" that speaks their cultural heritage (Chatterjee 1989; Kelley 1994; Mani 1989)—and as active guardians of the national culture. Women, more than men, are expected to preserve and pass on the national language; enact the national religion; make, wear, and wash the national costume; learn the national dances; prepare the home-cooked portions of the national dishes; and clean up after the national festivals. Although the workload in Los Olivos did seem fairly balanced, for men cooked some of the special foods, made the spiked punch, and did most of the work associated with putting on a bullfight, hiring a band, and organizing the procession of carts, the background work of ensuring that picnics were made, costumes were clean, and everything got home again fell on women's shoulders.

Because "modern" people are required to think for themselves, and thus to want to do what they do, women usually find it hard to evade— or even to complain about—the burden of enacting national traditions. The depiction of home as a place of rest and leisure may fit the experience of male breadwinners better than that of female homemakers, but women, too, find it hard to evade the image of home as a place where people can relax, free from state interference, the demands of employers, and the iron laws of the market. Because no policeman or boss seems to be telling a housewife to cook the dinner or wash the clothes, she must be doing these things because she, herself, decided to do them. Similarly, women who spend hours preparing national dishes, sewing and caring for national costumes, studying national dances, and exhibiting religious devotion seem be doing these things because they "want" to.

It is, of course, true that women often do want to enact the national heritage. But I have also heard women from Los Olivos complain about how long it takes to make *cocido* (the regional dish of chickpeas, vegetables, and sausages), how boring it is to sew endless ruffles on flamenco dresses, how hard it is to remove the horse stains from men's flamenco costumes, and how, maybe, they would really like to sit out this pilgrimage, resting at home in front of the television set. Whereas men from Los Olivos could decide for themselves whether they wanted to devote their free time to participating in a pilgrimage, women seemed to find themselves participating whether they wanted to or not. And, of course, in the end, women really did "want" to participate, in the sense that women usually produced personal reasons to explain why they, as individuals who thought for themselves, had decided to join. After all— women would explain to me—*cocido* is a nourishing dish, a daughter really should have her own flamenco dress rather than wearing an older cousin's hand-me-down, a son should be able to ride a horse if all his friends were doing so, and a husband might have worse passions than wanting to participate in local pilgrimages.

The gendered contradictions inherent in modern nationalism were summed up for me in a picture published in the *Gran enciclopedia de Andalucía* under the entry on *Andalucismo* (Andalusianism). The picture portrayed young people on a country picnic. They were all dressed in blue jeans. One young man was playing a guitar, a young woman was dancing a *sevillana*, and the rest were clapping. The caption read, "Andalusianism is something more than the political dimension of an idea: it is a powerful sentiment whose roots lie in folklore and which expresses itself spontaneously on every occasion when two or more Andalusians come together."[14] The dancing, I realized, had to be "spontaneous" in order to meet the requirement that modern nationalists simultaneously "think for themselves" and "obey only their own 'inner' voice." At the same time, however, I knew from experience that it took years of practice before a young woman could "spontaneously" perform a *sevillana* without making a fool of herself.

## CHOOSING TRADITION

As the example of the pictured teenagers reveals, Andalusian traditions, like all modern traditions, are less "spontaneous" enactments of a people's ethnic "essence" than cultural rituals whose repeated enactment requires learning, practice, commitment, and the expenditure of resources. But if modernity requires people to have, and to enact, cultural traditions, it also constructs tradition as a site for resisting modernity's impersonal rationalization of social life. My experiences in Los Olivos convinced me that modern people cherish their traditions not simply because they are required to do so by the modern ideology of nationalism but because people experience traditions as crucial resources in their struggles to preserve "self-respect, autonomy, and a life with meaning" (Jackson 1995, 18).

In his book tracing shifts in the "politics of tradition" in the market center of Aracena, Richard Maddox argues that "tradition" has always been a vibrant discourse in the Sierra de Aracena. But he observes that there have been shifts in the articulation of traditional discourses "with day-to-day social practices and hegemonic strategies of domination." A particularly important shift occurred with

> the emergence, rise, and triumph of the rationalized and impersonal modes of cultural authority involved in the development of modern bureaucracies and technologies, large scale capitalist corporations, and the nation-state. As social life has become increasingly subject to secular, instrumental, and objectified forms of knowledge and techniques of management and control, tradition has been gradually transformed from a repository of revelatory truths about the human condition and the character of social order into one among a number of cultural alternatives and possible value orientations that address problems of meaning, shape motives, guide actions, and construct specific visions of the good life. (1993, 263)

Because I too have argued that "tradition" lost its status as a repository of divine wisdom, I share Maddox's concern for exploring why "tradition" remains vibrant within modernity. Like him, I want to counteract the discrediting and trivializing of tradition that results from its double connotation as modernity's devalued opposite and as merely one possible value orientation among many.[15] In the previous section, I suggested that tradition remains vibrant because modern discourses of nationalism require people to have traditions. I observed that women, in particular, not only have to enact traditions but must want to do so. Such arguments, however, tend to portray traditions as enforced. They fail to capture the sense in which Andalusians in the 1980s were actively using tradition to "resist the increasing rationalization and homogenization of contemporary life" (Maddox 1993, 22).

In this final section, therefore, I turn to exploring why "tradition" provides such an effective tool for modern people to resist the increasingly "secular, instrumental and objectified . . . techniques of management and control" exercised by "modern bureaucracies, large scale capitalist corporations, and the nation-state" (Maddox 1993, 263). Tradition, I suggest, appears to offer a humane alternative because of its relationship to ethnicity and modern notions of the family. Many authors have observed that nationalism builds on ideas of kinship. Ethnic groups are families writ large. The family, however, has not always provided a site for resisting oppressive social hierarchies. When people from Los Olivos lived in a social world where status appeared to be inherited, families were sites for reproducing unequal social relations. It was through preserving family inheritances that people maintained their places in the social hierarchy. But when former villagers began to participate in the national market for jobs and commodities, they remade their families into sites of leisure and desire, apparently outside and apart from, the status competition of public life. They thus constituted their families— along with traditions preserved in the home—as sites for creating lives with meaning in an increasingly rationalized and homogenized world.

Throughout this book, I have used the philosophical definition of "tradition"—as a historical mode of thought that determines what counts as rationality—to suggest that "modernity," like "tradition," is best seen as a subtradition of a wider post-Enlightenment European cultural tradition (Tambiah 1990; Herzfeld 1992). The younger villagers I met in the 1980s may have imagined that they had abandoned the "backward" village customs of their parents and grandparents in favor of doing what any normal person would do. But, as I have tried to show, "normality" too is a historical tradition, in the sense that "normality" is imagined—as "tradition" once was—as a repository of "revelatory truths about the human condition and the character of social order" (Maddox 1993, 263). When social contract theory triumphed over earlier political theories of divinely ordained kingship, nature replaced God as the author of human possibilities.

I have used this understanding of modernity to suggest that commonsense explanations for the changes I observed in Los Olivos cannot fully account for them. Emigration, for example, seems to provide an obvious explanation for the fact that by the 1980s most of the people born in Los Olivos tended to identify themselves as Andalusians, or as from the Sierra de Aracena. Anthropologists have long known that people's statements about who they are, in terms of where they come from, tend to vary according to their current locations (Evans-Pritchard 1940). During both my visits to Los Olivos, a woman who was born in the village could have identified herself as a Spaniard if outside Spain, as an Andalusian if in Catalonia, as from the Sierra de Aracena if in Seville, or as from Los Olivos if in another Sierra de Aracena town. Villagers' adoption of a regional identity could thus be taken to reflect the simple fact that by 1980 more than half of the people who had been born in Los Olivos were living outside it. But emigration cannot explain why people who remained in Los Olivos also stressed their identity as Andalusians. The most fervent enactments of Andalusian identity that I observed all took place within Andalusia.[16]

Nor do I want to attribute villagers' adoption of an Andalusian identity to the fact that most of the people who left Los Olivos moved to cities. No one can deny that city life differs from village life. Rural-urban differences matter. But I have tried, in each chapter of this book, to show how the differences between urban and rural living cannot explain why love replaced expected inheritances as the most important factor determining whether young people's initial attraction would develop into a lasting marriage; why everyone thought that husbands and wives had become more equal; why children needed to be "prepared" rather than "subjugated"; and why young women thought it "served no purpose" to dress in black after the death of a close relative. Similarly, people's celebration of Andalusian traditions cannot be explained by the simple idea that emigrants pulled from their rural villages had to develop another basis for identity (see also Hirschon 1989). As I just noted, people who remained in Los Olivos—if they belonged to the generation born after the civil war—seemed as eager as their urban relatives to reclaim their Andalusian heritage.

I have also been arguing against explanations for change that attribute the shifts I observed to the fact that television, along with emigration, opened villagers' eyes and minds to new possibilities. I do not deny that the spread of television sets increased villagers' exposure to different ways of talking and acting. But I have continually questioned the simple idea that once country folk have been exposed to urban customs, they immediately want to adopt them.[17] The villagers I met in the 1960s knew a great deal about "modern" ways. They also had very good reasons for "not wanting to be the first person in Los Olivos" to adopt them, as the woman in mourning put it. No one can deny that television has played a major role in fostering national identities in Spain. Spanish television has broadcast endless programs depicting the festivals, dances, music, costumes, cuisines, and folklore of Andalusians, Catalonians, Basques, Galicians, and others. But television alone cannot explain why people from Los Olivos began to identify themselves as Andalusians, particularly since many, if not most, of the traditions depicted as Andalusian were not ones they or their immediate forebears had enacted.

Finally, in this section, I want to argue against the simple idea that Andalusians are reviving and elaborating their traditions because tradition, as modernity's opposite, provides an ideal tool for people to use in resisting the rationalization and homogenization of contemporary life. I do not deny that Andalusians are reworking "tradition" into an effective language and practice of resistance, as Maddox shows in the final chapters of his book (1993). But I do question whether tradition is modernity's opposite. Tradition, I have argued, is modern as well.[18] Throughout this book, I have explored how people who experience social status as determined by individuals' achievements in markets organized by secularized and rationalized techniques of modern management and control construct their families—and the ethnic groups that are families writ large—as sites of leisure, nature, and desire. It is modernity itself that makes tradition a crucial resource for modern subjects to use in their struggles to preserve "self-respect, autonomy, and a life with meaning" (Jackson 1995, 18). Power, as Foucault observed, constructs the sites for its own resistance (1978; see also Abu-Lughod 1990).

Sylvia Yanagisako, in a multiply authored essay, argues that "what gives shape to our (modern) conception of The Family is its symbolic opposition to work and business." Family, she writes, evokes "a certain kind of relationship: a relationship that entails affection and love, that is based on cooperation as opposed to competition, that is enduring rather than temporary, that is noncontingent rather than contingent upon performance, and that is governed by feeling and morality instead of law and contract" (Collier, Rosaldo, and Yanagisako 1982, 34). For people who live in a social world where individual achievement appears more important than inheritance for determining social status, the private sphere of home, family, and tradition offers not only a space where individuals can maximize such values as love, cooperation, and morality—instead of the selfishness, competition, and legalism required for success in the public sphere of capitalist markets and republican politics—but also a space where individuals can relax and be loved for who they are rather than for what they do. Modernity may compel "man to face the task of producing himself" rather than "liberate man in his own being"

(Foucault 1984, 42), but the private sphere constructed by modern forms of rationalized power promises precisely this vision of "liberation." Safe among those who love one simply for who one is, the modern subject is free just to be.

This sense of "liberation" was dramatically brought home to me by two incidents I observed on returning to Los Olivos in the 1980s. Stepping out my front door one hot summer morning, I encountered the teenage daughter of my neighbor, dressed only in baby-doll pajamas. I was stunned. In the 1960s, no one—particularly a young woman—would have appeared in the street in pajamas, to say nothing of such skimpy ones. Did this teenager have no shame? Did she not worry about what the neighbors would say? The answer to these questions was suggested by a later incident, in which I watched the mother in a vacationing emigrant family plead with her twenty-year-old son to trade his short shorts and ragged top for long pants and a proper shirt. The mother told her son that he should look nice when he went out in the evening. Her son, in reply, asked why he should bother to dress up, since everyone in the village was family.

People from Los Olivos had, of course, long affirmed that everyone in the village was family. But these incidents reveal that the family imagined by young people in the 1980s was a very different family from the one experienced by villagers in the 1960s. No longer did membership in a family impose onerous obligations, such as the duty to protect the family's property and reputation from envious and gossiping neighbors. Instead, the family offered a "haven" from the "heartless world" of capitalist competition (Lasch 1977). It was a space where individuals could relax, secure in the knowledge that relatives had to accept them for who they were rather than for what they did.

By promising unconditional acceptance, the modern family offers individuals a haven from the obligation to choose. Modern subjects, as Giddens observes, may "have no choice but to choose" (1991, 81), but modernity's construction of the family as based on "natural" rather than "contractual" bonds holds out the promise of relationships that exist prior to, and in spite of, the choices an individual makes. The attraction of unchosen relationships is revealed in the comments of Eduardo, a man from Los Olivos who spent most of his life in the city of Huelva. Even though Eduardo's family suffered terribly during the repression following the Spanish civil war, he said he wanted to retire in the village. When asked why, he said he felt at home there. To explain what he meant, Eduardo contrasted his experience patronizing bars in Huelva, where he had to choose among bars and drinking companions, with his experience in Los Olivos, where—he said—the men accepted him simply because he was one of them and they had all known each other from

childhood. Although Eduardo had undoubtedly experienced cooperative and caring relationships in his employment and among bar patrons
in Huelva, he had also spent most of his life in a social world where the
employers who determined his income and lifestyle claimed to base their
decisions on rational cost-benefit assessments of his performance. No
wonder he and other emigrants of his generation experienced the promise of enduring and noncontingent relationships as more truly "human"
than relationships grounded in the "mechanics" of market rationality.

When Jean Jackson observes that people elaborate "tradition" in their
struggles to preserve "self-respect, autonomy, and a life with meaning"
(1995, 18), she captures the sense in which modern people experience
ethnicity as a tool for resisting modern forms of rationalized power. In
a social world where inequality appears to be determined by competition
among individuals for jobs and commodities, cultural traditions do offer
people more than simply one possible vision of the good life. They offer
the most compelling vision of what a life governed by moral principles
(rather than amoral greed) might encompass. Moreover, traditional cultures promise to "liberate" people in their own being by releasing them
from the modern requirement to "produce themselves." Free to relax
among those who must accept one for who one is rather than for what
one does, the modern subject can finally experience an authentic self.

Jean Jackson's observation, however, also reveals that ethnic traditions do not free modern subjects from the requirement to choose. In
contrast to "traditional" subjects, who could "resign" themselves to
fulfilling the obligations associated with the station in life to which God
had assigned them, "modern" subjects must take charge of their lives.
They have to struggle to create "lives with meaning." When Eduardo
explained why he wanted to retire in Los Olivos, he did not report that
all his age-mates were doing so and would criticize him if he did not
follow their example. Rather, he produced a worse alternative as evidence that he thought for himself rather than allowing others to think
for him. Similarly, when people from Los Olivos embraced Andalusian
traditions, they could not resign themselves to doing what their ancestors had always done. Rather, they had to actively seek their ethnic
traditions in the writings of intellectuals. However lively and intelligent
Esteban's mother might have been, Esteban and his wife could not ask
her to teach her grandchildren about their Andalusian heritage. They
had to buy the *Gran enciclopedia de Andalucía* instead.

# Notes

## Introduction

1. —¡De modo que para este ateo infame—exclamó con franca rabia—no hay conveniencias sociales, no hay nada más que capricho! (Pérez Galdós 1983, 184).

2. These sentences are my translations from notes I took in Spanish on the front matter of the first volume of the *Enciclopedia*. The Spanish words I recorded are "Andalucía fué hasta hoy un puro sentimiento romántico." The population of the region "se siente andaluz—pero sin más conexiones de origen tipo y sin elementos para 'fijar' su identidad regional." "La Enciclopedia inicia la tarea de 'dotar de alma' a la región andaluza proporcionándole aceso a sus contenidos culturales propios. Si no lo hacemos, los andaluces caeremos en una peligrosa frustración al comprobar que carecemos de base de identidad para el pueblo andaluz."

3. As will become clear in the final chapter, I think the argument that village customs in the 1960s reflected Castilian domination is better understood as a rationalization than as a reason for their rejection by Andalusian nationalists.

4. The hitchhiker actually said, "Ya no se aguanta la gente; aguantaba más antes" [People no longer endure (things); they endured more before], suggesting that people in the 1980s thought they had the right to refuse onerous social obligations they formerly accepted without question.

5. The young man made this observation to Richard Price, as recorded in his field notes for the summer of 1964. Richard Price's field notes continue: "The problem, [the young man] said, was that you could not discuss these things with others. He said that he considered most of what went on in the church *tonterías* (stupidities), and that many other men agreed. But they still went [to church]." When Richard Price mentioned to the young man that he "had seen [a notoriously irreligious youth] of all people, kiss the Canonigo's hand that morning," the young man replied, "'sure, I'd have done it too. You have to, but it doesn't mean anything really.'"

6. In writing about the nearby market town of Aracena, for example, Richard Maddox observes that "the most striking feature of working-class culture during the period [of agrarian capitalism] was the breadth and depth of concern expressed for understanding what people owed and could expect of one another. Notions of honor, personal integrity, and reputation were heavily influenced by a moral economy of *obligaciones* (obligations) and *deberes* (duties)" (1993, 137).

7. Although villagers in Los Olivos resemble people elsewhere in having replaced apparently authoritarian and hierarchical families with apparently affectionate, egalitarian ones, I do not think these changes occurred because industrialization, urbanization, and the spread of capitalist labor markets stripped the preindustrial peasant family of its productive and political functions, thereby reducing it to its affective core (see Shorter 1975; Goode 1970; Stone 1979;

Trumbach 1978, 1979). Such an explanation for family change rests on the questionable assumption that families everywhere have affective cores to which they can be reduced (Yanagisako 1979, Medick and Sabean 1984). I do not assume that family interactions inevitably generate affectionate feelings, which people will act upon when freed from social and economic constraints that prevent their expression. Rather, I plan to explore how changes in people's experiences of social inequality encouraged them to shift from talking about their obligations to talking about their feelings.

8. Among the Spaniards who have written about the derogatory views of Spanish and Andalusian culture propagated by anthropologists are Luque Baena (1981); and especially Moreno Navarro (1975, 1981, 1984).

9. English-speaking scholars have also written about the derogatory implications inherent in accounts of "Mediterranean" culture as "traditional" (e.g., Alberra 1988; Boissevain 1979; Cole 1977; Driessen 1981, 1984; Faubion 1993; Fernandez 1983; Gilmore 1982; Halpern 1980; Herzfeld 1980, 1984, 1987; Pina-Cabral 1989).

10. Because I believe that the two ways of imagining the relationship between desire and action implied in the contrast between following social conventions and thinking for oneself are best envisoned as subtraditions that developed in opposition to each other within the larger historical tradition of the European Enlightenment, I think they correspond most closely to "ideologies" as defined by Comaroff and Comaroff in their discussion of the terms "culture," "hegemony" and "ideology" (1991). Following Williams (1977), the Comaroffs use "ideology" to "describe 'an articulated system of meanings, values, and beliefs of a kind that can be abstracted as [the] "worldview" of any social grouping" (1991, 24). They observe that "as long as [an ideology] exists, it provides an organizing scheme (a master narrative?) for collective symbolic production" and "that while the nature and degree of its preeminence may vary, [an ideology] is likely to be protected, even enforced, to the full extent of the power of those who claim it for their own" (1991, 24). I envision the two subtraditions I analyze in this book as embodied in institutions and powerfully enforced. In this sense, they are more comparable to the contrasting ideologies of communism and capitalism than to opposing liberal and conservative positions within either regime. Not only did communism develop in opposition to capitalism as a distinct approach to realizing the Enlightenment ideal of human liberation but, for most of the twentieth century, the two ideologies were embodied in the social institutions of world regions and enforced by powerful states.

11. Berman, in his analysis of "modernity," describes its "second phase" as occurring in the aftermath of the American and French Revolutions, when "the nineteenth century modern public can remember what it is like to live, materially and spiritually, in worlds that are not modern at all. From this inner dichotomy, this sense of living in two worlds simultaneously, the ideas of modernization and modernism emerge and unfold" (1982, 17)—giving rise to an idea of "tradition" in the process.

12. In chapter 6, where I focus on the celebration of traditional festivals in Los Olivos in the 1980s, I consider another dilemma that anthropology's link with nationalism poses for anthropologists such as me who want to write about

the loss of tradition in the second sense, followed by the development of traditions in the third sense. Given nationalists' need for anthropologists to "scientifically" validate the authenticity of the traditions that establish their unique cultural heritage, how can an anthropologist write about the apparent "invention of traditions" without undermining, however unwillingly, political movements for self-determination that deserve support?

13. There is also a third way in which my situation as a "modern" person limited my understanding of the 1980s. Anthropology, as a product of the European Enlightenment and the nineteenth-century's romantic reaction to eighteenth-century rationalism, discouraged me from seeking explanations for behaviors that I shared with people born in Los Olivos. Not only did anthropology's links with folklore studies and nationalist politics define anthropology's mission as one of documenting cultural differences rather than exploring similarities, but anthropology's participation in creating the conceptual oppositions between subjectivity and objectivity, and between cultural beliefs and scientific truths, discouraged the development of concepts for exploring behaviors that were neither unique to particular peoples nor universally shared. Because the courting, child rearing, and mourning customs that villagers and I observed in the 1980s did not distinguish them from me, these customs could not be easily attributed to our subjective cultural heritages, even as our shared customs' lack of universality made it difficult to imagine that these customs reflected rational, objective, adaptive responses to universal human problems. Neither anthropology as a humanistic discipline focused on cultural differences nor anthropology as an objective science dedicated to discovering and promoting behaviors based on scientific truths encouraged anthropologists like me to treat "modern" behaviors as problematic.

14. Spanish friends who read earlier versions of this manuscript have kindly pointed out several such misunderstandings to me. Although I regret the errors that necessarily remain, I hope that my mistakes will alert others to questions I failed to ask.

15. The plan to compare Los Olivos to a Maya Indian hamlet proved misguided because the social consequences of six hundred people, an agricultural economy, and mountainous terrain were determined not by such supposed independent variables but by people's active participation in wider national and historical contexts.

16. I did not experience the people of Los Olivos as poor, probably because I met them after having done fieldwork in southern Mexico, where many people were far poorer by world standards. Everyone who lived in Los Olivos in the 1960s had a solid house and enough food to eat, even though they tended to lack cash and such modern conveniences as cars, gas stoves, washing machines, televisions, cameras, and so on. It is also true that, at the time, my husband and I owned fewer possessions than most villagers—although we did have more cash.

17. When doing fieldwork in Zinacantan, Chiapas, Mexico, I had been able to collect detailed case histories because senior North American anthropologists working in the region had developed the custom of paying informants a daily wage for the time they spent answering questions. When doing fieldwork in Los

Olivos, however, I not only lacked the money to pay people but knew they would be insulted if I should offer. I was therefore able to give only token gifts in thanks for people's kindness.

18. Michelle Rosaldo died in 1981. Although she wrote an unpublished essay on Los Olivos mourning customs shortly after her stay in the village, neither I nor members of her family have been able to find it among our papers.

19. My focus on commonsense understandings of how to get ahead is similar to the focus on "common sense understandings of human motivation" that Derné proposes as a way to explore the causal effects of "culture" (1994, 267). Like Derné, I turned from studying "values" to exploring common sense in order to understand how people who actively contest cultural norms are nevertheless constrained by them. And like him, I focus on the socially organized sanctions that constrain people by limiting the "strategies of action that individuals can use to buck social pressures" (1994, 274). Derné, for example, observes that because those "whose actions do not appear to fit the dominant framework may be mistrusted as lacking normal human attributes," people are constrained to at least justify their actions in terms of the dominant ideology (1994, 275).

My framework, however, differs from Derné's in at least two ways. First, my focus on wider systems of social inequality leads me to explore how "commonsense understandings of human motivation" are related to commonsense prescriptions for how to get ahead. In this book, for example, I explore how the motivations of "duty" and "desire" correlated with commonsense assumptions about status as inherited or achieved. Second, I believe that there are many more than "two general types of understanding" of human action (Derné 1994, 270). From the viewpoint of those who live within a cultural system where actions appear to be "chosen by individuals themselves," all other understandings of human action may appear to fall into the category of cultural systems where "actions seem to be driven by forces outside the individual" (Derné 1994, 270). Such a view, however, misses not only variations among "outside driven" systems but also the sense in which both "duty" and "desire"—and the concern for following caste and family dictates expressed by the Indian men Derné interviewed (1994)—presume a bounded "I" who wants and acts. The concept of a coherent, bounded, desiring self contrasts with concepts of permeable or partible selves that tend to be found primarily outside the former agrarian civilizations of Eurasia (see Strathern 1988; J. Collier 1988).

20. Foucault distinguished Kant's vision of enlightenment from "freedom of conscience: [defined as] the right to think as one pleases so long as one obeys as one must." Instead of arguing that people should be submissive in public while remaining free to think for themselves in private, Kant argued that people should be submissive in private but enjoy free use of reason in the public sphere (Foucault 1984, 36).

21. Giddens portrays women in "traditional cultures" as unable to realize their natural desire for sexual pleasure because "For most women, in most cultures, and throughout most periods of history, sexual pleasure, where possible, was intrinsically bound up with fear—of repetitive pregnancies, and therefore death. . . . The breaking of these connections was thus a phenomenon with truly radical implications" (1992, 27).

22. The focus on values and social integration prompted other scholars, particularly Gilmore (1980), to explore the class conflicts that characterized Andalusian communities (see also Martínez-Alier 1971).

23. Not all anthropologists from English-speaking countries worked in villages. Some worked in cities and factories (Benton 1990; Corbin and Corbin 1984, 1987; Kenny 1966; Kenny and Kertzer 1983; Gregory 1983; McDonogh 1986; Murphy 1983a, 1983b; Pi-Sunyer 1974; Press 1979).

24. Andalusian anthropologists also analyzed traditional festivals (e.g., Rodríguez Becerra 1980, 1985).

25. Galdós tells a very different story from the kind of romantic tales women from Los Olivos tended to read in the 1960s. In those tales, the motives of the characters were seldom in doubt. Heroines, in particular, always wanted to preserve their virtue. The question most such stories answered concerned not why people acted as they did but whether or not the characters could reconcile conflicting obligations. A very popular story line, for example, focused on whether, and how, the heroine could avoid succumbing to the villain's lustful advances while still managing to save her fiancé, father, brother, mother, sister, child, or whomever from death or disaster.

## Chapter One

1. Vea usted de qué le vale a mi hijo . . . el haber sacado tantas notas de sobresaliente y ser el primor y la gala de Orbajosa. . . . Se morirá de hambre, porque ya sabemos lo que da la abogacía, o tendrá que pedir a los diputados un destino en La Habana, donde le matará la fiebre amarilla . . . (Pérez Galdós 1983, 257).

2. Although many of the villagers I spoke with in the 1980s were the same ones I had interviewed twenty years earlier, the distributions of wealth they were called upon to explain had changed drastically between 1960 and 1980, as will become clear later in this chapter.

3. It would be very difficult for a researcher to decide if the system of social inequality in Los Olivos changed from one based on ascription to one based on achievement because a researcher who wanted to define "ascription" in terms of intergenerational continuity of social status and "achievement" in terms of intergenerational mobility would first have to confront the fact that the system for evaluating social status changed between 1960 and 1980.

4. Villagers also avoided emphasizing wealth distinctions. Even though one of the bars in town was called the *casino* (a term used in larger towns to label the gathering place of wealthy landowners in contrast to the simple bars patronized by working-class men), Richard Price noticed that village men usually visited both establishments every evening, ending up in the one nearest home (RSP field notes, summer 1964). Similarly, I noticed that our housekeeper took care to patronize both village stores, even though they sold the same items and shopping at the lower one involved less climbing.

5. Smuggling items—primarily coffee and tobacco—across the nearby border with Portugal was once, and might still have been, an important source of income for Los Olivos residents. We deliberately refrained from asking about illegal activities, however.

6. Even the unmarried children of elite families who moved away from the village to more important towns attended parties and dances with Los Olivos young people when they were in the village. No child of an elite family married a villager, however.

7. Richard and Sally Price (1966b:533) report that Los Olivos "informants consistently used four categories when asked to assess the wealth of individuals," suggesting the cultural salience of the three loosely bounded status groups (plus members of the regional elite) that I describe. The Prices' "very wealthy" category corresponds to those I label regional elites; their "wealthy" category to my *propietarios*; their "middling" category to my *autónomos*; and their "very poor" to my *jornaleros*. The Prices asked informants to rank individuals, rather than households, because they were interested in courtship patterns.

8. The figure of one hundred seventy-seven households does not include all the households in the 1950 census. The mayor did not rate some households, particularly those composed of a single person or belonging to families who had moved away by 1963.

9. I also learned that the history of Los Olivos paralleled that of many similar rural communities (see particularly Gilmore 1980; Kaplan 1977; Mintz 1982; Moreno Alonso 1979; Fraser 1973). Readers who want to learn more about the history of Los Olivos and about the wider political and economic context that shaped local events should consult G. Collier (1987) and Maddox (1993).

10. The two factions were, of course, not composed solely of landlords and workers respectively. In addition to many of the wealthier villagers and several *autónomos*, the landlord faction included some workers, particularly those who held permanent positions with individual proprietors. Similarly, the worker faction included some members of landed families and of families that owned stores and trucks, in addition to many landless workers. See G. Collier (1987, 39) for further information on faction membership.

11. There is no evidence that poor families actually faced starvation. Women—who were paid a fraction of what men earned—remember that there was always agricultural work available for them. Children, who were paid even less than women, could obtain employment running errands, guarding pigs (if they were boys), or watching toddlers (if they were girls). Unemployment was a problem primarily for adult men.

12. Socialist policies also threatened to undermine the moral as well as the economic and political superiority of landowners. By establishing employment as a worker's right, rather than a landowner's gift, the socialists sought to erase the distinction between men who could offer homage freely because they could meet their subsistence needs from their own estates and men who had to do others' bidding because they needed food. If workers had the right to a job paying enough to feed themselves and their families, they, like autonomous landowners, would be "free" to decide for themselves whether to accept or reject the requests of others. The socialist program thus constituted much more than an attack on landowners' freedom to run their estates as they chose. It threatened to destroy the moral significance of owning land.

13. Postwar processes also created the apparently timeless stratification pattern based on landownership. After taking control of the municipal government,

the victorious landowners, in conjunction with Franco regime propaganda, re-wrote village and Spanish history. In 1963, for example, the mayor described village events prior to the civil war as aberrant—as communist-inspired violence that ended as soon as Franco's forces chased the communists away. "Once the military passed through," he said, "order was restored, and little by little things have returned to normal" (quoted in G. Collier 1987, 165). Things did return to "normal" in the sense that landowners resumed control of the municipal gov-ernment they had dominated for at least a century before 1933. But in blaming opposition to their rule on communist agitators from outside, landowners re-wrote the long history of agrarian struggles in the village and in Andalusia gen-erally. They constructed their dominance as "normal" by inverting and silencing the discourse of class opposition invoked by pre-civil war socialists (G. Collier 1987, 166).

14. The quotation is from field notes recorded by George Collier in October 1963.

15. One young man, the only son of one of the major landowning families, said that he decided to emigrate in 1965 because, although "he liked agricul-ture, there were no opportunities in it." Agricultural work, he said, required human labor (rather than machines), and he wanted a better life—clearly imply-ing that he was not about to devote his body to working the soil. George Col-lier's field notes from this interview, recorded in Spanglish, describe this man as saying that "He liked the *campo*, but there were no *medios* there. All the work in the campo was *a base de cuerpo*, and he wanted a *vida más aprovechable*" (GAC interview notes, April 1983).

16. In 1963–64, the mayor reported that the minimum wage had just been raised to sixty *pesetas* a day.

17. I put the word "unskilled" in quotation marks because most of the men who left Los Olivos were, of course, very skilled farmers.

18. Even though events in Los Olivos paralleled those occurring in many rural communities (Aceves and Douglass 1976; Aceves 1971; Barrett 1974; Be-har 1986; Brandes 1975; Gregory 1978; Harding 1984; Martínez-Alier 1971), I focus on what happened in the village (see G. Collier 1987, 186–202).

19. I, of course, attribute this change in how people talked about gossip to the fact that in the 1960s people who talked about gossiping neighbors revealed their understanding of, and concern for, social conventions, whereas in the 1980s people who mentioned the neighbors' gossip could be accused of letting their actions be dictated by others rather than thinking for themselves.

20. Hooper (1994) observes that all Spaniards became wealthier during the economic boom years but that the status hierarchy did not change.

21. In the early 1980s, I read the phrase "tanto cobras, tanto vales" in a newspaper article. Unfortunately, I did not bother to cut out the article, nor did I note the newspaper or date, although I believe I found the article in the fea-tures section of *El País*. I remember that the author fulminated against the phrase, arguing that people's moral worth could not, and should not, be judged by their salaries. David Gilmore told me that he heard the phrase "tanto tienes, tanto vales" from landowners and agricultural workers in the Andalusian com-munity where he worked (personal communication).

22. As should be obvious, I am assuming that there is a relationship between stratification based on wealth and stratification based on virtue or honor. I know that some ethnographers of Spain argue that "'Prestige' derived from integrity has no connexion with economic power" (Lison-Tolosana 1966, 108). But I agree with John Davis that wealth and virtue are linked, even if some rich people are immoral and some poor people are saints (1977, 97). I am therefore not interested in asking whether wealth and virtue are linked, or even why they are linked. Rather, I want to explore differences in how the connection is made.

23. As Dahrendorf has observed, "In the last analysis, established norms are nothing but ruling norms, i.e., norms defended by the sanctioning agencies of society and those who control them" (1968, 174). In chapter 4 of my 1988 book, I explore Dahrendorf's argument more fully.

24. Social scientists have long known that market processes privilege the already wealthy (Weber 1966).

25. Lison-Tolosana, in his discussion of stratification in an Aragonese community, provides another example of how wealth might lead to virtue when he suggests that "the sense of shame and responsibility is . . . much more developed among the groups of high position than among those in lower levels [because] the eyes of the community as a whole are on them" (1966, 108).

26. I collected only a few employment histories from women, primarily because most of the women I interviewed did not hold jobs in the formal sector. Women, however successful they had been, tended to provide bare, factual accounts of the jobs they had held. A schoolteacher, who earned an excellent salary by village standards, told a simple story of expected career advancement. She talked about her education, the university and job entrance exams she had passed, and her teaching positions. She also mentioned that it had been easier to become a teacher at the time she entered the profession than it was in 1983. Another woman, who had migrated with her husband and small children to a northern city, simply listed the unskilled jobs she held as a cleaning lady for individuals, churches, and shops before finally obtaining a permanent position on the cleaning staff of a large company. She did mention, however, that she had obtained one cleaning job in a shop because the shopkeeper thought well of her. Another woman, who found work in a factory after the factory where she first worked had dismissed her in the process of cutting its labor force, mentioned that she refused to return to the first factory when it later offered her a job because the the second factory provided better benefits. Although women offered personal reasons for some of the job decisions they made, none of the women I interviewed told heroic sagas of obstacles overcome, skills acquired, and risks taken.

## Chapter Two

1. —Nadie se casa con la precipitación que tú deseas, y que daría lugar a interpretaciones, quizá desfavorables a la honra de mi querida hija . . . (Pérez Galdós 1983, 106–7).

2. Although I first accepted Conchi's observation at face value (for I, too, thought that the courting customs villagers had observed in the 1960s were not

"normal"), I soon put her words together with Foucault's analysis of "normaliz-ing discourses" (1977a, 1977b, 1978). The next day, as I wrote up my notes from the interview, I remember thinking, "Welcome to disciplinary society."

3. Villagers in the 1960s were too polite to ask why my husband and I had married so young. In any case, the answer must have seemed obvious: we had a baby. On the few occasions when I tried to tell friends that we had been married more than a year before the baby was born, they never questioned my story. Their faces, however, tended to assume an expression best described as a mixture of disbelief and pity. When I returned to Los Olivos in the 1980s, I no longer had to explain why I married young. Instead, most of the villagers and emigrants I interviewed were then wondering why they, or their senior relatives, had post-poned marriage for so long.

4. The Spanish phrases that I recorded in my field notes describing these changes in courtship customs were: "Antes no salían de la falda de la madre, ahora van solos a todos lados"; "Entonces la gente no le corría tanta prisa casarse, ahora ¡ que se casan el día que se ponen novios!"; "Antes los hombres no entraban sin pedir, ahora entran sin pedir"; "Antes los hombres respetaban a las mujeres, ahora hay menos respeto."

5. I developed the analysis of gender conceptions presented in this section with Michelle Zimbalist Rosaldo while we taught a course together at Stanford University on "Women in Cross-Cultural Perspective." The course was later re-named "Sex Roles and Society."

6. See also Hirschon (1978) about Greek ideas of women as "open."

7. The idea that men's bodies are (or should be) impenetrable suggests a reason why the anus, as a hole through which a man can be penetrated, might acquire special meaning (Spaniards tell endless *culo* [ass] jokes). It also suggests a reason why anal penetration might be perceived as the act that transforms a (superior) man into an (inferior) woman (see Brandes 1980, 95–96). In con-trast, people who use a discourse of occupational achievement tend to portray the act of sexually desiring a man, rather than the act of being penetrated, as the sign of (inferior) femininity.

8. Some ethnographers of Spain (e.g., Pitt-Rivers 1954, 96) suggest that men refuse to marry women who had former fiancés because they fear becoming "retrospective" cuckolds. I suggest that such men *are* cuckolds (rather than merely "retrospective" ones) because they have—by marrying a woman they did not have to marry—knowingly allowed their wives to sleep with other men.

9. Once again I do not want to trace a particular cultural tradition but rather to use a "destiny is anatomy" line of argument to suggest reasons why people who negotiate relations of social inequality by telling stories about individual achievements might invent, and continually reinvent, such gender stereotypes as emotional reproducers and rational producers—even though women also pro-duce goods and men help care for children.

10. Humans, including babies, cannot be marketed without blurring the crucial ideological distinction between people and things, a distinction vital to both capitalist and socialist political ideologies (Radin 1987). In reality, of course, the distinction is always blurred. Every day wage earners "sell" their bodies and minds to employers for several hours. And "free market"

ideologues do advocate the commercialization of such "services" as incubating embryos.

11. Laqueur has characterized this difference in gender conceptions as one between a "one-body model," in which women are imagined as inferior men, and a "two-body model," in which women are imagined as men's opposites (1990).

12. Humans, as I just noted, need to produce both babies and goods if they are to survive. People must care for one another without calculating costs, even as the (imagined) world scarcity of time and goods requires people to rationally calculate costs and benefits if they are not to end up hungry and despised. Altruism, however, always appears odd in a world dominated by market rationality. It seems irrational, and therefore incomprehensible. As a result, people who live in market-dominated societies, where people's actions testify to their intentions, inevitably try to find reasons for altruistic behavior. The "economic man" invented by economists has to have a "subjective" hierarchy of desires—fortunately discovered by psychologists.

13. I am implying that people who use a discourse of inherited property tend to define the good woman/bad woman opposition differently from those who use a discourse of occupational achievement. When people tell stories about inherited rights to property, they commonly focus on a woman's (reputation for) chastity: a good woman does not, a bad woman does. When people tell stories about occupational achievements, in contrast, they tend to focus on a woman's motives: a good woman succumbs to emotion even if she is not yet married to the man she loves; a bad woman calculates the costs and benefits of engaging in sexual intercourse. Lillian Rubin, who interviewed working-class Americans, characterized their understanding of the good woman/bad woman distinction this way: a good woman does, but does not plan; a bad woman does and plans (i.e., practices contraception) (1976, 63).

14. Durkheim, writing at the end of the nineteenth century, endorsed the argument of an evolutionist who claimed that women's brains had gotten smaller as men's brains had increased in size (1933, 60). Although Durkheim clearly believed that women's increasing stupidity contributed to social solidarity, he did not seem to think highly of silly Parisian women.

15. Doña Perfecta's and Pepe Rey's different understandings of the causes of social chaos are reflected in their preferred origin myths. Doña Perfecta subscribes to the biblical story of Adam and Eve in which a woman causes the Fall from Grace by succumbing to temptation. Pepe Rey subscribes to Darwin's theory of evolution in which—at least as I was taught the myth in college—men, who create society by inventing (bourgeois) marriage, can also destroy society by refusing to care for the helpless women they impregnate. But if dominant myths tend to blame one sex, subordinate narratives can reverse culpability. In Doña Perfecta's world, for example, people could blame cuckolds for causing chaos by allowing their women to mate promiscuously. In market societies, people can accuse "masculine" women of destroying society by failing to be lovable.

16. During both of my visits to Los Olivos, the people I spoke with often used a human/animal contrast to evaluate their own and others' behaviors. But between visits the criteria seem to have changed. In 1963–64, "animals" suc-

cumbed to carnal desires, "humans" understood social conventions. By 1983–84, "animals" followed the herd, "humans" thought for themselves. As this example suggests, people during both time periods disparaged animal behaviors. But over time their assumptions about the relationship between human and animal behaviors shifted. For those who invoked the human/animal contrast in 1963–64, humans did not succumb to carnal desires. If they did, they were "animals." In the 1980s, however, humans who would think for themselves could not disregard their animal instincts. They had to take them into account when deciding how to behave. In other words, as people from Los Olivos shifted their assumptions about how humans should deal with their animal natures, they also shifted their assumptions about the nature of animals.

17. "Nature," of course, is always culturally defined. Whether or not "woman" is everywhere associated with "nature" rather than "culture" (Ortner 1974), the "nature" that correlates with conceptions of femininity varies spatially and historically—as does the idea of "culture" associated with conceptions of masculinity (MacCormack and Strathern 1980).

18. An interesting thing about this and other stories of broken courtship told to the Prices is what their informants did not say. In many cases, the person who was deemed too poor or immoral belonged to a socialist family, but the Prices' informants never mentioned prewar political affiliation (G. Collier 1987, 183).

19. In the early 1960s, villagers—particularly the elders who controlled courtships—assessed wealth primarily in terms of property ownership. When describing someone who was rich, villagers would say "es muy rico/a" [s/he is very rich], "tiene mucho capital" [s/he has lots of capital], or, more informally, "tiene mucha tela" [s/he has lots of cloth/folding stuff], or, still more informally, hold up a hand and rub the fingers together to suggest money.

20. Many ethnographers of Spain and other southern European countries describe the custom of drawing lots to equalize the inheritance shares of siblings (e.g., Behar 1986; Friedl 1962; Campbell 1964).

21. RSP field notes, July 1964.

22. RSP field notes, July 1964.

23. RSP field notes, July 1964. In the article he later wrote with Sally Price, they summarize young men's reasons for wanting to cut short the intermediate stages of courtship: "Boys do not like to linger at this stage, partly because the pre-dinner visits coincide with the evening drinking hours of adult men. Furthermore, these *novios* have little to do after dinner when all the older boys are visiting their formal *novias*. Only upon asking entrance can a boy participate in the usual daily round for men" (1966a, 308).

24. RSP field notes, June 1964.

25. RSP field notes, July 1964.

26. RSP field notes, June 1964.

27. RSP field notes, June 1964.

28. RSP field notes, July 1964.

29. To my knowledge, none of the village's unwed mothers had been impregnated by a village man.

30. RSP field notes, July 1964.

31. One woman, for example, told Shelly that a woman "is never free" [nunca es libre] whereas "a man can do what he wants even if he acts without thinking" [lleva siempre su razón aunque vaya sin ella] (MZ formal interview 23, 1965).

32. MZ formal interview 22, 1965.

33. MZ and SS formal interview 35, 1965.

34. RSP field notes, July 1964. When trying to explain why there were so many spinsters in Los Olivos, the mayor told George Collier that "Spanish men will not marry just any woman: a man will not consider marrying a girl who has been had by another man. He said that he knew of cases where a girl had been kissed at a dance and thereafter could not marry" (GAC field notes, October 1964).

35. It is little wonder that villagers were very suspicious of women from other towns who married (or were engaged to) men from Los Olivos.

36. RSP field notes, July 1964.

37. MZ field notes, June 1965.

38. MZ field notes, June 1965.

39. MZ formal interview 23, 1965.

40. Because I never heard any villager say anything nice about the accused murderess, she may indeed have been guilty. Nevertheless, her fate provided a graphic demonstration of how vulnerable a woman could become if she lost her honor.

41. MZ formal interview 35, 1965.

42. MZ field notes, July 1965. Older women also enjoyed bawdy jokes. In the summer of 1964, Richard Price was walking with Manuel when they came upon "three old women shrouded in black sitting in a doorway." Manuel said, "very loudly, '*Aqui es la calle de las viejas*,' [Here is the street of old women] to which one of the women replied, '*Las gallinas viejas tienen la mejor carne*' [Old hens have the tastiest meat], and invited the young men to give them a try" (RSP field notes, July 1964).

43. RSP field notes, July 1964.

44. RSP field notes, July 1964.

45. RSP field notes, July 1964.

46. MZ field notes, June 1965.

47. When the Prices interviewed an old woman about sex during courtship, she said that she was like all girls; she wanted to do it too. Respect for her family kept her from taking this step (RSP field notes, July 1964).

48. SHP field notes, July 1964.

49. MZ field notes, June 1965. By the phrase "got married before she got married," the young woman obviously meant "had sexual intercourse before the wedding."

50. Although novias in Los Olivos were as vulnerable as those described by Pitt-Rivers (1954, 96–97), I have no evidence that Los Olivos novias who feared losing their novios used love magic as did novias in the village Pitt-Rivers studied. It is always difficult to prove an absence, but neither the Prices nor I, after repeated questioning, could find anyone who claimed to have used or to know about love magic. Richard Price, however, did elicit two stories involving con-

sultations with "wise people." A Los Olivos mother consulted a *sabia* from another town about her son's illness, and a woman visited a famous *sabio* near Seville to find out what had happened to her brothers who disappeared during the civil war (RSP field notes, July 1964).

51. RSP field notes, July 1964.

52. Spinsters who kept houses for their unmarried brothers could escape the fate of the overworked spinster I observed. As long as a woman assumed the duty of caring for an adult man—whether husband, brother, father, or son—she could politely refuse other women's requests for help by observing that she had to go home to fix her man's meals, wash his clothes, and so forth.

53. RSP field notes, July 1964.

54. MZ field notes, June 1965.

55. RSP field notes, June 1964.

56. RSP field notes, July 1964.

57. Despite the reported lack of formality, Richard Price concluded that the structural pattern of courtship fifty years before "was far closer to the Los Olivos ideal than is that of modern *noviazgo*. Adolescents had apparently sown enough of their wild oats in the socially sanctioned pre-*noviazgo* period so that only 1 in 10 formal *noviazgos*, once entered upon, did not end in marriage, compared to 1 in 2 today. Thus, prolonged 'playing the field' was followed by relatively late entrance into a formal *noviazgo* that had excellent chances of ending in marriage after four to six years" (Price 1964).

58. When Richard Price writes of "less formal families" he is probably echoing his informants' use of the word "formal," a word that implied high status and honorable behavior in the 1960s. For a villager to describe a family as less formal was to cast aspersions on the honor of its members.

59. It also made sense for poor women to appear chaste in order to merit the charity that they, and their poor families, needed to beg from elite property owners and power holders. Because members of the regional elite represented working-class women as guardians of family virtue and piety, in contrast to working-class men, whom they denigrated (see Maddox 1986, chap. 7), a poor woman who conformed to elite images of female modesty was more likely to be successful in begging aid for her impoverished kin than was a woman who appeared to embrace dangerous socialist doctrines.

60. In order to calculate the relationship between wealth and courtship history in Los Olivos, the Prices created two groups: the "rich," comprising 20 percent of individuals of courting age between 1945 and 1964, and the "poor," comprising the other 80 percent of such individuals (1966b, 533).

61. The Prices calculated a higher celibacy rate for children of wealthy families than for children from poor ones—20 percent for rich adolescents compared with 15 percent for the poor. Although they cite "idiosyncratic shortcomings" as the main reason why "rich" adolescents failed to find partners, George Collier notes that some of the supposedly "loose" or "domineering" women and the "shy" or "homosexual" men were from merchant families that had supported the socialist cause before the war—a fact never mentioned by villagers who discussed broken courtships with the Prices in 1964 (1987, 183).

62. The dominant landowners created an environment that not only fostered increasingly "formal" courtship customs but also encouraged the denigration of outsiders and the postponement of marriage. Villagers who contrasted their "formal" courtship customs with the "lax morals" of outsiders preserved scarce municipal lands for people born in Los Olivos by encouraging endogamous marriages. And not only were young couples expected to acquire and furnish a complete house before the wedding (as I discuss in the next chapter), but both parents and suitors benefited from prolonging a girl's (supposed) freedom from adult obligations.

63. I actually have information on twenty men who were born between 1945 and 1949. But I have left out of my calculations one man who finally married at the age of forty, long after everyone who knew him expected him to remain a bachelor. The other nineteen men born in this period married in their twenties.

64. I do not know enough about people's use of birth control to speculate on the relationship between age of marriage and the use or availability of birth control. If I had to guess, however, I would suggest that the dropping age of marriage led to the increased use of birth control rather than the increased availability of birth control contributing to the declining age of marriage. After all, the average age at marriage for women fell most dramatically for the cohort of women born between 1935 and 1939, who reached childbearing age at a time when the Franco regime was still strong, and the Catholic Church limited the availability of most forms of birth control.

65. By the 1980s, Los Olivos had become a place for youngsters brought up in urban areas to seek potential mates. Many migrants from the Sierra de Aracena returned to their natal villages in the summer, particularly during the holiday month of August, bringing their adolescent children, and even the children of friends, to meet other young people who shared their accent and cultural heritage. When we interviewed migrants in 1983, for example, we noticed that many of their children had married, or were engaged to, young people who had been born in, or to parents from, Los Olivos and nearby Sierra communities. In the 1980s, villagers and migrants were far more likely to stress similarities among Sierra de Aracena towns than to point out the lax morals of neighbors. Instead of criticizing nearby communities, people from Sierra de Aracena communities tended to join together in emphasizing the differences between their wholesome rural pleasures and the dissolute entertainments pursued by urban youth.

66. Urbano reported that "ya me pelaba las piernas trás ella" [I was already running after her] (GAC field notes, May 1983).

67. The Spanish phrase she used was "Este es pa' mi," a phrase I also heard from other people.

68. No longer could a man's visits to prostitutes signify his respect for his novia. Rather, a man insulted his novia by openly visiting prostitutes and called into question the depth of his affection for her.

69. The people I interviewed recognized, of course, that men also "have" children. But the phrase, when applied to men, lost the implications of "bearing" and "nurturing" that it had when applied to women.

70. The widow and her daughter also expressed different views of why one of the unwed mothers never married, despite having received several offers from

other men. The widow said she refused marriage because she did not want her child to have a stepfather. The daughter said she never married because having found her true love she could never love someone else. The widow and her daughter also expressed contradictory views of abortion, then a hot topic in Spain. The widow was against abortion for any reason, even to save the mother's life. Her daughter said that since rich women were going to obtain abortions anyway, by going abroad, Spain should legalize the procedure and make it available through social security hospitals so that the poor would have equal access with the rich.

## Chapter Three

1. Doña Perfecta's husband "tenía tanta hacienda como buena mano para gastarla. El juego y las mujeres cautivaban de tal modo el corazón de Manuel María José, que habría dado en tierra con toda su fortuna si más pronto que él para derrocharla no estuviera la muerte para llevársele a él" (Pérez Galdós 1983, 28).

2. I have been amazed at the similarities between the household and farm utensils used by Los Olivos villagers in the 1960s and the items displayed at colonial museums in the United States, such as Mount Vernon and period homes in Philadelphia.

3. Just as I argue that the change from co-owners to coworkers does not reflect a shift from households as units of production to households as units of consumption, I do not want to suggest that it reflects a decline in landowner- ship. During both my periods of fieldwork, most of the people born in Los Oli- vos owned land even if not very much of it. What changed, therefore, was not the fact of having land but the role of land in determining family members' oc- cupations, incomes, and lifestyles.

4. I take the term "class-divided" from Giddens (1981, 7)

5. SHP field notes, July 1964.

6. Using the terminology for property transfers at marriage suggested by Davis (1977, 184), a Los Olivos groom received a "marriage gift" and a bride received "paraphernalia" at the time of the wedding.

7. In Spanish, they reported that a groom furnished "el dormitorio y la bodega," while the bride provided "todo lo demas."

8. The "bed and sausage" provided by a groom symbolized, of course, the site and the equipment for begetting legitimate heirs. In a village where men regularly visited prostitutes, the marital bed symbolically distinguished between uses of the "sausage": a "sausage" produced legitimate heirs when used in the marriage bed, illegitimate bastards when used outside it. It is thus no accident that a groom was expected to provide the "dormitorio."

9. Some male ethnographers of Mediterranean communities have stressed the role of fathers, rather than mothers, in providing their children's wedding goods (see Pina-Cabral 1986, 51). I do not know whether this emphasis reflects regional variations or the fact that ethnographers tend to hang out with people of their own sex.

10. When I toured the wedding house shortly before we left Los Olivos, my hosts proudly displayed the groom's new clothing, which included several sets of summer and winter underwear, each piece neatly monogrammed with his initials.

11. RSP field notes, June 1964.

12. SHP field notes, June 1964.

13. SHP field notes, July 1964.

14. Although villagers portrayed parenthood as requiring "sacrifices," childlessness was clearly worse. Without children, a married couple was deprived of the ability to act "for others," as well as deprived of the most important standard for assessing the success or failure of their actions. Couples without children appeared to be acting only for themselves, and thus inevitably selfish.

15. Actually, the custom of wearing a black wedding dress was dying out. The first village bride to wear a white wedding dress married in 1959; the bride who married in 1964 also wore white.

16. MZ formal interview 1, 1965. In Los Olivos, employers who wanted to hire female wage workers went, or sent messengers, to women's houses.

17. JFC field notes, December 1963.

18. Corbin and Corbin, in their study of the Andalusian town of Ronda, suggest that "the poor are unable to pursue the logic of class without ambivalence" because "the premiss of class politics is contrary to that of the politics of honour. . . . Mobilization in class terms requires people to act in public not as whole men but on class status alone" (1987, 146). Poor men in Los Olivos, however, do not seem to have suffered from such ambivalence. Instead of mobilizing in "class" terms as coworkers subject to employers, village men before 1965 appear to have mobilized in "status group" terms as independent managers of family estates who had been deprived, by political coercion rather than weak economic bargaining position, not of their fair share of the products of their labor but of their rightful access to productive resources.

19. When I first visited Los Olivos, I noticed that people seemed to make an implicit distinction between jobs "owned" by workers and jobs "owned" by employers. A friend, for example, spoke of the *peón caminero* (the government employee charged with maintaining the local highway) and his family as if they were autonomous property owners whose household assets enabled family members to support themselves without having to work for others. Like landowners who had undisputed rights to the crops that grew in their fields, the roadworker—in this woman's view—had an undisputed right to the wages (and house) that symbolically grew on his stretch of highway. She even expected the roadworker to bestow productive highways on his sons and sons-in-law (through his political connections), just as landowners bestowed fields on their heirs (through their politically enforced ownership of private property). In my friend's view, the roadworker occupied a very different social position from agricultural day laborers who had to demean themselves by begging landowners to allot them, and their family members, jobs in the landowners' possession.

20. This urban wife's wedding furniture, made by Sierra de Aracena carpenters in the 1950s, did look heavy and out of place in the cramped, working-class apartment where she lived. I wondered, however, if the furniture she despised

might not seem valuable to someone from the upper classes who would recognize her pieces as superb examples of Spanish rural craftmanship.

21. After listing the drawbacks of urban living, several of the urban housewives I interviewed did defend their lifestyles by listing some disadvantages of rural life. They pointed out that old village houses required more care and upkeep than recently built apartments, and that village houses tended to lack the kitchen and bathroom appliances commonly found in urban dwellings. Some women also observed that although rural life might be "tranquil," they preferred the bustle and excitement of urban life. Several parents pointed out that urban schools offered children a wider range of educational opportunities than were available in the small village school.

22. I do not think that there were fewer daughters in the 1980s than in the 1960s. The demographic shift to fewer children occurred earlier in the century. When I first visited Los Olivos in the 1960s, there were a couple of large families. But, as I discuss later, the parents were disparaged as "animals" who had been unable to restrain their sexual appetites. "Good parents" in the 1960s consciously limited the number of heirs who would have to split limited properties.

23. Some emigrants working in the private sector were employed by local businesses, such as bus lines or small construction or janitorial firms. But most of those I interviewed seemed to work in factories owned by multinational corporations or in construction and transportation firms that were national rather than local in scope. It is also true that people preferred to work for the government or for large businesses because such jobs tended to provide better benefits and to offer more secure employment.

24. Although I never heard villagers in the 1980s distinguish between "productive" and "reproductive" labor, I think the social world they lived in encouraged a cultural distinction between work that earned money and work that saved money—between labor that earned wages or produced profits because it was done for exchange in the market and labor that did not earn money because it was done for oneself in the home.

25. Unfortunately, I was never able to find out how people from Los Olivos would have responded to my pessimistic analysis of women's declining power since I was never able to take charge of conversations long enough to state my argument clearly. I also developed my analysis away from Los Olivos.

26. I cannot recall any of the people from Los Olivos contrasting *trabajo* with *ocio* (pleasure), although this cultural contrast was propagated by newspapers and magazines advertising paid entertainment, such as films, theaters, nightclubs, restaurants, etc.

27. In her field notes from 1964, Sally Price reported a young woman's statement "that her parents talk very little together" and commented, "From what we have seen, this is completely true—they almost never say much more than *Buenos Días!*" (SHP field notes, July 1964). Rereading this quote from her field notes in the late 1980s, Sally Price observed that "this now strikes me as a rather gross overstatement."

28. JFC formal interview, February 1983.

29. JFC formal interview, April 1983.

30. In the 1980s, I noticed that bars in Los Olivos had become more hospitable to women. The girlie pictures that decorated their walls in the 1960s had disappeared.

31. JFC interview notes, February 1983.

32. JFC interview notes, February 1983.

33. JFC interview notes, April 1983.

34. JFC formal interview 4, 1964.

35. JFC interview notes, February 1983.

36. Andrés said that he worked hard to *poner la casa* (JFC interview notes, April 1983).

37. One older woman I spoke with in 1983 made the link between a husband's salary and his family's lifestyle when she observed that her former neighbors were having difficulty making ends meet because the husband's salary was so low. When I asked her if her son's family also had trouble making ends meet on his salary, she replied that they were doing well because her son earned more money than the former neighbor she was pitying.

38. GAC interview notes, April 1983.

39. The word she used was "aburrida" (JFC field notes, February 1983).

40. I thus became a witting, rather than an unwitting, beneficiary of the status implications of housework in Los Olivos. I have never lived in such a well-kept house, before or since.

41. MZ field notes, June 1965.

42. MZ formal interview 23, 1965.

43. MZ formal interview 25, 1965.

44. Pina-Cabral tells of an old woman in northern Portugal who used the myth of Adam and Eve to argue that women's "unhappy lot" began at "the start of the world." In the view of this woman, "women have always been morally weak while men, who know what is right, are controlled and tempted by women into evil acts" (1986, 82).

45. Corbin and Corbin (1987) observe that women's talk appears to be "gossip" because women exchange information about other people, whereas men, instead of seeking information about others, try to display their own knowledge and potency.

46. MZ formal interview 25, 1965.

47. As recorded in my field notes for October 1963. At the time, I thought that perhaps married women in Los Olivos complained of their hard lot because most of them had to do agricultural work in the fields during summer months. I no longer think this was the case. I noticed, for example, that even during the peak labor times of winter, such as the olive harvest, women tended to spend only a few long days in the fields. The rest of the time they stayed home.

48. After noticing that the doctor's waiting room was always full of married women complaining of various aches and pains, I finally realized that illness played an important role in women's lives. Not only did illness testify to a mother's sufferings (she had ruined her health in sacrificing herself for her children), but a woman had to get sick from time to time in order to participate in women's networks. Only by becoming ill herself could a woman allow her friends to repay the visits she had paid them when they were ill.

49. Actually, husbands did not get control over all of a wife's property. During the Franco regime, a woman's property was legally divided into three conceptual categories: the *estimada* portion of her dowry, over which her husband assumed complete control, the *inestimada* portion, which "was presumably under her control" but which she could not sell or mortgage except with her husband's permission, and her *parafernales*, which were not considered part of her dowry and over which she had special privileges (Sponsler 1982, 1610).

50. It is also true that divorce was illegal at that time in Spain. Nevertheless, I did hear about four couples who had separated. In two of the cases, the men involved had taken up with other women. In the other two, the couple held periodic reconciliations.

51. JFC field notes, November 1963.

52. Rogers's (1985) discussion of a wife's subordinate status in a French peasant community with stem families suggests that women may have difficulty claiming de facto authority on the basis of their "sacrifices" when impartible inheritance casts them in the role of contributing little property to the estate that determines the family's social status.

53. JFC field notes, April 1983.

54. JFC field notes, January 1983.

55. Certainly the men I saw interacting outside bars exhibited the aggressive-defensive stance described by those ethnographers. Men actively asserted their views and appeared constantly wary of being tricked or put down. When village men carried the Virgin's float through the streets during Holy Week in 1964, for example, they halted the procession for half an hour while they argued over how to pass the Virgin's canopy under low electric wires. The Virgin bobbed up and down as each man asserted his opinion and refused to listen to anyone else's. The rest of us enjoyed the show.

56. Whereas Papataxiarchis (1991) treats the differences between male friendship and kinship in Greece as evidence for the fact that they are unrelated, I draw the opposite conclusion. Although I would not put kinship and friendship on a continuum, I would argue that it is the importance of kinship for determining social status that gives male friendship its special qualities. In societies where inherited property appears to be the most important determinant of social inequality, kinship constructs friendship as its imagined opposite. Just as "modern" business practices, which claim to reward people for the value of their labor, construct the family as a haven of noncontingent acceptance and love (Collier, Rosaldo, and Yanagisako 1982), so inherited property, which establishes a hierarchical social order, constructs same-sex friendship as a haven of egalitarianism.

57. During working hours, wage laborers might have to submit to employers and overseers, but after work, a man could seek companionship from those who treated him as equal. In many Andalusian communities, bars attracted different clienteles, stratified by wealth (see Maddox 1993, 136). Los Olivos was too small to support many bars. It had only two and men commonly patronized both.

58. The many similarities between men's "don't fool with me" stance in what I call "brideservice" societies and men's aggressive-defensive stance in stratified, class-divided societies where people use a discourse of inherited status

result, I suggest, from the fact that men in both types of societies have to worry primarily about losing status relative to other men (see J. Collier 1988; Collier and Rosaldo 1981).

59. Some married men did, of course, actually waste the family estates they were charged with managing. Two women born before 1920 blamed their poverty on their fathers. One woman described her father as a bad businessman who had had to sell off his wife's inherited land to pay his debts. Another woman told us that her father had been tricked by gambling buddies into losing a large tract of land.

60. JFC field notes, June 1983.

61. JFC field notes, April 1983.

62. JFC field notes, February 1964. I doubted this statement at the time I heard it. In my field notes, I observed that "This is what [the woman] said, but it is questionable how true it is."

63. People assured me that in the 1960s employers usually gave the wages earned by unmarried children directly to their parents. The children then obtained spending money from their mothers.

64. My handwritten notes, taken during the interview itself, record his words as "los andaluces tienen más machismo." (JFC formal interview, May 1983).

65. Even at the time I wrote up my field notes, I disputed Jose's assumption that Andalusian husbands could dispose of a wife's property. In my field notes, I added in parentheses, after his statement, "I don't think this is true, legally, given that a widower has only usufruct of his wife's property unless she wills it to him specifically."

66. "Trabaja en la calle, la pobre." As should be obvious, Pilar was worried about Clara because in a social world where people's status is determined by inherited property, women who had to work in the "street" were far more likely to be dishonored than women who were able to remain in the family "house." When I lived in Los Olivos in the 1960s, it was indeed a tragedy for a woman who had once been able to work at home to have to work in the street.

## Chapter Four

1. —Yo te enseñaré los deberes de hija, que has olvidado (Pérez Galdós 1983, 286).

2. JFC field notes, February 1983. This woman continued by stating, "Now María's daughter collects her own wages for agricultural work. But when I was young and my parents took me into the country to work, my father collected the wages for the whole family."

3. JFC field notes, January 1983.

4. JFC field notes, February 1983.

5. Indeed, Pepe Rey did grow up to be an engineer. Galdós observed that "Years passed, and then more years. The boy grew and continued to draw lines. Finally, he drew one called the Tarragona-Mont Blanch [railroad] line. His first real toy was the 120-meter bridge over the Francolí River" (Pérez Galdós 1960, 19).

6. Villagers' treatment of infants also differed from what George Collier and I had observed among the Maya Indians of Zinacantan, Chiapas, Mexico. Zina-

canteco adults usually spoke softly to infants and avoided overexciting them. But Zinacantecos did not share Dr. Spock's vision of infants as autonomous individuals whose needs and desires deserved equal consideration with those of adults. Instead, Zinacantecos believed that infants' souls were easily dislodged from their bodies, causing illness and death. They thus avoided any actions that might frighten or startle an infant.

7. No villager actually told us that small children were seen as toys, as reported by Hirschon in relation to Greece (1992, 37).

8. SHP field notes, July 1964.

9. RSP field notes, August 1964.

10. MZ formal interview 16, 1965.

11. By suggesting that these *loca* girls would attract gossip, even though they might be *buenas* (good), this woman implied that outward behavior—specifically, conformity to social rules—was a more important determinant of a person's reputation (and hence life chances) than inward qualities or personal capacities.

12. See also Campbell (1964, 158) on how children learn by watching and imitating. Once, during Mass in the Los Olivos church, I observed a little boy pretend to wash a handkerchief, perfectly imitating the actions of an adult woman at the washing fountain. When he accidently dropped the handkerchief, he exclaimed, "Ay, se me cayó al agua" [Oh, it fell in the water] in exactly the tone of voice that women used. There were audible titters from the pews behind.

13. GAC field notes, March 1983.

14. JFC field notes, February 1964.

15. The Prices, for example, were amazed when none of the children in a family told their mother about a large hole one sister had burned in an expensive blanket. They concluded that "apparently no one has the courage to inform [the mother] of household accidents, . . . they just let her find out for herself, which she often probably doesn't at all" (RSP field notes, July 1964).

16. JFC field notes, February 1964. Given young people's defiance of social rules, I was skeptical when, in 1983, an older woman declared that "if parents in the old days told their children that the children could not go to a fiesta that the children wanted to go to, then the children simply did not go" (JFC field notes, February 1983).

17. Many a mother told me, with evident pride, that her little darling was "más malo(a) para comer."

18. JFC field notes, March 1983. When I asked a friend if television was responsible for convincing mothers in the 1980s that infants and toddlers needed yogurt, she replied that she thought doctors were recommending it.

19. JFC interview notes, March 1983.

20. JFC formal interview, February 1983.

21. JFC interview notes, March 1983.

22. GAC interview notes, June 1983. The notes, as recorded in Spanglish, actually said: "We have been *pobre*, but we have *aprovechared tiempo al máximo*. We have had no *lujo*, no *privilegio*, except for the *hijos: colegio, colegio*. I don't want them to be like me [i.e., an unskilled laborer]. That is my point of view. *Lujo pa' mi no existe. Aun desprecio el lujo*."

23. Indeed, I was surprised that many emigrant parents sent their children to private, parochial schools. Because none of the families I interviewed were rich by national standards, their expenditures on education represented a major portion of their income. One man said that his wife's entire salary as a nurse went to pay for their children's private schooling.

24. JFC formal interview, May 1983.

25. JFC field notes, July 1980.

26. The contrast, in Spanish, was between those who had "cultura" and those who remained "brutos."

27. JFC field notes, May 1983.

28. GAC formal interview, June 1983.

29. GAC field notes, March 1983.

30. GAC formal interview, June 1983.

31. JFC field notes, June 1983.

32. JFC interview notes, February 1983.

33. GAC interview notes, July 1983. In Spain, students who hope to attend a university must obtain appropriate scores on nationwide university entrance exams.

34. JFC formal interview, June 1983.

35. GAC formal interview, February 1983.

36. JFC formal interview, May 1983.

37. Even parents who had built successful small businesses appeared to feel cheated if their children dropped out of school to work. One couple, who ran a bar, said that they wanted their children to attend a university even though the parents would then lose their children's help. These parents spoke of their small business primarily as an insurance policy. "If [we] were to die now," they said, "[we] would at least leave [our children] a going business. The bar is all paid for and is successful. [Our children] will thus have an inheritance, which is something [we] did not have when [we] started out with nothing" (GAC formal interview, May 1983). I believe that parents with small businesses did not want their children to succeed them because their enterprises were so small and labor-intensive. The one emigrant who ran a more capital-intensive enterprise was unfortunately childless. I therefore do not know if he would have prepared a child to succeed him.

38. JFC formal interview, June 1983. One woman expressed the depth of her parental anxiety and guilt when she observed that she did not want her children to be able to say that their parents had not done everything they could for them (JFC field notes, April 1983).

39. GAC field notes, February 1983.

40. GAC formal interview, February 1983.

41. JFC formal interview, March 1983.

42. JFC field notes, August 1984.

43. JFC field notes, March 1983. I wonder if the term *confianza* had acquired a new significance in the 1980s. My notes from the 1960s suggest that, at that time, a person of *confianza* was a friend who could be trusted not to repeat confidential information to others. As a result, one could speak openly to him or her. The mother I spoke with in 1983, however, did not mention repeat-

ing information to outsiders. She implied that a person shared confidences because the confidant shared confidences in return.

44. Perhaps the general experience of upward mobility is partly responsible for the strong parent-child bonds we observed. In 1983, most parents of teenage and young adult children successfully provided their children with more education and better job opportunities than the parents experienced as young adults. In 1983, parental sacrifices—and pressures to study—visibly paid off. Most children, particularly those who had obtained higher education, were appropriately grateful. But what will happen to parent-child relations if the economic situation deteriorates and most children find themselves condemned to the lowly class position of their parents?

45. JFC field notes, May 1983.

46. Although my husband and I tried to interview people about birth control in the 1980s, we learned very little because both we and those we interviewed found the topic embarrassing. Most couples refused to talk about their own practices but rather told us that "people" tended to use withdrawal (*echarse pa' atrás*). They also said that "people" knew about the pill and condoms. One couple mentioned using what I understood as "Ogino-Knaus," a calendar method advocated by the Catholic Church. In 1964, Richard Price reported that

> Last night I talked with Juan [an unmarried man] for about an hour about birth control . . . three methods are known here [in Los Olivos]; condoms can be bought in any pharmacy for 8–10 pesetas each; some people practice rhythm; and many men go "*por atrás*" (i.e., practice "withdrawal"). Condoms are known by men starting in their teens and are usually, though not always, used with prostitutes to prevent disease, which is officially why they are sold publicly. Men know, however, that they provide the best protection available for casual encounters and many carry them in their wallets. Married people often do not use them because of their expense. Besides, many married people are content to have babies as soon as they happen to come along. As Juan said, by the time a woman has had three, if she married at 28–9, she is already pretty old, her husband comes home tired from work in the fields, and sex becomes very infrequent. . . . Rhythm is used by many couples and fits in well with the pattern of fairly limited sex which Juan indicated existed by the time people have had a couple of kids and start to think about birth control. Withdrawal is the oldest and best known and most widely practiced method by married couples, Juan thinks. (RSP field notes, July 1964)

47. It is also true that in the 1960s the personal pleasures that parents sacrificed earned them the respect of neighbors who would have criticized them had they indulged personal whims. In the 1980s, in contrast, the pleasures that parents renounced were activities that media advertisements, in particular, urged adults to enjoy.

During neither period of fieldwork did parents seem to expect children to support them in old age. As I discuss in the next chapter, elders in the 1960s expected to retain control over their property until they died, forcing their heirs to rent the lands and houses they would eventually inherit. Parents in the 1980s seemed to expect to provide for their own retirement, with help from the state system of social security. But if parents in neither period expected money from their children, they did expect their children to take physical care of them in old age.

Nor did the Spanish parents I interviewed think of education as comparable to inheritance or dowry, as has been reported for "modern" parents in Greece (du Boulay 1974; Allen 1986, 3).

48. JFC field notes, April 1983.

49. JFC formal interview, May 1983.

50. JFC interview notes, March 1983.

51. JFC field notes, March 1983.

52. JFC field notes, April 1983.

53. One could, of course, ask why fathers did not feel a similar need to personally provide the daily, individualized care they thought young children required. None of the people I met from Los Olivos, however, asked this feminist question.

54. JFC field notes, March 1983.

55. JFC formal interview, April 1983.

56. JFC field notes, June 1983.

57. GAC formal interview, March 1983.

58. GAC formal interview, February 1983.

59. JFC field notes, July 1984.

60. My admiration for Spanish concepts of child development led me to wonder if their failure to blame parents for children's problems might be related to the historical failure of bourgeois culture to achieve dominance in Spain. Because Spanish proponents of Enlightenment values were always contesting powerful "traditionalists," they never had to justify their rule. As a result, they could claim credit for successes and blame failures on the "harmful" ideas of their enemies. Nor did Spain develop a bourgeois class, separate from the aristocracy, whose women, deprived of the "productive activities" bourgeois men used to justify their dominance, might find comfort in the idea that women "produced" children in the same sense that men "produced" goods—i.e, by molding "raw materials" into finished products whose value reflected the quality of labor invested.

## Chapter Five

1. Vestía siempre de luto, a pesar de que su viudez era ya cuenta muy larga (Pérez Galdós 1983, 248–249).

2. JFC formal interview, February 1983.

3. JFC field notes, June 1983.

4. JFC formal interview, February 1983.

5. The histories of elderly people I collected tended to confirm, or at least not to contradict, the idea that old men were more reluctant than old women to leave the village. Of the eleven men born between 1900 and 1909, only one, who emigrated in young adulthood, settled permanently outside the village. Seven remained in the village, even if they had to live alone, and three others,

who had emigrated when younger, returned or planned to return in old age. Of the fourteen women born between 1900 and 1909, in contrast, only six stayed in the village. The others moved away to live with a daughter (six cases) or, lacking a daughter, to live with a niece or daughter-in-law.

6. JFC field notes, November 1963.

7. RSP field notes, July 1964.

8. Although this young man emigrated, he moved to a nearby city. Whereas young men tended to emigrate, I did find that several women had postponed emigrating with their husbands and teenage children in order to care for aging parents in the village.

9. In another case, some nephews whose wives did not want to provide care for their elderly aunt paid a servant to nurse the dying woman, thus retaining their right to inherit her property (according to villagers who discussed the case).

10. MZ formal interview 2.

11. Villagers assumed that daughters provided better and more loving care than daughters-in-law or more distant relatives. One older friend who had no daughter was obsessed with the question of what would happen to her when she became too sick or feeble to care for herself. She fervently hoped her son would marry a "good" woman, but feared that he would be misled by a pretty face. She often spoke enviously of her age-mates who had daughters, telling me that they did not have to worry about who would care for them in old age. Indeed, I found that of the twenty-five elders in the birth cohort just before hers—those born between 1900 and 1909—everyone who had a daughter lived with her or expected to rely on her for care, even if the elder also had a son.

12. These thirty-two elders born before 1900, as well as the elders in other birth cohorts, do not represent either complete or random samples of the people born in those years. Not only were more people born than lived into old age, but the numbers represent only those older people whose whereabouts I could trace.

13. Of the twenty-seven elders who had been able to remain in the village, eighteen were living in their own homes, cared for by an unmarried daughter, married children, a maid, or a younger female relative. In 1983, one widow without daughters was living alone in her house, but she was cared for by her three daughters-in-law, who each took week-long turns dressing and feeding her and sending a child to spend the night with her. Of the nine elders who stayed in the village but who had to move from their own homes, seven lived with a married or widowed daughter in her house, one widower lived with his only son and his son's wife, and another widower who had divided his property among his three sons took turns living with each.

14. Of the nine elders who were able to remain in the village, four were women and five were men. Two of the women were widows who lived with their married daughters, one was an elderly spinster who lived with a spinster niece, and one was a childless widow who lived alone but expected to receive help from a nearby niece when she needed it. All five of the elderly men lived alone. Three single men and one childless widower were tended by nearby younger sisters, and one elderly widower with sisters in the village also lived alone because, people said, he refused to live where his unmarried only daughter worked. (When he

became terminally ill, his daughter took a leave of absence from her job to care for him.) Of the four elders who had left the village but hoped to return there to die, two traveled among their geographically dispersed children spending a few months with each. Both hoped to spend their final days in Los Olivos, tended by married daughters who lived there. The other two who hoped to die in Los Olivos were childless widowers who had emigrated as young men. By 1984, one had already returned to the village to live near his only sister. The other expected to move in with his village niece when he could no longer care for himself. Finally, twelve elders had little hope of being able to spend their final days in the village. Three of these twelve were still living in the village in 1983, but they expected to join their emigrated children when they could no longer care for themselves. The remaining nine had already left. Five were women who had gone to live with their emigrant daughters when widowed and four others, who had emigrated as middle-aged adults, continued to live with or near their urban children after retirement.

15. Of the sixteen who stayed in Los Olivos, only six lived with relatives—two with unmarried daughters in their own homes; three, all bachelors, with younger unmarried or widowed sisters; and one active widow kept house for her bachelor son. Of the ten elders who lived alone, nine were men, three of whom had children living elsewhere. One of them was a widower who had gone to live with his only daughter in Madrid but returned to the village within the year, telling his neighbors that he felt lonely and trapped in the city.

16. JFC field notes, February 1983.

17. JFC field notes, November 1963.

18. Villagers said that girls under fourteen were "put into" mourning costume (*se le pone ropa negra*), whereas girls and women over fourteen "donned" mourning costume (*se lleva ropa negra*).

19. One childless woman who lost a parent in the early 1960s told me that she spent her years of required mourning reading novels. Evidently this quiet pastime escaped the ban placed on more audible amusements such as listening to the radio or watching television.

20. When Shelly Zimbalist asked an older villager why a woman in deep mourning was allowed to leave her house to visit the sick, the villager replied, "because visiting a sick person is not going anywhere" (MZ formal interview 27, 1965).

21. MZ formal interview 1, 1965. When Shelly asked a man why men mourned less than women, he replied, "because a man has another thing, another kind of freedom; [men] are not as sentimental as women; and because [a man] meets his friends and, without intending, goes to the movies" (MZ formal interview 36, 1965).

22. MZ field notes, June 1965.

23. When I returned to Los Olivos in the 1980s, I noticed that a few of the oldest women, who had been born around the turn of the century, were still wearing the *pañuelo*.

24. Despite villagers' impression that mourning requirements were becoming more relaxed in the 1960s, the lists Michelle Zimbalist collected from older

and younger people in 1965 suggest that periods of required mourning had not noticeably shortened over the previous twenty years. Villagers, however, may have thought requirements were once stricter because older women were more likely to be wearing black than younger ones. In addition, women had more occasions to mourn in the past because families were larger and the death rate was higher. Mourning may have been more obvious in the years following the civil war because the socialist men assassinated in 1936 and 1937 left many mourning widows, mothers, sisters, and daughters.

25. MZ field notes, July 1965.

26. JFC field notes, December 1963.

27. MZ field notes, July 1965.

28. MZ field notes, July 1965.

29. MZ field notes, August 1965.

30. In the 1960s, some people also complained that mourning serves no purpose. Shelly, for example, talked with a woman who observed that "once someone has died, what are we to do? We have to live, to enjoy ourselves as well" (MZ field notes, July 1965). But in the 1960s, such observations were about what people thought underneath as they outwardly conformed to social conventions.

31. JFC field notes, February 1983.

32. Danforth (1982) treats mourning rituals as rites of passage for the mourners, which fits with my analysis of mourning dress in the 1960s as signifying the passage of inheritances.

33. MZ formal interview 19, 1965.

34. MZ field notes, July 1965.

35. MZ formal interview 22, 1965.

36. MZ formal interview 19, 1965.

37. Josefa went on to demonstrate her point that touching and feeling did not necessarily coincide by observing that if a woman indicated "más ganas de divertirse . . . yendo al baile, al paseo, a la televisión" [that she wanted to have fun—to go dancing, attend paseos, or watch television], then people would infer that "lo siente menos que le toca" [she felt the death less than it touched her] (MZ formal interview 19, 1965).

38. Villagers also distinguished between "natural" and "unnatural" deaths, between those who died in old age of illness in bed, and those who died before their time or of unnatural causes, such as murder or accidents. Villagers expected mourners to feel an unnatural death more than a natural one.

39. MZ formal interview 19, 1965. The woman who told Shelly Zimbalist about the disinherited cousins described the unmarried siblings who died as "un poco locos" [a bit crazy] because "instead of asking a woman of their family for help, they asked a stranger; and in less than three months (three of the four) died, and they disinherited the brother, and the woman took all the inheritance" (MZ formal interview 19, 1965). Another woman, however, told Shelly that "according to the will, [the woman who inherited from the deceased] had to take care of their very old brother for as long as he lives" (MZ formal interview 2, 1965).

40. MZ field notes, June 1965.

41. MZ formal interview 19, 1965. Only legitimate children had inheritance rights, however. A man could disinherit an illegitimate child. One wealthy merchant whose wife bore no children reportedly left some money to his illegitimate daughter, but willed the bulk of his estate to the niece who cared for him in old age. I never heard of a woman disinheriting an illegitimate child, but all the women who bore illegitimate children never married (and all were poor). They also lived with their children, receiving care from them in old age.

42. MZ formal interview 19, 1965. Although villagers said that parents divided their property equally among all children, the shares occasionally varied. Parents often left more property (particularly houses and furniture) to unmarried children, arguing that such children had never drawn on the family estate to set up a marital household and that they had contributed more years of labor to the parental estate. Unmarried daughters who remained at home caring for their aging parents were particularly likely to inherit the parents' house and furniture as well as an equal share of the remaining family properties.

43. Villagers said that the property a deceased person inherited from his or her natal family should revert to that family if the deceased died childless, but they were less certain about the proper disposal of property the deceased had acquired on his or her own. Some villagers, for example, considering the question of who would inherit the property of a childless man, refused to speculate because, they said, although he had several nieces and nephews, he had acquired most of his property with money he earned working abroad.

44. JFC field notes, April 1983.

45. MZ formal interview 2, 1965.

46. Grandchildren inherited indirectly through their parents. The children of a dead person's siblings inherited even more indirectly, through their grandparents and parents, if the deceased died without children. A woman participated in the inheritance of her parents-in-law through her husband, but she held only usufruct rights for her lifetime. After her death, the property passed to her husband's heirs (who might be her children). First cousins inherited only if both the deceased and his or her siblings died childless.

47. MZ formal interview 2, 1965.

48. MZ formal interview 1, 1965.

49. MZ formal interview 19, 1965.

50. JFC field notes, February 1983.

51. JFC interview notes, May 1983.

## Chapter Six

1. El resumen de todos los debates era siempre la supremacía de Orbajosa y de sus habitantes sobre los demás pueblos y gentes de la tierra (Pérez Galdós 1983, 102).

2. The three Americans in our group were, as far as I could tell, the only foreigners present. Almost all of the Spaniards who attended the pilgrimage had been born in nearby communities.

3. Although the people of Los Olivos called the costume *traje de flamenco*, it also has other names. Murphy (1994), writing about the famous pilgrimage to the shrine of the Virgen del Rocío, notes that the women's version of *traje corto* is known as "the *traje de faralaes* or the *traje de gitana*" and he cites several sources.

4. RSP field notes, June 1964.

5. The Prices report that some of the wives of the Guardia Civil who were stationed in the village did join the dancing and did recruit men as partners.

6. Murphy (1994, 53) provides a fuller description of this male costume and observes that it is known as "*traje corto.*" He also observes that both the male and female versions of *traje corto* have their origins in elite attire and are associated with the Andalusian landed class, the *señoritos.*

7. The fandango is the form of flamenco music associated with the province of Huelva.

8. I, of course, have also portrayed the "traditional" customs I observed in Los Olivos in the 1960s as reflecting Castilian domination. Village courtship and mourning customs, in particular, were developed and practiced by people who were trying to preserve their rights to land in a social world dominated by agrarian elites who needed landless laborers to work their large estates. Although the landed elites who dominated the Sierra de Aracena may have been born in Andalusia, they were closely allied with political forces in Madrid both before and after Franco's victory in the civil war. After all, they relied on the national corps of Civil Guards to enforce the property and wage laws that ensured them a steady supply of very cheap labor.

9. I owe this insight to Michael Herzfeld. The impossibility of "having traditions" without "being traditional" is nicely illustrated in a recent editorial by Andalusian writer Antonio Muñoz Molina, published in *El País*, March 13, 1996. Titled "*Andalucía obligatoria*," the editorial criticizes the government of the Andalusian Autonomous Region for requiring communities to put on an endless round of folkloristic fairs, festivals, and pilgrimages. Instead of tackling Andalusia's real social problems, such as the high rate of unemployment, the autonomous government wastes money in propagating the "two principal vices" of the old landed upper classes: "religious/folkloristic fanaticism and disdain for work." As a result, the author claims, Andalusia is falling farther and farther "behind" other regions of Spain.

10. David Sutton (1994) discusses many of these issues when analyzing the sliding boundary between "tradition" and "modernity" on a Greek island.

11. Members of Antonio's and Esteban's generation fondly remembered the picnics, dances, and festivals they had attended as young people, even as they disparaged the long courtships and extended mourning periods that—in the 1960s—they had themselves enacted as proof that they were capable of recognizing and fulfilling adult "obligations."

12. Herzfeld (1992, 17–18) phrases the Enlightenment contrast that I have labeled as between reason and superstition as one between reason and ritual. Both these characterizations capture Antonio's distinction between thinking for oneself and letting others think for one.

13. Obviously I have been arguing throughout this book against representations of women and the home as being "insulated" from wider social and economic changes (Yanagisako and Collier 1987).

14. El andalucismo es algo más que la dimensión politica de un ideal: es un sentimiento desabordante que asume las raices vivas del folklore popular y se expresa con espontaneidad en cualquier ocasión en que se encuentra más de un andaluz (Gran enciclopedia de Andalucía 1979, 1: 195).

15. In the introduction to his book, Maddox suggests that the main value of his historical ethnography "may be to undermine the reifying tendencies of both the folkloric and dependency views of tradition" (1993, 22). By demonstrating the changing politics of tradition through time, Maddox hopes to avoid "reinforcing the sort of folklorism that represents local cultural traditions as worthy of preservation largely because they attract tourists and add a touch of historical color to national life." Similarly, he hopes to counter the vision of "traditions" as "vehicles of a culture of dependency that has to be overcome in the interests of material progress and sociopolitical liberation" by showing how Andalusians in the 1980s were using tradition to "resist the increasing rationalization and homogenization of contemporary life" (1993, 22).

16. I do not think that people's enactments of Andalusian identity were stimulated by my presence as a foreigner. They dressed in Andalusian costumes, danced Andalusian dances, and participated in local pilgrimages for their own benefit.

17. Bourdieu, arguing that the "economic attitudes" of Algerians had to be understood in terms of their objective economic situations, presents a devastating critique of sociologists studying "modernization" who proceeded "as if the adoption of a modern way of life were the result of a free choice" (1979, 32).

18. Maddox (1993) also argues that "tradition," as practiced by the people of Aracena in the 1980s, was a modern discourse rather than a traditional one.

# References Cited

Abu-Lughod, Lila
 1990 "The Romance of Resistance: Tracing Transformations of Power through Bedouin Women." *American Ethnologist* 17(1):41–55.
Aceves, Joseph
 1971 *Social Change in a Spanish Village.* Cambridge, MA: Schenkman Publishing.
Aceves, Joseph, and William Douglass (eds.)
 1976 *The Changing Faces of Rural Spain.* Cambridge, MA: Schenkman Publishing.
Aceves, Joseph B., E. C. Hansen, and G. Levitas (eds.)
 1976 *Economic Transformation and Steady-State Values: Essays in the Ethnography of Spain.* New York: Queens College Publications in Anthropology, no. 2.
Acosta Sánchez, José
 1979 *Historia y cultura del pueblo andaluz.* Barcelona: Editorial Anagrama.
Aguilar Criado, Encarnación
 1990 *Cultura popular y folklore en Andalucía (Los orígines de la antropología).* Sevilla: Diputación Provincial Sevilla.
Aguilera, Francisco Enrique
 1978 *Santa Eulalia's People: Ritual Structure and Process in an Andalucian Multicommunity.* St. Paul, MN: West Publishing.
Alberra, Dionigi
 1988 "Open Systems and Closed Minds: The Limitations of Naïvety in Social Anthropology—A Native's View." *Man* (NS) 23:435–452.
Allen, Peter
 1986 "Female Inheritance, Housing, and Urbanization in Greece." *Anthropology* 10:1–18.
Anderson, Benedict
 1983 *Imagined Communities: Reflections on the Origin and Spread of Nationalism.* London: Verso.
Appadurai, Arjun
 1990 "Disjuncture and Difference in the Global Cultural Economy." *Public Culture* 2:1–24.
Asad, Talal
 1993 *Genealogies of Religion: Discipline and Reasons of Power in Christianity and Islam.* Baltimore, MD: Johns Hopkins University Press.
Barrett, Richard A.
 1974 *Benabarre: The Modernization of a Spanish Village.* New York: Holt, Rinehart and Winston.
Behar, Ruth
 1986 *The Presence of the Past in a Spanish Village: Santa María del Monte.* Princeton, NJ: Princeton University Press.

Benton, Lauren
1990 *Invisible Factories: The Informal Economy and Industrial Development in Spain.* Albany: State University of New York Press.
Berman, Marshall
1982 *All That Is Solid Melts into Air: The Experience of Modernity.* New York: Simon and Schuster.
Boissevain, Jeremy
1979 "Towards a Social Anthropology of the Mediterranean." *Current Anthropology* 20:81–93.
Boissevain, Jeremy (ed.)
1992 *Revitalizing European Rituals.* London: Routledge.
Bourdieu, Pierre
1977 *Outline of a Theory of Practice.* Cambridge: Cambridge University Press.
1979 *Algeria 1960.* Cambridge: Cambridge University Press.
Brandes, Stanley
1975 *Migration, Kinship, and Community: Tradition and Transition in a Spanish Village.* New York: Academic Press.
1980 *Metaphors of Masculinity: Sex and Status in Andalusian Folklore.* Philadelphia: University of Pennsylvania Press.
Brennan, Gerald
1950 *The Face of Spain.* London: Penguin.
1967 *The Spanish Labyrinth.* Cambridge: Cambridge University Press.
Briggs, Charles L.
1996 "The Politics of Discursive Authority in Research on the 'Invention of Tradition.'" *Cultural Anthropology* 11(4): 435–469.
Burchell, Graham
1993 "Liberal Government and Techniques of the Self." *Economy and Society* 22(3):267–282.
Campbell, John K.
1964 *Honour, Family, and Patronage.* Oxford: Clarendon Press.
Carr, Raymond, and Juan Pablo Fusi
1981 *Spain: Dictatorship to Democracy.* 2d. ed. London: Allen and Unwin.
Cazorla, José
1980 "Mentalidad 'modernizante': Trabajo y cambio en los retornados andaluces." *Revista Española de Investigaciones Sociológicas* 11:29–53.
Chatterjee, Partha
1989 "Colonialism, Nationalism, and Colonized Women: The Contest in India." *American Ethnologist* 16(4):622–633.
Cole, John W.
1977 "Anthropology Comes Part-Way Home: Community Studies in Europe." *Annual Review of Anthropology*, 6:349–378.
Collier, George A.
1987 *Socialists of Rural Andalusia: Unacknowledged Revolutionaries of the Second Republic.* Stanford, CA: Stanford University Press.
Collier, Jane F.
1974 "Women in Politics." Pp. 89–96 in *Woman, Culture, and Society,*

Michelle Z. Rosaldo and Louise Lamphere, eds. Stanford, CA: Stanford University Press.

1986  "From Mary to Modern Woman." *American Ethnologist* 13(1):100–107.

1988  *Marriage and Inequality in Classless Societies*. Stanford, CA: Stanford University Press.

Collier, Jane, Bill Maurer, and Liliana Suárez-Navaz
1995  "Sanctioned Identities: Legal Constructions of 'Modern' Personhood." *Identities: Global Studies in Culture and Power* 2(1–2)1–27.

Collier, Jane F., and Michelle Z. Rosaldo
1981  "Politics and Gender in 'Simple' Societies." Pp. 275–329 in *Sexual Meanings*, Sherry Ortner and Harriet Whitehead, eds. Cambridge: Cambridge University Press.

Collier, Jane F., Michelle Z. Rosaldo, and Sylvia Yanagisako
1982  "Is There a Family?: New Anthropological Views." Pp. 25–39 in *Rethinking the Family: Some Feminist Questions*, Barrie Thorne, ed. with Marilyn Yalom. New York: Longman.

Collier, Jane, and Sylvia Yanagisako
1989  "Theory in Anthropology Since Feminist Practice." *Critique of Anthropology* 9(2):27–37.

Comaroff, Jean, and John Comaroff
1991  *Of Revelation and Revolution: Christianity, Colonialism, and Consciousness in South Africa*. Vol. 1. Chicago: University of Chicago Press.

Comaroff, Jean, and John Comaroff (eds.)
1993  *Modernity and Its Malcontents: Ritual and Power in Postcolonial Africa*. Chicago: University of Chicago Press.

Corbin, John R., and Marie P. Corbin
1984  *Compromising Relations: Kith, Kin, and Class in Andalusia*. Hampshire, England: Gower Publishing.

1987  *Urbane Thought: Culture and Class in an Andalusian City*. Hampshire, England: Gower Publishing.

Cowan, Jane K.
1990  *Dance and the Body Politic in Northern Greece*. Princeton, NJ: Princeton University Press.

Crain, Mary
1992  "Pilgrims, 'Yuppies,' and Media Men: The Transformation of an Andalusian Pilgrimage." Pp. 95–112 in *Revitalizing European Rituals*, Jeremy Boissevain, ed. London: Routledge.

Creighton, Colin
1996  "The Rise of the Male Breadwinner Family: A Reappraisal." *Comparative Studies in Society and History* 38:310–337.

Dahrendorf, Ralf
1968  *Essays in the Theory of Society*. Stanford, CA: Stanford University Press.

Danforth, Loring M.
1982  *The Death Rituals of Rural Greece*. Princeton, NJ: Princeton University Press.

Davis, John
    1977    *The People of the Mediterranean: An Essay in Comparative Social An-thropology.* London: Routledge and Kegan Paul.
D'Emilio, John, and Estelle B. Freedman
    1988    *Intimate Matters: A History of Sexuality in America.* New York: Harper and Row.
de Onís, Harriet
    1960    "Benito Pérez Galdós (1843–1920)." Pp. v–xvi in *Doña Perfecta.* Translation and Introduction by Harriet de Onís. Woodbury, NY: Barron's Educational Series.
Derné, Steve
    1994    "Cultural Conceptions of Human Motivation and Their Significance for Culture Theory." Pp. 267–287 in *The Sociology of Culture: Emerging Theoretical Perspectives,* Diana Crane, ed. Oxford: Blackwell.
Dirks, Nicholas B.
    1990    "History as a Sign of the Modern." *Public Culture* 2:25–32.
Douglass, William A.
    1975    *Echalar and Murelaga: Opportunity and Rural Exodus in Two Basque Villages.* New York: St. Martin's Press.
Doumanis, Mariella
    1983    *Mothering in Greece: From Collectivism to Individualism.* New York: Academic Press.
Driessen, Henk
    1981    "Anthropologists in Andalusia: The Use and Comparison of History." *Man* 16:451–462.
    1983    "Male Sociability and Rituals of Masculinity in Rural Andalusia." *Anthropological Quarterly* 56:125–133.
    1984    "Andalusian Ethnography." *Man* (NS) 19:665–666.
Dubisch, Jill
    1995    *In a Different Place: Pilgrims, Gender, and Politics at a Greek Island Shrine.* Princeton, NJ: Princeton University Press.
Dubisch, Jill (ed.)
    1986    *Gender and Power in Rural Greece.* Princeton, NJ: Princeton University Press.
du Boulay, Juliet
    1974    *Portrait of a Greek Mountain Village.* Oxford: Clarendon Press.
Durkheim, Emile
    1933    *The Division of Labor in Society.* Translated by George Simpson. Glencoe, IL: The Free Press. (Fourth printing, 1960.)
Evans-Pritchard, E. E.
    1940    *The Nuer.* Oxford: Oxford University Press.
Faubion, James
    1993    *Modern Greek Lessons: A Primer in Historical Constructivism.* Princeton, NJ: Princeton University Press.
Fernandez, James D.
    1983    "Consciousness and Class Consciousness in Southern Spain." *American Ethnologist* 10(1):165–173.

Foucault, Michel
1973   *The Order of Things.* New York: Vintage Books.
1975   *The Birth of the Clinic.* New York: Vintage Books.
1977a  *Discipline and Punish.* New York: Random House.
1977b  *Madness and Civilization.* London: Harper and Row.
1978   *The History of Sexuality.* Vol. 1, *An Introduction.* New York: Random House.
1980   "Truth and Subjectivity." The Howison Lecture, Berkeley, CA. (Mimeo, mentioned in Burchell 1993.)
1984   "What Is Enlightenment?" Pp. 32–50 in *The Foucault Reader,* Paul Rabinow, ed. New York: Random House.
Fraser, Ronald
1973   *Tajos: The Story of a Village on the Costa del Sol.* New York: Pantheon.
Freeman, Susan Tax
1970   *Neighbors: The Social Contract in a Castillian Hamlet.* Chicago: University of Chicago Press.
Friedan, Betty
1963   *The Feminine Mystique.* New York: Dell Publishing.
Friedl, Ernestine
1962   *Vasilika: A Village in Modern Greece.* New York: Holt, Rinehart and Winston.
1967   "The Position of Women: Appearance and Reality." *Anthropological Quarterly* 40:97–108.
Friedman, Jonathan
1992   "The Past in the Future: History and the Politics of Identity." *American Anthropologist* 94:837–859.
Frigolé Reixach, Joan
1983   "Religión y política en un pueblo murciano entre 1966–1976." *Revista Española de Investigaciones Sociológicas* 23:77–126.
Gellner, Ernest
1983   *Nations and Nationalism.* Ithaca, NY: Cornell University Press.
Giddens, Anthony
1981   *A Contemporary Critique of Historical Materialism.* Berkeley: University of California Press.
1984   *The Constitution of Society.* Berkeley: University of California Press.
1991   *Modernity and Self-Identity: Self and Society in the Late Modern Age.* Stanford, CA: Stanford University Press.
1992   *The Transformation of Intimacy: Sexuality, Love, and Eroticism in Modern Societies.* Stanford, CA: Stanford University Press.
Gilmore, David
1980   *The People of the Plain.* New York: Columbia University Press.
1982   "Anthropology of the Mediterranean Area." *Annual Review of Anthropology* 11:175–205.
1987   *Aggression and Community: Paradoxes of Andalusian Culture.* New Haven, CT: Yale University Press.
Gilmore, David (ed.)
1987   *Honor and Shame and the Unity of the Mediterranean.* Washington, DC: American Anthropological Association.

Goode, William J.
1970   *World Revolution and Family Patterns.* New York: Free Press.
Greenwood, Davydd
1976   *Unrewarding Wealth: The Commercialization and Collapse of Agriculture in a Spanish Basque Town.* Cambridge: Cambridge University Press.
Gregory, David
1978   *La odisea andalusa.* Madrid: Tecnos.
1983   "The Meaning of Urban Life: Pluralization of Life Worlds in Seville." Pp. 253–272 in *Urban Life in Mediterranean Europe.* Michael Kenny and David Kertzer, eds. Chicago: University of Illinois Press.
Hall, Catherine
1994   "Rethinking Imperial Histories: The Reform Act of 1867." *New Left Review* 208:3–29.
Hall, Stuart
1992   "The Question of Cultural Identity." Pp. 274–325 in *Modernity and Its Futures,* Stuart Hall, David Held, and Tony McCrew, eds. Cambridge: Polity Press.
Halpern, Joel
1980   "European and Mediterranean Studies; An Overview." *American Anthropologist* 82:108–113.
Handler, Richard
1988   *Nationalism and the Politics of Culture in Quebec.* Madison: University of Wisconsin Press.
Handler, Richard, and Jocelyn Linnekin
1984   "Tradition, Genuine or Spurious." *Journal of American Folklore* 97: 273–290.
Harding, Susan
1984   *Remaking Ibieca: Rural Life in Aragon under Franco.* Chapel Hill: University of North Carolina Press.
Herr, Richard
1971   *An Historical Essay on Modern Spain.* Berkeley: University of California Press.
Herzfeld, Michael
1980   "Honour and Shame: Problems in the Analysis of Moral Systems." *Man* (NS) 15:339–351.
1982   *Ours Once More: Folklore, Ideology, and the Making of Modern Greece.* Austin: University of Texas Press.
1984   "The Horns of the Mediterraneanist Dilemma." *American Ethnologist* 11(3):439–454.
1985   *The Poetics of Manhood.* Princeton, NJ: Princeton University Press.
1987   *Anthropology through the Looking Glass.* Cambridge: Cambridge University Press.
1991   *A Place in History: Social and Monumental Time in a Cretan Town.* Princeton, NJ: Princeton University Press.
1992   *The Social Production of Indifference: Exploring the Symbolic Roots of Western Bureaucracy.* New York: Berg.

Hirschon, Renée B.
1978   "Open Body/Closed Space: The Transformation of Female Sexuality." Pp. 66–88 in *Defining Females: The Nature of Women in Society*, Shirley Ardener, ed. London: Croom Helm.
1989   *Heirs of the Greek Catastrophe: The Social Life of Asia Minor Refugees in Piraeus*. Oxford: Clarendon Press.
1992   "Greek Adults' Verbal Play: Or, How to Train for Caution." *Journal of Modern Greek Studies* 10:35–56.
Hobbes, Thomas
1991   *Leviathan*. Cambridge: Cambridge University Press. (First published 1651.)
Hobsbawm, Eric J.
1990   *Nations and Nationalism Since 1780*. New York: Cambridge University Press.
Hobsbawm, Eric, and Terence Ranger (eds.)
1983   *The Invention of Tradition*. Cambridge: Cambridge University Press.
Hooper, John
1994   *The Spaniards: A Portrait of the New Spain*. New York: Viking Press. (First edition, 1986.)
Hutchinson, John, and Anthony D. Smith
1994   "Introduction." Pp. 3–13 in *Nationalism*, John Hutchinson and Anthony D. Smith, eds. Oxford: Oxford University Press.
Jackson, Jean
1995   "Culture, Genuine and Spurious: The Politics of Indianness in the Vaupés, Colombia." *American Ethnologist* 22(1):3–27.
Kaplan, Temma
1977   *Anarchists of Andalusia, 1868–1903*. Princeton, NJ: Princeton University Press.
Kelley, Heidi
1994   "The Myth of Matriarchy: Symbols of Womanhood in Galician Regional Identity." *Anthropological Quarterly* 67:71–80.
Kenny, Michael
1966   *A Spanish Tapestry: Town and Country in Castile*. New York: Harper Colophon Books.
Kenny, Michael, and David Kertzer (eds.)
1983   *Urban Life in Mediterranean Europe: Anthropological Perspectives*. Urbana: University of Illinois Press.
Kristeva, Julia
1991   *Strangers to Ourselves*. Translated by Leon S. Roudiez. New York: Columbia University Press.
Laqueur, Thomas
1990   *Making Sex: Body and Gender from the Greeks to Freud*. Cambridge, MA: Harvard University Press.
Lasch, Christopher
1977   *Haven in a Heartless World: The Family Besieged*. New York: Basic Books.

Latour, Bruno
1993    *We Have Never Been Modern.* Cambridge, MA: Harvard University Press.
Leavitt, John
1996    "Meaning and Feeling in the Anthropology of Emotions." *American Ethnologist* 23(3):514–539.
Lison-Tolosana, Carmelo
1966    *Belmonte de los Caballeros.* Oxford: Clarendon Press. (Reprinted by Princeton University Press, 1983.)
Llobera, Josep R.
1994    *The God of Modernity: The Development of Nationalism in Western Europe.* Oxford: Berg.
Luque Baena, E.
1974    *Estudio antropológico social de un pueblo del sur.* Madrid: Tecnos.
1981    "Perspectivas antropológicas sobre Andalucía." *Papers* 16:13–52.
MacCormack, Carol, and Marilyn Strathern (eds.)
1980    *Nature, Culture, and Gender.* Cambridge: Cambridge University Press.
MacIntyre, Alasdair
1970    "The Idea of a Social Science." Pp. 112–130 in *Rationality*, Bryan R. Wilson, ed. Oxford: Basil Blackwell.
Maddox, Richard
1986    "Religion, Honor, and Patronage: A Study of Culture and Power in an Andalusian Town." Ph.D. diss., Stanford University.
1993    *El Castillo: The Politics of Tradition in an Andalusian Town.* Urbana: University of Illinois Press.
Mani, Lata
1989    "Contentious Traditions: The Debate on Sati in Colonial India. Pp. 88–126 in *Recasting Women: Essays in Indian Colonial History*, Kumkum Sangari and Sudesh Vaid, eds. New Delhi: Kali for Women.
Martínez-Alier, Juan
1971    *Labourers and Landowners in Southern Spain.* London: Allen and Unwin.
McDonogh, Gary
1986    *Good Families of Barcelona.* Princeton, NJ: Princeton University Press.
Medick, Hans, and David Warren Sabean (eds.)
1984    *Interest and Emotion: Essays on the Study of Family and Kinship.* Cambridge: Cambridge University Press.
Mintz, Jerome
1982    *The Anarchists of Casas Viejas.* Chicago: University of Chicago Press.
Mitchell, Timothy
1990    *Passional Culture: Emotion, Religion, and Society in Southern Spain.* Philadelphia: University of Pennsylvania Press.
1991    *Blood Sport: A Social History of the Bullfight.* Philadelphia: University of Pennsylvania Press.

Moreno Alonso, Manuel
  1979   *La vida rural en la sierra de Huelva: Alájar.* Huelva: Instituto de Estudios Onubenses "Padre Marchena."
Moreno Navarro, Isidoro
  1972   *Propiedad, clases sociales, y hermandades en la Baja Andalucía: La estructura social de un pueblo del Aljarafe.* Madrid: Siglo Veintiuno.
  1975   "La antropología en Andalucía: Desarrollo histórico y estado actual de las investigaciones." *Etnica* 1:109–144.
  1977   *Andalucía: Subdesarrollo, clases sociales y regionalismo.* Madrid: Manifesto.
  1981   "Rechazo de la dependencia y afirmación de la identidad: Las bases del nacionalismo andaluz." In *Jornadas de estudios socioeconómicas de las comunidades autónomas,* vol. 3, 87–106. Seville: Universidad de Sevilla.
  1984   "La antropología cultural en Andalucía: Estado actual y perspectiva de futuro." In *Antropología cultural de Andalucía,* Salvador Rodríguez Becerra, ed. Seville: Consejería de Cultura, Junta de Andalucía.
Muñoz Molina, Antonio
  1996   "Andalucía obligatoria." *El País,* March 13, 1996: 38. Madrid, Spain.
Murphy, Michael D.
  1983a  "Coming of Age in Seville: The Structuring of a Riteless Passage to Manhood." *Journal of Anthropological Research* 39(4):376–392.
  1983b  "Emotional Confrontations between Sevillano Fathers and Sons." *American Ethnologist* 10(4):650–664.
  1994   "Class, Community, and Costume in an Andalusian Pilgrimage." *Anthropological Quarterly* 67:49–61.
Nadel-Klein, Jane
  1991   "Reweaving the Fringe: Localism, Tradition, and Representation in British Ethnography." *American Ethnologist* 18(3):500–517.
Navarro Alcala-Zamora, P.
  1979   *Mencina: La cambiante estructura social de un pueblo de la Alpujarra.* Madrid: Centro de Investigaciones Sociológicas.
Ortner, Sherry
  1974   "Is Female to Male as Nature Is to Culture?" Pp. 67–88 in *Woman, Culture, and Society,* Michelle Z. Rosaldo and Louise Lamphere, eds. Stanford, CA: Stanford University Press.
  1976   "The Virgin and the State." Michigan Discussions in Anthropology 2:1–16; reprinted 1978 in *Feminist Studies* 4:19–36 and in 1996 in *Making Gender: The Politics and Erotics of Culture,* by Sherry B. Ortner. Boston: Beacon Press.
  1984   "Theory in Anthropology Since the Sixties." *Comparative Studies in Society and History* 26:126–166.
Papataxiarchis, Evthymios
  1991   "Friends of the Heart: Male Commensal Solidarity, Gender, and Kinship in Aegean Greece." Pp. 156–179 in *Contested Identities: Gender and Kinship in Modern Greece,* Peter Loizos and Evthymios Papataxiarchis, eds. Princeton, NJ: Princeton University Press.

Pérez Díaz, Victor
1974   *Pueblos y clases sociales en el campo español.* Madrid: Siglo Veintiuno.
1976   "Processes of Change in Rural Castilian Communities." Pp. 115–135 in *The Changing Faces of Rural Spain,* Joseph Aceves and William Douglass, eds. New York: Schenkman Publishing.
Pérez Galdós, Benito
1960   *Doña Perfecta.* (English Translation by Harriet de Onís.) Woodbury, NY: Barron's Educational Series.
1983   *Doña Perfecta.* Madrid: Alianza Editorial. (First published in 1876.)
Peristiany, J. G. (ed.)
1965   *Honour and Shame: The Values of Mediterranean Society.* London: Weidenfeld and Nicolson.
Pina-Cabral, João de
1986   *Sons of Adam, Daughters of Eve.* Chicago: University of Chicago Press.
1989   "The Mediterranean as a Category of Regional Comparison: A Critical View." *Current Anthropology* 30:399–405.
Pi-Sunyer, O.
1974   "Elites and Noncorporate Groups in the European Mediterranean: A Reconsideration of the Catalan Case." *Comparative Studies in Society and History* 16:117–131.
Pitt-Rivers, Julian
1954   *The People of the Sierra.* Chicago: University of Chicago Press.
1965   "Honour and Social Status." Pp. 19–77 in *Honour and Shame: The Values of Mediterranean Society,* J. G. Peristiany, ed. London: Weidenfeld and Nicolson.
1976   "Preface." Pp. vii–x in *The Changing Faces of Rural Spain,* Joseph Aceves and William Douglass, eds. Cambridge, MA: Schenkman Publishing.
1977   *The Fate of Shechem, or the Politics of Sex.* Cambridge: Cambridge University Press.
Press, Irwin
1979   *The City as Context: Urbanism and Behavioral Constraints in Seville.* Urbana: University of Illinois Press.
Price, Richard
1964   "A Glance at the Past." Typescript in Jane Collier's possession.
Price, Richard, and Sally Price
1966a   "Noviazgo in an Andalusian Pueblo." *Southwestern Journal of Anthropology* 22:302–322.
1966b   "Stratification and Courtship in an Andalusian Village." *Man* 1:526–533.
Radin, Margaret Jane
1987   "Market-Inalienability." *Harvard Law Review* 100(8):1849–1937.
Riegelhaupt, J.
1967   "Saloio Women: An Analysis of Informal and Formal Political and Economic Roles of Portuguese Peasant Women." *Anthropological Quarterly* 40:109–126.

Rodríguez Becerra, Salvador (ed.)
1980 "Cultura popular y fiestas." Pp. 447–494 in *Los andaluces*, M. Drain et al., eds. Seville: Universidad de Sevilla.
1985 *Las fiestas de Andalucía: Una aproximación desde la antropología cultural.* Seville: Biblioteca de la Cultura Andaluza.

Roediger, David R.
1991 *The Wages of Whiteness: Race and the Making of the American Working Class.* London: Verso.

Rogers, Susan Carol
1975 "Female Forms of Power and the Myth of Male Dominance: A Model of Female/Male Interaction in Peasant Society." *American Ethnologist* 2(4):727–756.
1985 "Gender in Southwestern France: The Myth of Male Dominance Revisited." *Anthropology* 9:65–86.

Rubin, Lillian
1976 *Worlds of Pain: Life in the Working Class Family.* New York: Basic Books.

Salamone, S. D., and J. B. Stanton
1986 "Introducing the *Nikokyra*: Ideality and Reality in Social Process." Pp. 97–120 in *Gender and Power in Rural Greece*, Jill Dubisch, ed. Princeton, NJ: Princeton University Press.

Schneider, Jane
1971 "Of Vigilance and Virgins: Honour, Shame, and Access to Resources in Mediterranean Societies." *Ethnology* 9: 101–124.

Schneider, Jane, and Peter Schneider
1976 *Culture and Political Economy in Western Sicily.* New York: Academic Press.

Seccombe, Wally
1992 *A Millenium of Family Change.* London: Verso.

Shorter, Edward
1975 *The Making of the Modern Family.* New York: Basic Books.

Shubert, Adrian
1990 *A Social History of Modern Spain.* London: Unwin Hyman.

Spock, Benjamin
1957 *Baby and Child Care.* New York: Simon and Schuster. (First published in 1946 under the title *The Common Sense Book of Baby and Child Care.*)

Sponsler, Lucy A.
1982 "The Status of Married Women under the Legal System of Spain." *Louisiana Law Review* 42(5):1599–1628.

Stocking, George
1979 "Anthropology as Kulturkampf: Science and Politics in the Career of Franz Boas." Pp. 33–50 in *The Uses of Anthropology*, Walter Goldschmidt, ed. Special Publication, No. 11 of the American Anthropological Association.

Stone, Lawrence
1979 *The Family, Sex, and Marriage in England, 1500–1800.* New York: Harper and Row.

Strathern, Marilyn
  1988  *The Gender of the Gift.* Berkeley: University of California Press.
Sutton, David E.
  1994  " 'Tradition and Modernity': Kalymnian Constructions of Identity and Otherness." *Journal of Modern Greek Studies* 12:239–260.
Sutton, Susan
  1986  "Family and Work: New Patterns for Village Women in Athens." *Journal of Modern Greek Studies* 4:33–49.
Tambiah, Stanley J.
  1989  "Ethnic Conflict in the World Today." *American Ethnologist* 16(2):335–349.
  1990  *Magic, Science, Religion, and the Scope of Rationality.* New York: Cambridge University Press.
Tannen, Deborah, and Christina Kakava
  1992  "Power and Solidarity in Modern Greek Conversation: Disagreeing to Agree." *Journal of Modern Greek Studies* 10:11–34.
Trumbach, Randolph
  1978  *The Rise of the Egalitarian Family: Aristocratic Kinship and Domestic Relations in Eighteenth-Century England.* New York: Academic Press.
  1979  "The Family, Sex, and Marriage in England, 1500–1800." (Review article.) *Journal of Social History* 13(1):136–143.
Vogt, Evon Z.
  1994  *Fieldwork among the Maya: Reflections on the Harvard Chiapas Project.* Albuquerque: University of New Mexico Press.
Weber, Max
  1966  "Class, Status and Party." Pp. 21–36 in *Class, Status, and Power: Social Stratification in Comparative Perspective*, Reinhard Bendix and Seymour Martin Lipset, eds. 2d ed. New York: Free Press.
Williams, Raymond
  1977  *Marxism and Culture.* Oxford: Oxford University Press.
Winch, Peter
  1970  "Understanding a Primitive Society." Pp. 78–111 in *Rationality*, Bryan R. Wilson, ed. Oxford: Basil Blackwell.
Yanagisako, Sylvia
  1979  "Family and Household: The Analysis of Domestic Groups." *Annual Review of Anthropology* 8:161–205.
Yanagisako, Sylvia J., and Jane F. Collier
  1987  "Toward a Unified Analysis of Gender and Kinship." Pp. 14–50 in *Gender and Kinship: Essays toward a Unified Analysis*, Jane F. Collier and Sylvia J. Yanagisako, eds. Stanford, CA: Stanford University Press.

# Index

adultery, 126, 149–50
agriculture, 35–36, 40, 42, 44; collapse of, 33, 44, 47
*ajuar*, 90, 119–20
*amarrado/libre* contrast, 91–92, 138, 230n. 31
amusements, 208–10; during mourning, 184–85, 191, 244n. 19
Andalusian identity, 3–4, 115–16, 199–202, 211–17
animal/human contrast, 76, 155, 169, 228n. 16
anthropology, 10, 13–15, 18, 28, 201–5, 221n. 13
Aracena, 18, 35, 55, 65, 78, 84, 94, 96, 144, 186, 212, 219n. 6; secondary school in, 100, 164, 167; Sierra de, 38–40, 42, 55, 123, 162, 195, 198, 214
authority, in the family, 8, 116, 128, 141–44, 147, 151
*autónomos*, 38–41
autonomous regions, 3–4, 201–2

Barcelona, 3, 23, 43–44, 100, 133
bars, 19, 20, 36, 46, 223n. 4, 236n. 30; men in, 121–22, 129, 132–33, 141–42, 144–47, 179, 185, 216, 237nn. 56 and 57; women in, 114, 130, 132–33, 197–98
bastards, 72, 138, 149. *See also* illegitimate children; unwed mothers
birth control, 169, 232n. 64, 241n. 46
Boas, Franz, 14–15, 204–5
Bourdieu, Pierre, 12, 24
breadwinner, 116, 122, 126, 128–30, 211
budget, family, 118–20, 147–48, 167–68, 238n. 2
bullfight, 197–99, 207, 211

*casa/calle* contrast, 50, 91, 130–31, 136. *See also* public/private contrast
Castilian domination of Andalusia, 4, 202, 219n. 3, 247n. 8
Catalonia, 4, 43–44, 150, 199, 201–2
celibacy, 98, 148, 230n. 34, 231n. 61
cemetery, 56, 187

census, 20, 22–23, 38–39, 181
chaperon, 67, 81, 88–89, 92–93, 100, 104–6
charity, 41, 231n. 59
chastity, 70–72, 90–91, 98–99, 107, 109, 126. *See also* virginity
child care, 125, 137, 142, 156, 175–76
childhood, stages of, 157–59, 184
childlessness, 148, 180–81, 190–91, 234n. 14
choice, 26, 46–47, 115, 212, 215–17; of occupation, 36, 46–47, 57–61, 163–66, 223n. 5; of spouse, 69, 74–75, 77, 79–80, 82–83, 102
church, 6–7, 20, 35–37, 78, 84, 144, 159, 197–98, 219n. 5; schools run by, 161–62, 240n. 23
civil war, 23, 28, 32, 40–42, 48, 97–99, 122, 162–63, 224n. 13
class, 19, 37–42, 49–53, 55, 65; as principle of stratification, 145–46, 234n. 18
class differences: in courtship, 97–98; in marriage, 115–16; in schooling, 156–57, 161–64
cliches, 5–6, 51, 144
cohort analysis, 23–24, 62, 97–100, 181–82
Collier, George A., 20–23, 37, 39–45, 89, 92, 97–98, 122, 161–63
conversational style, 22–23, 151
cost/benefit analysis, 74–75, 77, 105–6, 139–40, 209, 217
courtship histories, 81–83, 85, 102
cuckold, 72–73, 90, 92, 126, 146, 227n. 8, 230n. 34
culture, concept of 201–5
customs: backward, 9, 28, 46, 177, 187; change in, 45–47, 67–68, 96–100, 120, 183–86; loss of, 9, 28–29, 100–107, 130, 177–78; modern, 9, 17–18, 100–101, 104–8, 183, 186, 195–200

dances, 3 7, 77, 84, 96, 98–99, 185, 191, 224n. 6; Andalusian, 30, 133, 198, 200, 211–12

PRINCETON STUDIES IN
CULTURE/POWER/HISTORY

The Savage Freud and Other Essays on Possible and Retrievable Selves *by Ashis Nandy*

Children and the Politics of Culture *edited by Sharon Stephens*

Intimacy and Exclusion: Religious Politics in Pre-Revolutionary Baden *by Dagmar Herzog*

What Was Socialism, and What Comes Next? *by Katherine Verdery*

Citizen and Subject: Contemporary Africa and the Legacy of Late Colonialism *by Mahmood Mamdani*

Colonialism and Its Forms of Knowledge: The British in India *by Bernard S. Cohn*

Charred Lullabies: Chapters in an Anthropography of Violence *by E. Valentine Daniel*

Theft of an Idol: Text and Context in the Representation of Collective Violence *by Paul R. Brass*

Essays on the Anthropology of Reason *by Paul Rabinow*

Vision, Race, and Modernity: A Visual Economy of the Andean Image World *by Deborah Poole*

Children in "Moral Danger" and the Problem of Government in Third Republic France *by Sylvia Schafer*

Settling Accounts: Violence, Justice, and Accountability in Postsocialist Europe *by John Borneman*

From Duty to Desire: Remaking Families in a Spanish Village *by Jane Fishburne Collier*

About the Author

JANE FISHBURNE COLLIER is Professor of Anthropology at Stanford University. She is the author of *Law and Social Changes in Zinacantan* and *Marriage and Inequality in Classless Societies.*